Yoga for the

Modern World

By the same author

Freedom through Self-Realisation

Yoga for the Modern World

*Nineteen lectures on the
relevance of Yoga for
modern Western society*

A M Halliday

SHANTI SADAN
LONDON

First published in 2000 by Shanti Sadan

Copyright © Shanti Sadan 2000
29 Chepstow Villas
London W11 3DR

All rights reserved.
*No part of this publication may
be translated, reproduced or transmitted
in any form or by any means without the
written permission of the publisher.*

ISBN 0-85424-051-9

Printed and bound by
J W Arrowsmith Ltd., Bristol BS3 2NT

CONTENTS

		page
	Introduction	vii
1	The Relevance of Yoga for Modern Western Society	1
2	The Religion of the Future	14
3	The Vedantic View of the World	29
4	The Inner Enquiry	42
5	Attentive Silence	60
6	The Meaning of Life	72
7	No Time Like the Present	84
8	Exchanging Complements	100
9	A Good Koan	115
10	Reconciling the Contradictions	131
11	An Example of Greatness	147
12	Seeing is Believing	172
13	Tolstoi's Questions	211
14	Living in Truth	236
15	Learning from Experience	261
16	The Mind in Society	278
17	A Critical Ailment	292
18	Time for Thought	312
19	Searching for the Good Life	333
	Notes	351
	Index	368

Introduction

AS MODERN MAN prepares to enter the new millennium, there is an increasing sense of the fragmentation of human culture and of the urgent need to find a way forward which will satisfy both the yearning of the human heart for beauty, peace and love, and the demand of the intellect for a clear understanding of truth. For Leonardo da Vinci in the fifteenth century, there was no conflict or barrier between the pursuit of beauty through artistic creation and the pursuit of scientific truth through his own research; but modern man is haunted by the sense of a great divide between these two cultures, and his inner life is consequently stunted and fragmented.

There has perhaps never been a greater need to find a way of reconciling the wisdom of the great spiritual traditions and the validity of scientific knowledge in its approach to objective truth. Even sceptical philosophers like Bertrand Russell have stressed the difference between knowledge and wisdom, and have lamented the lack of wisdom in the way modern man manages his affairs. Ethics has been largely discounted in modern philosophy and has been dismissed as something concerned only with value judgements and not with truth. But, as the philosopher F H Bradley demonstrated, the fact is that ethics is based on man's quest for self-realization. It is a recognition of the discrepancy which he feels within his own personality, between what he ought to be and what he feels he is. Only through the insight of the great spiritual teachings can this fundamental dichotomy, which leaves the individual divided against himself, be faced and overcome by a deeper understanding of man's nature. An understanding of the good life is as vital to man's well-being as the pursuit of

Introduction

truth. Keynes spoke of the way his generation had lived on the spiritual and ethical legacy of its Victorian predecessors, but had done nothing to cherish or supplement it and was, as a consequence, heading for ethical bankruptcy.

The teachings of Yoga offer a peculiarly apt contribution to dealing with this situation. Yoga has been rightly described by one of its leading exponents as 'experimental religion', and he said that it should be approached in the same spirit as we approach chemistry or physics, not taking things on faith, but putting the results and insights reported by the competent yogis to the test of verification in our own experience. It offers the possibility of extending the sphere of investigation from the outer objective world to the inner world of the mind and the subject of experience. It is particularly relevant to current thought, in view of the awakening interest among leading scientists in investigating the nature of consciousness.

This book contains a further selection of lectures, given on behalf of Shanti Sadan between 1965 and 1994, in an attempt to present aspects of the teachings of the Yoga of Self-Knowledge to audiences made up largely of those with a Western upbringing and background. Most of these talks have already appeared in print in past numbers of the quarterly journal *Self-Knowledge,* which has been published by Shanti Sadan since 1950.

Not surprisingly in a series of lectures given by the same individual over a period of more than thirty years, there are one or two places where the same quotations from other authors have been cited in different contexts. These repetitions have been left unaltered, rather than risking a certain loss of continuity in the original lectures by excision.

Introduction

It is hoped that the reader will tolerantly overlook them.

The author's thanks are due to those writers and thinkers whose works have been quoted, often extensively, in the course of these lectures; and in particular to Václav Havel for giving him permission to quote at length from his book, *Letters to Olga*, in the lecture 'Living in Truth', and to Professor William McNeill, who has been equally generous in permitting the use of much material from his biography of Arnold Toynbee in the lecture on 'Learning from Experience'.

The author's greatest debt of gratitude is owed to Dr Hari Prasad Shastri, who came to England in 1929 and founded Shanti Sadan as a traditional school of Yoga in 1933. It was from him that he had the inestimable privilege of learning of these spiritual teachings both in theory and practice, from 1936 until his death in 1956.

August 1999
London

The following sources of the photographs on the cover are gratefully acknowledged: The central figure of the Lohan is used by kind permission of the British Museum; the picture of Arnold Toynbee was provided by Camera Press; that of F H Bradley was generously made available by its owner, Bradley's great, great, great nephew, Dr Tom Whinnicroft; and the remaining pictures of Havel, Tolstoi, Faraday, Russell, Wittgenstein and Schrödinger were provided by the Hulton Getty Picture Collection.

1

The Relevance of Yoga
for Modern Western Society*

One of the difficulties of speaking in public on a religious subject nowadays is that the audience expects the speaker who comes to them to be already committed—as indeed he is likely to be. When we listen to a salesman we are, not unwisely, suspicious of what he has to say. We think we shall hear all about the advantages of the goods he is selling and none of the snags. As a consequence many of us would much prefer to have a report from *Which?* considering all the possibilities and recommending the best buy! It is not that one would regard *Which?* as an infallible guide (a kind of substitute Pope for the scientific age), but simply that one is more likely to get the true answer from a source which tries to be impartial.

It is worth asking why it is so difficult to get this sort of impartiality in the sphere of religion, and one of the answers must surely be that it is because as soon as the topic is raised, feelings are deeply roused (not only *for*, let us add, but also *against*). It appears to be too uncomfortably 'near home' for impartiality: the whole topic needles us out of our plush seat in an imaginary Olympian grandstand of scientific objectivity. The questions raised, whether to govern our life with idealism or expediency, with self-sacrifice or self-indulgence, concern us deeply and intimately, and the way we answer

* A lecture delivered to the Progressive League on 15th June 1965.

them threatens to change us. Even irreligiousness changes us. We can't avoid it. The dilemma is one on whose horns we are precariously driven forward whether we will or no. To decide even *not* to take an interest is to decide on a definite course. For this reason the religious questions, in their broader context, are always intensely relevant to life, and in the modern secularized society we are not really avoiding them, we are simply answering them in a different way.

It is, of course, a truism that the dominant outlook of Western society today is more secular (or at least more professedly secular) than it has ever been, and that this position is related to the rise of the physical sciences and the success of modern technology. For many people religion has reached an impasse. It appears to offer an act of irrational faith which you either take or leave at your choice. But there is no real basis for a dialogue thereafter between those who take it and those who leave it, and there appears to be no real test of its validity other than a purely pragmatic one. The individual can say: 'My faith has transformed my life and made it joyful and meaningful, where it was unhappy and meaningless before', but this statement, even if it is true for a given individual, has no necessary relationship with the truth of the religious belief which has produced that change. This has convinced some people that religion is in no way concerned with truth, and can only be understood or valued at the pragmatic level. It is, they would maintain, on a level with one's attitude to great art or classical music. One may have a taste for it or not, and the justification for its existence is simply that there are a number of people whose lives are enriched by it. It has little to do with reality.

Philosophy is also at an impasse, at least in this field, because any useful progress in metaphysics is generally held to be impossible. Immanuel Kant, in answering Hume, himself successfully demolished the possibility of using reason or intellectual knowledge as the basis for arriving at metaphysical truth, and metaphysics has never recovered from this mortal blow. Since then we have had, on the one hand, a series of anti-intellectual movements stemming from such thinkers as Schopenhauer, Bergson, William James and the existentialists and, on the other hand, the claims made for reason or intellectual knowledge by the philosophical schools that have still remained faithful to it. But amongst the latter, the claims made by such leading schools as the logical positivists or the advocates of logical analysis like Russell are now very modest indeed. They no longer hold that reason can give us any new knowledge; its rôle is at best to sort out muddled thinking and to correct errors due to faulty logic or the misleading use of language. Meanwhile scientific investigation has gone from strength to strength and is generally regarded as the only valid means to discover new truths.

I have begun by sketching in these well-known features of contemporary thought in modern Western society because it is against this background that we have to consider the relevance of the teachings of Yoga. A great deal of nonsense is nowadays talked about Yoga and you will see it advocated in the popular press as if it were a means to prolong youth or health or as a kind of glorified pelmanism to improve the powers of memory and concentration and ensure success in business. It is hardly necessary to say that much of this stems from cheap attempts by mountebanks to cash in on the gullibility of the public. A good many of the articles which recommend courses of Yoga exercises seem to be well-meaning and perhaps harmless attempts to make physical jerks more interesting and attractive by surrounding them with something of the aura of the mysterious East. But it is not for any of these reasons that Yoga deserves attention.

What is unique and important about the claim of the real Yoga in this day and age is that it is (as one of its leading modern exponents has expressed it) 'experimental religion' in the strict and proper sense of that term. In other words it offers not a static faith or even a way of life, but a technique of experimental verification of the truths which it teaches, which can be tested by the individual himself in the laboratory of his own personality. This is a claim easily made, but difficult to substantiate. So I want in this talk to try and consider some few aspects of the teachings of the Yoga of Self-knowledge so that you can get a clearer idea of its claims and presuppositions. I speak to you, not as an expert, but as one who was fortunate enough to have the opportunity of studying for many years under someone who undoubtedly was, Dr Hari Prasad Shastri.

Historically, the tradition of Yoga arises in the Hindu culture and first finds expression in the Upanishads which form the last part of the Vedas. Vedanta, the philosophy of Yoga, means literally the end of the Vedas in the sense of both the last part and the culmination of the Vedic teaching. The Indian tradition gave rise to a rich variety of philosophical schools expressing every kind of opinion from the most materialistic, represented by the Charvakas at one extreme, to the Advaita Vedanta schools whose most illustrious exponent was the philosopher Shankara Acharya who lived in about the eighth century AD. One of the most admirable features of the tradition was the practice of holding free public debates between the different schools, where criticisms could be freely made in an atmosphere of tolerance and respect for the truth.

Adhyatma Yoga follows the Advaita Vedanta tradition. It is of considerable interest that at the time of Shankara a very influential rival school of Vedanta, the Karma Mimamsakas, held that the sole function of the Vedic teaching was pragmatic. The individual was regarded as a man acting in the world in order to achieve the objects of his various desires. The rôle of the religious teaching in the Veda was simply to tell him of certain rituals and sacrifices by which he could achieve certain definite fruits either in this world or in the next. As against this view, the Advaita claimed that the teachings of Vedanta have a cognitive as well as a pragmatic value, that they have something to teach the individual about the nature of the reality behind the world and, above all, about his own nature. It was pre-eminently through the practice of Yoga that this knowledge was to be revealed.

This at once raises for the modern mind the question of what kind of knowledge could be provided in this way and of the relationship of such knowledge, if such there be, to the knowledge provided by science and empirical observation. This in turn brings up the question of verification. These are not easy questions to deal with briefly, but one important point can be made at the outset, because it is both obviously relevant and also a point usually totally ignored in Western thought.

It is this: Yoga stresses that the quality of our knowledge or of our vision of truth depends intimately on the state of our instruments of cognition, and that we have to examine the competence of the mind to arrive at a knowledge of the truth and also to find out the influences which disturb it or lead to its malfunctioning. Eddington reminds us of the dependence of our knowledge on the quality of our mind when he gives the example of the fishermen who go out to discover the nature of the creatures living in the ocean. After extensive investigation, they come to two conclusions:

(a) that all sea creatures are at least one inch in size and

(b) that all sea creatures have gills.

Both conclusions are, of course, wrong, though the data they had collected showed both to be correct without any exception. The first was simply a function of the size of the holes in their net, and the second followed from the fact that all sea creatures without gills happen to be smaller than this!

The point of the story is that it is perilous, even in empirical investigation, to ignore the limitations of our instruments. This is a point which is made by many mystics, not only of the Indian tradition. We would not dream of using a microscope or a telescope which we knew to be badly made or which had unevenly ground lenses, because they will distort anything we want to look at. But the yogis tell us that the mind can distort truth just as badly if it is dominated by prejudice and irrational impulses (the so-called vasanas or latent impurities). It is of great interest that many centuries before Freud they recognized that these latent deposits were stored in an unconscious part of the mind, behind the waking or dreaming experience, and were liable to emerge into our conscious mental life as overpowering passions or delusions.

Quite apart from such gross distortions, the lenses which we want to use to make accurate observations must be cleaned or they will not transmit light without obscuring and distorting it. In an analogous way the yogis say that we must refine and tranquillize the mind or it will not function well in grasping a subtle truth. An important defect in the mind is an inability to concentrate it, which again is related both to the presence of the disturbing irrational influences, likes and dislikes (mainly stemming from narrow self-interest) and also to our failure to cultivate the habit of controlling the mind. In the yogic literature the raw and uncontrolled mind is often compared to a wild horse which has not been broken in or disciplined and which, though potentially a fine mettlesome steed, is of little practical use to us until it has been brought under control and subjected to the bit and the spur so that we can direct it where we will. Even in the empirical sphere it is clear that the scientific ideal of an impartial observer is hardly attainable so long as the mind is not under our control. Unless we can concentrate it and direct it at will, and unless its innate irrational tendencies are curbed, it is not likely to be a very reliable guide to truth.

This teaching of Yoga has two important corollaries. It means that, although the Yoga aims to lead us to a deeper understanding of truth, we have got to set about changing ourselves, or at least our mental instruments of cognition, in order to bring it about, and it at once makes the inner life of feeling and ethical struggle relevant to the search for truth. This, of course, is quite alien to the now fashionable view, which regards all moral questions as ultimately a matter of feeling, and maintains that ethics are therefore utterly divorced from any relevance to truth or knowledge. Yoga on the other hand regards them as questions of vision, of our view of ourselves. In this respect, as in many others, Advaita Vedanta is much nearer the philosophical position of F H Bradley than of most other Western thinkers, though it would be wrong not to mention that there are important differences between the Bradleyan and Advaitic views of the world.

Moral questions are not simply problems of aesthetics or custom or the arbitrary conventions of society; they arise out of a conflict of desires within the individual, a conflict between what man feels that he is empirically and what he feels that he should be ideally. In other words they arise essentially out of a confused self-knowledge. Man does not know what he is (say the yogis); he is in a state of ignorance as to his own nature. Moral conflicts within his own being which testify to this uncertainty point beyond themselves to metaphysical and religious questions and pre-eminently to the question 'What am I?' The yogis anticipated William James and others in stressing the illusory nature of the many empirical selves which a man possesses as different aspects of his personality, the social selves which he presents to his family or his business associates or different circles of friends. All these have something of the quality of a rôle taken on, like the part assumed by an actor in a play, and they can hardly be called the essential Self of the individual. But, unlike David Hume or the Buddhist philosophers, Advaita Vedanta maintains that there *is* a real core within the personality, a true Self which can be known and realized in experience, though not as an object, which is one with the spiritual reality beyond the universe.

Most religious and spiritual traditions agree that the metaphysical truth which their doctrines teach is beyond comprehension by man's unaided mind. The Vedanta is no exception. It speaks of the spiritual reality behind the world, man's real Self, as beyond the reach of the intellect and speech. But it adds two important corollaries: first, that it is at the very core of the personality, within the mind of each and every man, and, secondly, that it can be known by direct experience, by what the yogis call enlightenment or knowledge (*jnana*). The *Kena Upanishad* says: 'That reality can neither be expressed in speech, nor thought of by the intellect, but it is that by which the mind thinks and speech is spoken. Know that to be God and not that which is worshipped as God by the people at large'.

There is good evidence that this knowledge of which the yogis speak has been gained by many of the greatest mystics in other traditions quite outside that of Yoga. This is indeed what we might expect, for, if the experience is possible, we should expect that the genuine and persistent seeker in any time and place will be a finder. But in many other religious traditions, not only is this knowledge not considered to be accessible to mankind at large, it is also regarded as a (to some extent) arbitrary result of the grace of the Deity. Moreover there is very little agreement about what exactly it is or how it is achieved and, above all, there is no evidence that there has ever been a genuine attempt in the West to treat this knowledge with scrutiny as a subject for philosophical enquiry and to try and find out its place in a philosophical system.

In India, Yoga and enlightenment has, on the contrary, been the central topic of interest in a long tradition of philosophical discussion and debate over many hundreds, if not thousands, of years, and many of the important questions concerning it have already been raised and considered in great detail. The interest of Yoga is therefore twofold: firstly, it claims a new source of knowledge which can be verified in practice and which promises to restore metaphysics as a fertile field of study for the human mind, and, secondly, it does this with the backing of an acute and subtle philosophy which allows the reasonableness of its claims to be considered objectively and with precision. It may be a mystical tradition, and it is certainly a religious one, but it is not vague or woolly-minded, and its claims (if they are accepted) are not merely of theoretical interest.

It is because of the great interest of Yoga philosophically that it has appealed to so many great minds in our

Western tradition who, even when they have had no intention of practising Yoga for themselves, have been deeply impressed by its philosophy. Schopenhauer said of the Upanishads 'They have been the solace of my life and they will be the solace of my death', and other great philosophical figures, like Deussen and Max Müller, were no less enthusiastic after a lifetime's study. But it is not only the philosophers who have been impressed by the teachings of Yoga. In this century one remembers a host of writers who have been deeply influenced by Vedantic thought, authors like Aldous Huxley, Gerald Heard, and even Isherwood and Somerset Maugham. Maugham is recorded as having said that though he himself was of the earth, earthy, the religious philosophy of Yoga was the only one which he thought merited serious consideration.

However, today it is rather to the scientists that we look as the guardians of truth. Even in this field one finds some of the greatest figures deeply impressed and influenced by Vedantic thought. Robert Oppenheimer is a case in point; but perhaps the best example is Erwin Schrödinger, the father of Quantum Mechanics and Nobel prize-winner who is an avowed believer in the philosophy of Advaita Vedanta. I think Schrödinger's writings on this subject have a particular interest in that he was led to believe in the Vedantic view by a consideration of the scientific evidence, in particular by what he calls the arithmetical paradox of the oneness of mind. Objectively we seem to have a plurality of egos, a multiplicity of conscious individuals and yet consciousness is never experienced in the plural. As he says:

> There is obviously only one alternative [to Leibniz's world-picture of a multiplicity of isolated, self-conscious monads], namely the unification of minds or consciousnesses. Their multiplicity is only apparent, in truth there is only one mind. This is the doctrine of the Upanishads. And not only of the Upanishads. The mystically experienced union with God regularly entails this attitude unless it is opposed by strong existing prejudices; and this means that it is less easily accepted in the West than in the East. Let me quote as an example outside the Upanishads, an Islamic-Persian mystic of the thirteenth century, Aziz Nasafi. I am taking it from a paper by Fritz Meyer and translating from his German translation:
>
>> 'On the death of any living creature the spirit returns to the spiritual world, the body to the bodily world. In this however only the bodies are subject to change. The spiritual world is one single spirit who stands like unto light behind the bodily world and who, when any single creature comes into being, shines through it as through a window. According to the kind and size of the window less or more light enters the world. The light itself however remains unchanged.'[1]
>
> He goes on to cite the surprising unanimity of mystics all over the world on their experience:
>
>> Ten years ago Aldous Huxley published a precious volume which he called *The Perennial Philosophy*[2] and which is an anthology from the mystics of the most various periods and the most various peoples. Open it where you will and you will find many beautiful utterances of a similar kind. You are struck by the

miraculous agreement between humans of different race, different religion, knowing nothing about each other's existence, separated by centuries and millenia, and by the greatest distances that there are on our globe.

Still, it must be said that to Western thought this doctrine has little appeal, it is unpalatable, it is dubbed fantastic, unscientific. Well, so it is, because our science—Greek science—is based on objectivation, whereby it has cut itself off from an adequate understanding of the Subject of Cognizance, of the mind. But I do believe that this is precisely the point where our present way of thinking does need to be amended, perhaps by a bit of blood-transfusion from Eastern thought. That will not be easy, we must beware of blunders—blood-transfusion always needs great precaution to prevent clotting. We do not wish to lose the logical precision that our scientific thought has reached, and that is unparalleled anywhere at any epoch.[3]

This passage makes it clear how relevant Erwin Schrödinger thinks the philosophy and teaching of Yoga is to modern Western society, and one could hardly cite a more impressive authority in science or Western thought.

2

The Religion of the Future*

There has been much talk in the last few years about the death of God and about the West having entered the post-Christian era. A prevalent (or perhaps one should rather say fashionable) view is that man has now outgrown religion which (it is said) was really only a feature of the more childish stages of human development. Of course, Sigmund Freud many years ago had already called religion an illusion, and the doctrine of materialism and atheism goes back much further than that, at least as far as the ancient Indian school of Charvakas or materialists who were flourishing—if one *can* flourish on this doctrine—at the time when the other schools of philosophy of Vedanta were being taught. But whereas Freud could write even forty years ago of *The Future of an Illusion*[1], there are many people nowadays who feel that it has no future at all.

What have the teachings of Yoga and Vedanta got to say on this subject? The Vedanta philosophy, on which Yoga is based, arose in a world very different from that in which we now live. At that time there was no question of any contact with modern scientific thought. But fortunately we have the authoritative view of someone who was well acquainted with both Yoga and science, because, early in 1902, one of the great modern yogis, Swami Rama Tirtha, went from India, first to Japan and then to America, to lecture on the teachings of Yoga and

* A lecture given on 29th March 1968.

Vedanta. In the course of that journey he said a great deal on the relevance of Yoga to the scientific thought of the modern world. In this lecture it is therefore proposed to consider in some detail the conclusions which he reaches. And it is worth remembering that we have here, not simply an opinion of one man rather than another, but the view of one who was himself an acknowledged master of Yoga and also an ex-professor of mathematics at an Indian University and a man who was very widely read in Western science and philosophy.

In almost the first lecture that he gave in Japan, Swami Rama said:

> The religion that Rama brings to Japan is virtually the same as was brought centuries ago by the followers of the holy Buddha. But the same religion requires to be dealt with from an entirely different standpoint to suit it to the needs of the present age. It requires to be blazoned forth in the light of Western science and philosophy.[2]

What Swami Rama is saying here is that the essential teaching of the Vedanta is as relevant as ever, but that its form of expression will need some modification to fit it for a scientific age.

Of course, you may say that Swami Rama speaks as an exponent of a system with which he is identified and naturally he is going to say that it is relevant to modern thought. As a committed adherent he is bound to regard it more favourably than any impartial outsider would. But I don't think this is necessarily the case. In this connection it is interesting to compare the comments on Vedanta written by a Western thinker who had all the impartiality and objectivity developed by his training as a High Court Judge in the British administration in India. Sir John Woodroffe became interested in the Vedanta philosophy, and particularly in that branch of it called Shaktivada, because he said it was something that he, as an Anglo-Indian, was always hearing being widely abused by people. And his training as a judge had taught him (he said) that whenever something was very extravagantly praised or extravagantly abused it was wise to examine the evidence more carefully to try and find out where the truth lay. As a result of his study he became a recognized authority on this particular branch of Vedanta. At the same time he became more and more convinced of its interest and subtlety and its relevance to modern thought, so much so that he was able to write in 1921:

> Indian philosophy and religion are too often treated in an archaeological way as things which have been and are gone, unrelated to and without value for current thought, and they do not receive the attention and respect which is their due. My own conviction is that an examination of the Indian Vedanta doctrine shows that it is in conformity with the most advanced scientific and philosophic thought of the West and that where this is not so, it is science which will go to Vedanta and not the reverse.[3]

Here, then, is someone completely outside the tradition (and a practising Catholic to boot, incidentally) who came to essentially the same conclusion which Swami Rama Tirtha had enunciated some twenty years before.

It is one of the doctrines of the *Bhagavad Gita* that

every object in the world partakes of a dual nature, being compounded of a mixture of the perishable and the imperishable. In other words, there is in each and every object an element which is passing and adventitious and also another element which is eternal. Swami Rama Tirtha is saying that the religious teaching is no exception to this principle. There is in it something which is of permanent value, a truth which will always be valid, but it is mixed with elements which are incidental and peculiar to the time and place in which the teaching was given. It is because of this passing and perishable element that the religious truths have to be expressed anew in each age.

Another teacher of Yoga, Shri Dadaji, a Brahmin by birth, clearly made a similar distinction when he taught that there is an essential central core of truth in all the great religious traditions, but that it is clothed in an outer tradition embodying various customs and rituals which owe much to the temporary historical conditions in which each of them first arose. He told his listeners:

> Islam is as true a religion as Hinduism. There cannot be uniformity of worship in mankind. There is no uniformity of dress, of ways of eating or of greeting, of marriage or of funeral rites... Why then should people quarrel with those who worship God in a different way from their own? Allah of the Koran is the same as Hari of Shrimata Bhagawata. The Hindus worship the Lord of the universe by using sacred images as their symbols; the symbol of Islam is an arch in empty space, but their God is one and the same. Different religions are different approaches to the same Deity. Their fundamental truths are

common. All great religions teach devotion, asceticism, charity and the importance of knowledge of God.[4]

The core of religion is one and the same in each and every great tradition. It is the passing and incidental dogmas which divide one religion from another. But what is the core of truth? This is what Swami Rama Tirtha has to say:

> Religion as distinguished from theology and divested of its dogmatic excrescences is essentially a mysterious process by which the mind or intellect reaches back and loses itself in the inscrutable source, the great beyond.... Not *a* religion, but *the* religion which is the soul of Islam, Hinduism or Christianity is, strictly speaking, that indescribable realisation of the unknowable where all distinction of caste, colour and creed, all dogmas and theories, the body and mind, time, space, and causality, together with all that is contained therein, this world and all other imaginable worlds are washed clean off into that which no words can reach. Is it mystifying? Not at all. Let any person of real religious experience refer to his moment of what is called communion and assert whether any idea of God, not to say of himself or the world, subsists there. In true realisation there is no *meum* and *tuum*, no trace of subject and object. Any systematic attempt leading to this goal is religious.[5]

This represents religion at its peak, the real object for which the saints and the incarnations have come to teach. But Swami Rama is not blind to the darker side of the history of religions. Where the perishable element takes precedence, religions can become a divisive force, stirring up conflict and enmity and dividing man from man. What *should* lead to a feeling of unity with all, leads to enmity and division. People often argue that if Vedanta were a source of valuable truth, India should not have been reduced to the state in which we find it. But Swami Rama says that it is precisely because India has failed to follow the real spirit of Vedanta that it has degenerated. He deplores the narrow sectarianism which characterized the India of his time, which denied the spirit of brotherhood and universal love, and compares it unfavourably with America, where, in spite of the existence of quite as many, if not more, sects and cults, the thought never replaces or subordinates the feeling of 'fellow-countrymanship' in the people at large. By contrast, in India, he says, religious sectarianism had clouded manhood in the people and eclipsed the sense of common nationality. The cause was 'blind identification with the dead forms of the past and abject slavery to the fantastic superstitions preached in the name of religion. In other words, spiritual suicide glossed over under the plausible name of obedience to authority.'[6]

Swami Rama has a good deal to say about the attitude to authority. For him (and he says it time and time again) the only real authority is truth verified directly for oneself in one's own experience. What one has tested in the fire of one's own life is what one ultimately believes in. This is not to say, of course, that one does not have to learn from others, from books and from example. But here modern man is in a different position. One should listen to what is said and judge it on its merits, adopting it as a working hypothesis, as one adopts the teachings of a book on chemistry or physics. The spiritual classics are authoritative in their field simply because they embody that personal spiritual experience of the sages which has given them an insight into the highest truth. The real Shruti, the genuine scriptural authority, is the direct knowledge (*jnana*) of the sages.

In this iconoclastic attitude to authority Swami Rama has truly adopted the attitude of Western science, well expressed by one of the greatest of nineteenth century physicists, James Clerk Maxwell, who was himself somewhat of a mystic. Clerk Maxwell said of authority: 'Nothing is to be *holy ground* consecrated to Stationary Faith, whether positive or negative'. And later, 'Again, I assert the Right of Trespass on any plot of Holy Ground which any man has set apart.'[7] What Clerk Maxwell is saying here is that one should be allowed to question, to investigate and to experiment in any region of truth.

Swami Rama Tirtha goes so far as to say that if religious teachings are adopted, it should be as a working hypothesis to be put into practice in one's own life, and not simply as an article of faith. The throwing over of the authority of the mediaeval Church was followed in Western history by an emphasis on the right of the individual to judge right and wrong in the light of his own conscience and to rely for revelation of the spiritual truth on that inner light of which the Quakers speak as the element of God hidden in each and every man. Swami Rama too indicates that man, in rejecting external authority, has to look for positive guidance to the light of mystical experience within his own being, obtained through meditation and the practice of Yoga. The truth will be revealed to him ultimately, not by any book or outer teaching. These are only aids. Swami Rama Tirtha is somewhat unorthodox and radical in the way he expresses this, compared with the earlier Advaitins. But Shri Shankara and his followers of the Advaita Vedanta school, also maintained that, as expressed in the spiritual classics, the truth could only be hinted at or indicated indirectly by words and that, no matter how inspired the book was, it could never directly express the truth. It could only be pointed at, so to speak. Nonetheless, Shri Shankara held that Shruti (scripture) was an authoritative source of spiritual knowledge for the ordinary man until it was superseded by direct experience.

Swami Rama Tirtha is more radical. In replying to a letter asking his opinion about the desirability of reviving the old *Yajna* ceremonies of the Vedas[8], he insists that we cannot return to old religious forms. We must not put the study of books above the study of facts.

> Shri Shankara's great mistake was in not emphasizing direct personal experience, than which there is no higher authority, in hiding his light beneath a bushel, in wasting his time torturing old texts to squeeze out of them the truth which he himself knew as a matter of personal realisation. Others came and did the same, but forcing their own meaning out of the helpless words of the same texts, the march of truth being hindered rather than helped thereby, making the living Self a slave to the ghosts of old books. Textual arguments, logic-chopping and chewing the dry bones of words were the result, and everyone

passes off what he has to say in the name of Shruti. O sages and seers of ancient Ind, has it come to this: that your sons shall have to settle questions concerning their immediate wants and present facts about themselves by the rules of grammar pertaining to a language no longer spoken! Laws and institutions are for man and not *vice versa*. Commenting on the old texts will not solve the difficulty. Too many patches and stitches are already added to the old garment. Can the discoveries of science be tacked on to the dogmas of the Christian Bible or other religious works as commentary? The original texts should be allowed to speak for themselves. Authority cannot establish truth. A simple mathematical truth gains no more weight if Christ, Muhammed, Buddha, Zoroaster, the Vedas and everyone else testify to it. The truth is to be known directly not to be believed in.[9]

At the beginning of the scientific tradition in the West Leonardo da Vinci expressed the same faith in experience as the test of truth when he said:

> Wisdom is the daughter of experience. First I shall test by experiment before I proceed further, because my intention is to consult experience first and then by reasoning show why such experience is bound to operate in such a way. And this is the true rule by which those who analyse the effects of nature must proceed.

Swami Rama extends the same principle not only to the effects of Nature but to the spiritual and religious sphere. One of the five points in which he summarized his teaching in America was:

> The sacred scriptures of all the world should be taken

in the same spirit as one studies chemistry, holding our own experience for ultimate authority.[10]

In a lecture delivered in San Francisco on January 26th 1903, a few weeks after his arrival in America, he urged his audience to take truth on its own merits, remembering that it is nobody's property. A religion should be accepted, not on account of its age, nor its newness, nor because it is believed by the vast majority of mankind, nor because it is held by some select minority, nor because it is held by a great renunciate (an ascetic), nor because it is held by a king, nor because it comes from a man of the highest character. We should accept a thing and believe in it, whether it is a religion or something else, on its own merits and see if it works. Examine it yourself, sift it (he says). The teachings of Buddha, Christ and Muhammed suited their times, not ours. Sell not your liberty to them. Be free to look at everything by your own light. Rama brings you Vedanta, not to name you Vedantins, but as a religion which is not only found in the Bible and in the most ancient scriptures but also in the latest works on philosophy and science, a matter of your whole life, the secret of success.[11]

When he was asked by one of the audience at a lecture in America if the future would see the emergence of one religion ruling all mankind[12], Swami Rama Tirtha first answered that religion should not rule, it should serve mankind, and then that there would indeed be one religion but that it would have no name. For names are precisely that which divides one religion from another. But whatever it is named, the religion of the future would be in essence the Vedanta, the religion of science, the universal religion, as he called it. But he added that man must not cling desperately even to the name Vedanta and what would be adopted would be the core of practical experience and the means to mystical experience in the teaching of Vedanta. He said that those who still believed in the idea of religion as a fixed dogma, a dogma which cannot change, should wake up, because religion in this sense will soon cease to exist. The study of science has opened people's eyes to what is going on in the higher spheres of knowledge, and such people have been freed from all subservience to creeds and dogmas. True religion is to free us not to bind us, he says. Rules represent just that element in religion which is perishable and must inevitably change if it is not to ossify and to degenerate. Unless renewed by experience, the form of a religious teaching becomes like a dead and lifeless carcass.

It is names in religions, he says, which lead to quarrels and misunderstandings. The prejudice against the name Vedanta or Yoga or the name Buddha, prevents people listening to the teachings, but in the twentieth century it is high time to rise above names. Names in religion are working great evil in the world. Buddhism has split India into four sects, China into seven. A man who says he is a Hindu will fight with a Christian or a Moslem simply because he wants to uphold the name Hindu, and so on. The modern scientific bent of mind can free man from this preoccupation with inessentials, if he will listen to it, and direct his mind to the essential experience which underlies true religion.

No sect or religion that has not come to an

understanding with the healthy humanising results of present day scientific research has the least right to prey upon its foolish votaries. Most of the different sets of religious dogmas and practices of the past were no more than the dictates of the known Science of the times. But as the fates would have it, these were received at first with bitter opposition, then with over-enthusiasm, so much so that the *mother* which gave birth to them, namely, independent thought and meditation, was ignored and killed in handling the child.

The teachings were gradually taken on trust; a boy found himself a Christian, Mohammedan, or Hindu before he was aware of being a man. Stagnation in the religious field was the natural consequence when, owing to the inertia and laziness of their followers, these dogmas and practices began to be accepted on the authority of personalities and volumes of paper, with little recognition or acceptance of the original research, diligence and concentration with which the original prophets had studied physical or spiritual nature and her laws. In time the teachings of the practical adherence to Christ's Sermon on the Mount or the Vedic Yajnas were in most cases discarded to all intents and purposes and their place taken by stronger allegiance to empty names. The spirit was actually driven out to worship the dead carcass.[13]

He goes on to say that the forms of the creed are not without their value in the economy of the world, but they are like the husk which is essential to the life and growth of the seed it covers during a certain stage of its development, but must be discarded or it becomes a choking prison for the germinating grain. The sprouting grain is of much greater value than the husk.

It was one of the tenets of the great German physicist, Max Planck, that science and religion were fighting a joint battle in human society, not with each other, but on the same side, 'a joint battle in an incessant, never-relaxing crusade against scepticism and against dogmatism, against disbelief and against superstition, and the rallying cry in this crusade has always been, and always will be: "On to God!"', meaning that truth or ultimate reality was the goal of both disciplines.[14] Religion is no true religion unless it teaches us that there is nothing sacred about our own particular prejudices.

Another final point in the teaching of Swami Rama Tirtha on this subject must be mentioned. Swami Rama says we are utterly wrong if we regard religion as one more thing that we can accumulate, as we accumulate property, skills, intellectual knowledge, or wealth, simply as an adornment or an unnecessary extra in our life. On the contrary, he says: 'Religion is as universal and as vitally connected with our being as the act of eating'.[15] And those who think that they are unconcerned with it and delude themselves that they are not religious because they are not interested in any institutionalized churches or creeds which may exist in the society in which they live, are quite wrong. For Yoga or Vedanta, the religious teaching concerns man's attitude and his understanding of his own nature, his belief about what sort of a being he is. And the truth of religion is the truth about his nature, a truth which exists independently of anything that he may choose to believe about it, but a truth which can be consciously investigated and discovered by him when he undertakes the enquiry into that nature through the practice of the Yoga of Self-knowledge.

In history one finds many great figures who have been deeply religious in this sense and yet have had no interest in any of the institutionalized religions of their day. Goethe for example was a deeply religious man as you can find through reading many of his works, but he had no use for the churches of his time. Beethoven was another very religious person who was not a member of any church or creed; but he had framed on his desk a text taken from an Egyptian source which in translation read: 'I am all that was, that is and that shall be; no one has ever lifted my veil'.

Some of you may have seen the programme on the Russian writer Boris Pasternak this week; someone again who, living in a materialistic society, was deeply imbued in his art and his work with the spirit of religion, but for whom the ordinary forms of religion had little value or meaning.

The atheist and the materialist, says Rama Tirtha, are like the man who doesn't know the process of his own digestion. He does digest food just like anybody else but he doesn't know about it. The life of which religion is speaking—the truth which it has to tell him about his own being—is there whether he is awake to it or not. But he is unaware that these laws of his being are operating and denies their existence.

One can appreciate from these words of Swami Rama Tirtha that, in the teaching of Vedanta, religion is not something which is confined to one little compartment of life, nor is it a faith which is adopted and accepted as a dogma to which one subscribes. It is an experimental science dealing with the investigation of man's own nature, concerned with answering the question 'What am I?' And it is the teaching of the Yoga that the answer to this question can be discovered in the being of man himself through traditional methods, and that this Self-realization brings inner balance and peace and the ability to transmit these to those around one and, in that way, to influence for good the whole world.

3

The Vedantic View of the World*

Slowly, almost unobserved, that spark of ancient Indian wisdom which the marvellous Rabbi had kindled to new flame beside the Jordan, flickered out. The light faded from the reborn Sun of Greece, whose rays had ripened the fruits we now enjoy. The people no longer know anything of these things; most of them have nothing to hold on to and no one to follow. They believe neither in God, nor gods. To them the Church is now only a political party, and morality nothing but a burdensome restriction which, without the support of those no longer credible bugbears on which it leant for so long, is now without any basis whatsoever. A sort of general atavism has set in. Western man is in danger of relapsing to an earlier level of development which he has never properly overcome. Crass unfettered egoism is raising its grinning head; and its fist, drawing irresistible strength from primitive habits, is reaching for the abandoned helm of our ship.

These words were written, in the autumn of 1925 by Erwin Schrödinger, one of the most creative and profound thinkers of our century. Since then it seems as if we have gone very much further down the slippery slope which Schrödinger is describing.

---

* A lecture given on 30th October 1970, based on some ideas from Erwin Schrödinger's early essay 'Seek for the Road', published in *My View of the World*, Cambridge University Press, 1964.

The Book of Exodus tells how, as soon as the children of Israel left Egypt, other troubles began, and, when Moses went up to the top of Sinai to commune with God, the people began to become restive. They went to Aaron, who was their leader at the time, and asked him: 'Make us gods to worship, for Moses has disappeared and we don't know what has happened to him'. And Aaron told them to bring all the gold and jewellery that they had, and melted it down, and fashioned it into a golden calf. And it was set up on the altar and worshipped. In many ways we are like the children of Israel today.

For the vast majority of mankind, spiritual wisdom, which Moses represented, has disappeared out of sight, and they no longer think anything of it, nor indeed about it. But they rush to the leaders and thinkers of the day and ask them to supply them with a substitute to worship, and from the material achievements of our technological society these leaders fashion some new graven image. They may be told to worship science; they may be told to worship the state; or they may be told, as they are by the humanists, that the object of their worship should be man—ordinary man as he is. They may be told to worship Chairman Mao or Che Guevara. And they are told by the people who give them this advice that these God-substitutes are the things which will bring them all the good and all the benefits that they require. And, of course, a lot of people bow down and worship before these idols.

One has to ask where these graven images are produced. Where is the mould which fashions these gods out of the melted-down substance of the world? And the answer quite clearly is that that mould is the mind of man. When it no longer recognizes the supremacy of the highest good, and does not turn towards the highest spiritual wisdom, then the Aaron of individualism takes over—not as a true leader, but as a misleader of men—and fashions from the materials at hand these false gods. And very often these gods are simply a cloak for the power desires or ambition of the person who has fashioned them. If one asks what was the real meaning and significance of the Nazi philosophy, it was largely a cloak for the ambition of Hitler and the thugs he collected around him. If one asks what is the real motive of the governments in the totalitarian states of the Soviet Empire, it is to serve the interests of the small oligarchic groups which rule these countries and allow them to maintain their power. So often the false gods are simply a façade behind which the few hide their self-interest, while they impose their will on the many.

One of the diagnostic signs of the human ego at work is its totalitarian tendency. Whenever one finds a philosophy which excuses intolerance on the grounds that its way is the only right way, and that all other ways are criminal and wrong, then one can readily discover, without much probing, the human ego lurking in hiding behind the mask. The façade may be very philosophical and superficially reasonable, but the driving force is that arch-tyrant—the raw and uncontrolled mind of man— which sees every object and every individual as useful, just in so far as they serve its own purposes. Even many 'movements' which start idealistically become corrupted in this way because their leaders have not got real spiritual insight. Because of the quality of their minds, they lack the wisdom necessary to sustain the idealism of the early founders of the movement.

This is certainly something of the explanation for the change which Schrödinger describes. What then are we to do? The answer is quite simple: it is to bring Moses back, to learn the importance and the value of the spiritual wisdom—not running to it like a coward simply from fear, to use it, as the children of Israel were willing to use Moses, when they found that things were not going well again, as a kind of lucky charm—but, by trying to follow and understand it, to gain the vision needed to deal with our present dilemma. And the first thing we have to do in order to achieve this, is to learn that we are subject to dangerous illusions.

Sigmund Freud was wrong in a vital respect in his attitude to religion. Freud said that religion was something which imposed an illusion on man, but the reality of the fact is that religion is the one force capable of freeing man from illusions—from the illusions of temporal power; from the illusions of ambition, the desire to achieve domination over our fellow men; from the illusions of achieving happiness through unlimited wealth, through unbridled individualism. The spiritual teaching is in fact the only really effective power to combat these serious misconceptions which the mind develops, when it banishes the Moses of wisdom and turns away from metaphysics.

Man must direct his mind towards this region of transcendence. The search for reality, for valid knowledge, whether it is in science or elsewhere, is a search for what is abiding. When the scientist in his laboratory seeks the scientific law, what he wants to find is the invariable in the variable, the universal in the particular. Newton, sitting in the orchard in Grantham in Lincolnshire, saw the apple fall from the tree. But, unlike most of us, he did not simply see it as a chance happening, just as another unremarkable incident—another windfall! He saw it as a manifestation of the same force which kept the planets on their courses round the sun, the same force which explained the phases of the moon, which accounted for the occurrence of the tides. There is one law, and in the unity of that law all these phenomena are predicted and explained. This is seeing the universal in the particular, the invariable in the variable. Hundreds of apples fall, but the law remains the same. So in Vedanta, in the Yoga philosophy, reality is defined as that which remains unchanged throughout the three divisions of time—the invariable element.

When the physicist asks the question: 'What is the nature of the world?', he is asking what it is made of—what is the real substance behind the appearances that we see around us? In the inorganic sphere the abiding element *prima facie* is matter. Whereas the particular forms that matter takes are transient and ephemeral, the matter itself is indestructible. The nineteenth century view was that the whole world is made up of the series of ninety-two indestructible elements, combined in different ways as molecules and compounds.

It is like the Vedantic simile of the ornaments made of gold. The substance, gold, abides unchanged, but the form in which we find it changes. It may be sometimes in the shape of an ornament; sometimes in the form of a necklace; sometimes in the form of a statue; but always the substance remains. However, further enquiry into the nature of matter reveals that the elements are not permanent, but that they are made up of entities which do seem to be permanent, namely the protons, the electrons and the neutrons. And then further analysis again suggests that even these entities are made up of yet smaller fundamental particles, the six varieties of quarks.

But when one turns from the inorganic world to the realm of living things the situation is completely different. If one asks then what is the essential nature of the living thing, the one thing that is quite clear is that it is *not* the matter of which it is composed. In fact the matter in the living creature continually changes. The substance of our body has virtually been replaced over the last few years—certainly it has changed many times during our life. Here, at first sight, it is not the substance which abides; it is the form which abides. And if we take an analogy from the inorganic world, then the living organism is in a sense like an individual wave passing over the surface of a pool of water. At any moment different particles of water are making up the crest or the trough of that wave, and the wave passes on, and other particles become the crest or the trough of the wave. But the wave has an individuality although the water of which it is made up is continually changing. It maintains its identity although it passes through and beyond any one particular part of the water and moves on to the next sequentially.

So in the living being, the matter of which its body is made up, like the particles of water in the wave, is continually changing. New atoms come and take the place of the present ones and in turn pass through. What seems to abide is the form of the body; but if one takes the analysis a stage further, even the physical form does not really abide. The organism is born, it grows, it passes through all the stages of life: infancy, childhood, youth, adulthood, and then on into old age. And so form too changes and is not really the persistent, *in*-variable element in the living thing. Some people may say: 'Ah, but you are missing the point. What really abides is the genetic blue-print. We now know that it is this little element in the nucleus which is the plan on which the whole individual is based.' Even if this were accepted (and the blue-print is not the person anyway) this too changes. There are many different ways in which the blue-print can change, well known to the geneticists.

What other candidates can we consider for the rôle of the abiding entity in the living thing? One to be seriously considered is thought, and, more particularly, memory. Thought sometimes lasts longer even than the individual body which is thinking it. The thought of people long since dead still influences us, because they have left it behind expressed and contained in their writings. So in that sense thought is very long-lasting. But even in the living person the world of thought persists, and it is particularly memory which gives an abiding unity to the contents of our experience in life. But even a moment's consideration reminds one that the form and content of thought is tremendously transient. It changes far faster than the body, for instance. The thoughts that we had yesterday, or last week, have gone, and we are thinking differently now. Much that we ought to remember has been forgotten, and our memory of our experiences or ideas is lost without our having lost our individuality, or our life. Moreover, if one tries to say that it is memory which gives identity to the individual, then one has to take into account that there is a very good case that some of our 'memories' are supra-individual. Instincts in animals are undoubtedly a form of race-memory. When a bird for the first time builds its nest, it may never have seen another bird building the nest, but it is (so to speak) remembering how to do it. There is something in the organism—a trace left from the past experience of the species—which leads to this wonderful memory, which allows it to build a nest which is exactly the right size, and of exactly the right properties for rearing the eggs which it may not yet have had experience of. This is an example of supra-individual memory. It may not be conscious (this is a different question) but it is a trace left from the past experience of other individuals in the make-up of the organism.

Thought and memory are transient and changing, and not abiding. And they don't provide the elements which we can identify as the invariable—the abiding element in the living organism. More fundamental than thought or memory is self-consciousness, the sense of 'I' which gives identity to the living thing and persists unchanged through its waking life. But what is the nature of this consciousness? What can we say about it if we approach it as the scientist approaches matter, or as the psychologist approaches mind? One thing we can certainly say about it is that consciousness is nowhere experienced in the plural. We may infer that there are other people who are also conscious, certainly, but it is never actually experienced in the plural. We certainly experience a plurality of bodies, in that we see many other bodies around us; and there is a plurality in the contents of our mind, in that we experience its many thoughts and moods, but consciousness itself is only experienced as a unique, non-plural and non-dual entity.

We have the idea that the unity of the self, of this self-consciousness, is dependent upon the unity of the body. This is the *prima facie* view. But we find that this idea leads to a series of paradoxical questions. The first one is: 'When did consciousness begin? At what moment in our life did consciousness start? Is it before the birth of the baby? Is it at some particular point after birth?' There seems to be a gradual awakening of consciousness in a baby, and there doesn't seem to be any reason why there should be a particular point where it begins. The germ plasms of the cells in the mother and the father join; they are living before they join, they are living after they join. And there is continuous development of those cells into the body of the child. There is no evidence of any discontinuity; nothing to correlate obviously with the appearance of the conscious individual. There is no sudden appearance of life, which continues uninterruptedly in parent and offspring.

Then we have another paradoxical question: 'When does consciousness cease to be associated with parts of the body, not only in death, but even during life?' Supposing we have a finger amputated; supposing we give a kidney for someone, perhaps a near and dear relative who needs a transplant in order to survive. Part of the living cells of our body have been transplanted into another body: is this organ suddenly deprived of the consciousness which we suppose to be associated with our body? Are there two consciousnesses in the person who has the transplant? These are paradoxical questions. Nowadays we can keep tissues alive in tissue culture indefinitely. A few cells from the skins of people have been kept alive and grown artificially long after they have died. How does one explain this, if the consciousness is simply associated with the body? This is another paradox.

Schrödinger says these sorts of questions have the mark of being pseudo-questions, because the premise on which we are basing these questions is wrong. It is not a fact that the idea of the unity of the self is dependent on the unity of the body. Consciousness is not dependent on the body. If you go to the very simple organisms like the hydra or planarians you find you can cut them in half again and again and each little bit will grow into a complete individual. Some people may say that there is no consciousness in a hydra, and it is fruitless to argue with them. But this again is another problem. When *are* living things conscious if you don't admit these primitive organisms have any consciousness? When did consciousness begin? Was it sudden? If we associate consciousness with the body we are landed continually with such problems, which are all to do with mathematics. If you say consciousness is 'here', and it is associated with this object, then when I cut the object in half there must be two consciousnesses. But it is not so, because there is no real multiplicity of consciousness—this is the Vedantic doctrine. Consciousness is never experienced in the plural because there is no real plurality of consciousness.

'Well', you may say, 'that's all very well, but I'm not aware of the thoughts going on in other people's minds. I only know the thoughts in my own mind; this proves that there is plurality in consciousness'. But it no more proves there is plurality in consciousness than the fact that there are many things in your own mind of which you are not conscious proves that you have more than one mind. Many memories are still lurking in your unconscious mind—many things which you have at present forgotten but which are part of your mind.

In the Vedantic view, as in modern science, the individual consciousness in the mind is a result of the possession of a central nervous system. It is only animals with a central nervous system which behave as self-conscious beings. The reason for this, in the old Vedantic terminology, is the possession of an *antahkarana*—an 'organ of inner experience', as the yogis call it. This *antahkarana* has the property of reflecting in the mind the consciousness which really transcends the mind. It is the reflection of consciousness in the many minds which are evolutes of subtle matter which gives the appearance of many egos in the world, which leads to the separate individualistic lives and to the appearance of a multiplicity of minds. And the aim of Yoga is to penetrate behind this apparently separate empirical consciousness to the underlying unity of the real Self, to the region of transcendence which is implicit in our experience but which we are unaware of until we turn towards it.

So, according to the Yoga, the essential abiding element behind both the living world and the non-living world is this transcendent element of awareness or Consciousness; not the empirical consciousness which changes and seems to come and go; not the consciousness which is now asleep, now awake, and now dreaming; but the underlying element—the real Consciousness behind the mind which, as the Upanishad says, 'is awake in those that sleep'.

What are the practical consequences of this metaphysical view? We have to seek this Reality. We have not to be led astray by the illusion, by the wrong suggestion of experience, by the Aarons who offer us the false gods. And there are very great ethical implications in this metaphysic. One can say that the ethical vision is only a reflection of the spiritual vision. The only really firm basis for ethics in human society is this spiritual vision, because it is an antidote for all the dangerous illusions that arise from rampant individualism. The spiritual vision is a vision of unity and transcendence, a recognition that we are all members one of another. It is for this reason that the enlightened man, according to the Yoga, cannot but live intent on the welfare of all beings. All beings *are* his Self. 'A man who sees his Self in all beings and yet feels that he has enemies, desires surely to make fire cold', says Shri Shankara. It is an impossibility. If a man has really penetrated to this Knowledge of Self, of the one

Consciousness in all beings, he doesn't have the feeling: 'Ah, over there is another person who threatens my interests, who is a potential enemy, who is a danger to me as an individual'. He doesn't feel this. He has the vision that all beings are One; that the same Self is the Self of all beings.

Man must ultimately take his stand on the spiritual Reality within him and recognize its realization as the most valuable achievement he can make, the real *summum bonum* of life, because where one's wealth is, there will one's heart be also. If man catches only a glimpse of this spiritual wealth then it will irresistibly attract him. One of the great modern yogis, Swami Rama Tirtha, says that effort must be made to instil into the hearts of all the awareness of this Divinity of the real Self. 'Let it sink deep into your hearts day by day', he says, 'let it penetrate your minds hour by hour, and you will see, according to the scientific laws, that this energy—this which appears to be vain speculation—will transform itself into the most noble activity on your part. And this knowledge you will see transforming itself into happiness and bliss for you'.

4

The Inner Enquiry*

One of the greatest benefits that modern man enjoys is the benefit of education, but there are two fundamentally opposed kinds of education which are current in the world today. There is the education which aims to inculcate useful knowledge, and to teach people what to think so that they can best serve the interests of the state and the rulers of society. Such education—and it is the education which is currently being provided, for instance, in Soviet Russia, or in Communist China—will provide man with many useful skills. It may be very efficient in making the population literate in reading, writing and arithmetic, and in teaching the more intellectually-gifted members of the population those technological skills which will enable them to be good servants of the community, in the factory, or even in government-directed research. But it will fail—and it will fail utterly—to make them really creative, particularly in the field of fundamental research and discovery. And it will do so for the very simple and definite reason that the deliberate policy of this type of education, overt or covert (for it may not willingly admit it), is to stifle the spirit of free enquiry.

Free enquiry represents, in the eyes of authority, something that is wasteful, inefficient, and disruptive of planned programmes and planned development. But in trying to stifle that spirit of free enquiry, this short-sighted policy cripples man by stunting the development of what

* A lecture given on 4th December 1970.

all the spiritual teachers in the Yoga tradition—and indeed many great thinkers in human history—have regarded as the highest and most typically human faculty—the desire to know. Aristotle says that the real feature which distinguishes man is this desire to know. So the most important feature of real education (of the second type of education as opposed to indoctrination) is to inculcate and develop this spirit of free enquiry, and to enable man to understand and create those conditions in which this enquiry can be effectively exercised.

Swami Rama Tirtha points out that education comes from the Latin roots '*ex*' and '*duco*'. It means to lead out; to draw out the hidden truth from the mind of man; not to indoctrinate, but to lead to this spirit of enquiry through which the truth can be sought and found.

The greatest discoveries of truth in human history are almost always unexpected. If you think about it and carefully examine the records, you will find that the really important discoveries have almost always been unpredicted. This does not mean to say that they were not prepared for. Their discovery is often the result of prolonged efforts of the human mind to grapple with the unsolved problems which face it, and of the willingness of the individual to question the accepted dogmas. Even the great technological discoveries of our own day, for instance, like jet air propulsion or television, which are a commonplace now and of which we all enjoy the fruits, began and remained for many years only the crazy, way-out enthusiasms of eccentric individuals, who devoted their lives to them because they believed in the development of these particular things. To develop television John Logie Baird worked on his own for years with very little money and under great difficulties because he believed in its possibility. If you go to the Science Museum you can still see the primitive equipment with which he first demonstrated it as a practical possibility. But it was not until many years later that these ideas were generally accepted and led to the world-wide television network which we now all make use of. Exactly the same thing is true of jet air travel. Originally it was regarded by many as a crazy, eccentric enthusiasm. Some of the older ones among us can still remember a time when Frank Whittle was known as someone who 'had a bee in his bonnet', because he believed in the future of jet travel. But now we all depend on it and take it for granted. So even in the purely technological field these things often arrive unexpectedly on our doorstep through the efforts of a few individuals who have unusual ideas which turn out, against all the predictions of the majority of the community or the authorities of the State, to be fruitful and successful and are then eagerly adopted.

The moral of this is that, whenever and wherever only officially approved thoughts are encouraged or allowed, the authorities become the enemies of the human spirit, whether they are theologians or dialectical materialists—it makes no difference! If this spirit of enquiry is stifled in man, then what follows is a kind of death for the human spirit. But the yogis tell us that, as well as authoritarian indoctrination by education or by propaganda, there are also inner enemies to this spirit of free enquiry. There is a lazy side of the mind which lulls us into an easy acceptance of comfortable prejudice.

Our teacher, Dr Shastri, used to say that when we

associate with our illusory desires, we begin to lose our inquisitiveness—our desire to know. And, as Socrates points out, that loss of the spirit of wanting to know is akin to a kind of death. The real 'opiate of the people' in the Marxian sense, is not so much religion, but the indulgence in sense-pleasures, because this indulgence diverts man into a kind of lotus-land of illusion, which is ultimately unproductive and unsatisfying. And it diverts him from this voyage of discovery which he has to make, through the spirit of enquiry. Man must be ever on the move to evolve through self-transcendence, by climbing higher and higher.

In the world today we are surrounded by many forms of creeping totalitarianism. The totalitarianism of the Right, and also the totalitarianism of the Left, and that other totalitarianism of the anarchists who want to totally destroy all institutions, whatever others may think or prefer. All these points of view may appear very arresting, dramatic, and even, to those who have not thought things out clearly, very interesting. But it is the less immediately interesting and arresting middle-way which marks out the only course of reason and sanity for mankind. According to the yogis, skilful living is balanced living. There is no future for man in the path of extremism or revolution. As the *Bhagavad Gita* says: 'Yoga is for him whose eating and recreation are moderate; who practises moderation in his actions, and in his sleep, and in his waking, and who above all maintains a balanced mind'.

Those who believe in this undramatic cultivation of equanimity and harmony may be accused by the revolutionaries, whether of the Right or Left, of hypocritical indifference to social ills, or indifference to the menace of revolution. But these are all unthought-out slogans. No possible good can come to man from extremes, whether such action succeeds or fails, and this can be clearly seen from the historical cases, not only of the French Revolution, but of the Russian Revolution, the Chinese, and many others. These revolutionary movements which started by aiming at freedom for the oppressed, invariably and inevitably ended by imposing something far worse, replacing what had been overthrown with a far more ruthless totalitarian tyranny than had existed before. All three ended in dictatorships—the French Revolution in Napoleon, the Russian in Stalin and the Chinese in Mao. It is worth remembering the bitter disillusionment of Beethoven who, when he thought that Napoleon was going to be the great champion of freedom in Europe, dedicated the Eroica Symphony to him. Then, shortly after he had finished it, he heard that Napoleon had had himself proclaimed Emperor, and he scored out the dedication in such fury that there is actually a hole in the title page of the manuscript score, where Beethoven has expressed the depth of his disillusionment, that what had started, as he had hoped, as a revolution for freedom had become merely another form of tyranny.

Therefore, the essential teaching of Yoga is that the highest activity which man can undertake, is what is called in Sanskrit, *vichara*, enquiry, and the supreme object of that enquiry is self-knowledge. One reason that enquiry must be free and open-ended, is that it needs a great effort to overcome the prejudices and preconceptions which already exist in our present empirical ways of thinking. The experts in any field are always deeply suspicious of any new idea. One cannot say it is wrong, because they know from personal experience how easy it is to make a mistake, and they cling to that body of solid and well-tried theory (not only theory, but also practical know-how) which they have accumulated and tested. But if advances are to be made, we have to have an open mind; we have to be open to new ideas, because no empirical knowledge is final. Revolutions in thinking are usually somewhat uncomfortable, which is another reason why people resist them. But unless Charles Darwin had been open to accept the evidence for evolution, which he saw on his voyage round the world, we might still be believing in the doctrine of special creation, and the whole of modern biology would not have taken place. Unless Michelson and Morley at the end of the last century had been open-minded enough to accurately observe, and accept the extraordinary phenomenon which their experiments disclosed, there would have been no Theory of Relativity by Einstein. As is well-known, Michelson and Morley in this experiment simply wanted to measure the speed of light through the ether, and they set up a very accurate experiment to do so. They planned to measure it in two directions: one when they were going towards the source of light, and the other case when they were going away from it (I am simplifying a little, but this is the essence of the experiment). And of course, as in passing another moving car, if the car is travelling towards you, then the relative speed is much higher than when you are travelling in the same direction as the car. So they expected to get two completely different measurements for the speed of light, according to whether they were going towards the source or away from the source, and their results were apparently nonsense. They found the speed of light was the same whichever way they went. This made absolutely no sense, and was such blatant nonsense according to current scientific orthodoxy, that it would undoubtedly have been unacceptable, not publishable, and instantly ridiculed in any totalitarian educational system. If they had worked in a system in which one was taught what is correct, there is no question that these results would not have been accepted. After they were published, they remained unexplained for many years. But it was as a result of this extraordinary and ridiculous state of affairs (a conclusion that even an intelligent child would not accept because it made such nonsense) that Einstein started thinking, and trying to puzzle out what on earth the results could mean. The data could be seen to have been well-measured, and repeated attempts had always arrived at the same result. As a result of this enquiry he produced his Theory of Relativity which completely exploded the, until then, universally accepted Newtonian picture of absolute space and time. It is a very good illustration of the need for free enquiry, and the need to be open to the results of careful observation and experiment; to accept the truth even when it conflicts with our preconceptions. The only thing in favour of the Michelson and Morley result was that it happened to be true.

According to the Yoga the same principle is no less true in the spiritual as in the scientific world. Yoga is concerned with the inner enquiry, and its aim is self-knowledge. And if the yogis are to be believed, its successful pursuit involves the overthrow of our most deeply entrenched preconceptions about our own nature: the preconception—if not the innate conviction—that we are the body, or the mind, and the accompanying belief that the world, as it appears to us empirically, is the ultimate reality.

But it must not be thought that because enquiry has to be free and untrammelled by the preconceptions in our mind, that there are therefore no qualifications for that enquiry—that everyone is equally able at any time to undertake the enquiry into truth. This is very far from the case. Enquiry demands as a prerequisite a prepared, controlled and purified mind. The raw mind is too full of prejudices and bad habits to be able to be focused properly on a problem in order to see it clearly. Therefore preparation and purification of the mind through meditation, and the discipline of mind-control, play a vital part in the life of the yogis, because of the need to prepare the mind for this enquiry.

Let us say something about meditation. According to our teacher, Dr Shastri, it involves three major factors: relaxation, concentration, and merging the mind in the enquiry into truth. It is not limited to those who practise Yoga. If one consults the accounts of how a really great mathematician sets about thinking about a problem, the first thing that he needs is relaxation. He needs inner peace. He cannot think creatively if his mind is in a state of agitation and turmoil. And until the mind is controlled—and in any great mathematician it is controlled through long practice of mathematics—the will is a captive to the wayward desires and impulses, thoughts and impressions, which bubble up in a never-ending stream from the unconscious. The greatest things in life, said our teacher, are achieved, not by strained effort, but by effortless effort—by self-forgetfulness, when the will has focused the mind and then abdicated. First of all, the will has to be brought into play to focus the mind, but then comes the stage where the mind has been focused effectively and the will can abdicate, leaving the field of mental consciousness to be totally absorbed in the object of contemplation. And when that state is reached—the state of the focused will-less mind (whether in the field of art, or mathematics, or, through Yoga, in the field of spiritual truth)—the mind achieves what is called 'effortless effort', and becomes really creative.

In the early stages of the Yoga practice, relaxation can be induced consciously in the mind by taking a few deep breaths, while counting each breath. The aim is to cultivate the natural, effortless concentration of the mind. But initially one has not yet achieved this, and one wants to acquire relaxation and loss of tension. So the method is to sit in the meditation posture and to breathe deeply in and out, and to count the breaths, say twenty-one times. In this way the mind is to a great extent pacified and relaxed, and then one can go on to further stages in the meditation, of concentration and merging.

You may ask: 'How can one achieve effortlessness by conscious efforts of will? Isn't it a contradiction in terms? Isn't it contradictory to talk about applying the will to the mind in meditation, and say that you want to achieve effortlessness?' But this question—this supposed difficulty—rests on a fallacy. If you go to see a very good juggler, the way in which he manages to keep all the balls in the air is apparently effortless. There is a sense of ease and effortlessness in it, although one knows perfectly well that this effortlessness is the result of long-continued practice, in the course of which he has had to make great efforts of will and successfully overcome many failures. If you go and hear a very great pianist playing a study of Liszt or Chopin, you hear with amazement the brilliant, effortless, fast finger work, which is sometimes hardly credible, particularly nowadays, when technique has reached such a peak of perfection. It sounds effortless, and it appears effortless. But one knows that this is only achieved by hours of long practice, often over weeks or years. So it is through the efforts of the will and long practice that the state of effortlessness is reached.

In the first chapter of the Yoga classic, *Panchadashi*, the process is described in this way:

> To find out the real meaning of the text 'That Thou Art', three methods are necessary. Enquiry and listening with reverence and faith to a traditional explanation of its meaning. Dwelling seriously on it and its explanation, and placing it under the scrutiny of reason in silence. And when enquiry and reflection bring about a firm and undoubted conviction, then allowing the mind to dwell constantly on the Self thus ascertained, in unbroken meditation. When the mind arrives at the higher stage of contemplation, it is like the flame of a lamp placed in a windless spot. All distinctions between the meditator and the meditation are merged in the one great object of meditation—that

is the Self. This state of super-consciousness is called *samadhi*. At the time of *samadhi* the will is not applied to the process of meditation on the Self. The mind achieves the state of *samadhi* as a result of the efforts of will made previously, prior to its achievement.

This passage puts the matter very clearly. Effort expended in the early stages of the practice of the meditation in Yoga, is designed to lead to that effortless mastery of the mind in the final stages of the practice.

St Teresa of Avila illustrates the same thing when she speaks of the soul as being like a garden, watered by the spiritual light, which keeps it verdant and is necessary to its growth and well-being. All that the garden produces is dependent on the supply of water which is brought to it. In this way, man is dependent spiritually on his contact with this water of spiritual knowledge and peace which comes from within his own being. At the beginning of his spiritual path, this water has to be brought very laboriously, carried by hand (as it were) with the expenditure of much hard effort. When we begin to meditate—as soon as the mind is restrained and focused—distractions start to arise. Some irrelevant idea intrudes itself into our consciousness, and the mind must again be focused by an effort of will and brought back gently to the meditation. This (says St Teresa) is like carrying the water from the well by hand in a bucket. It is very hard work. You bring the bucket, usually spilling some of the water on the way, and, when you get there, one bucket doesn't go very far. Very soon, if one doesn't expend a lot of energy and effort in going to and from the well to fetch more of the water, the garden grows dry again, and becomes unproductive.

This illustrates very well the early stages of the meditation, when we need to continually re-focus the mind again and again, while it strays away pursuing one distraction after another. But as the meditation deepens, the second stage is entered when one does not any longer need to bring the water by hand with a bucket. At this stage one has a water-wheel at the well with a whole series of buckets on it, feeding water into an irrigation canal. One still has to turn the wheel by hand, so effort is needed and the watering will only occur when the wheel is being actively turned. Every drop of water which comes up does so because of the effort expended in turning the wheel, but the whole process is much more efficient and effective. At this stage the will is exerted on the mind, and only while the will keeps the mind focused will the meditation yield results, but the same effort is much more productive, and the exertion much less onerous, than when the water was being carried in a single bucket.

In the third stage, as one gains more mastery of the technique, the meditation deepens and becomes habitual. It then becomes like watering the garden by simply diverting an already-flowing stream. All that is necessary is to divert the stream in the right direction, and once it has been actively diverted, then the watering goes on automatically without further effort. At this stage an effort of will is still needed to begin the meditation, but once the mind has been focused and the meditation begun, it does not need any further effort of will to maintain it. There are no distractions and the meditator is becoming really expert. But this (St Teresa says) is still not the final stage of meditation. The final stage (which is spoken of in Yoga as *samadhi*—the state of super-consciousness) is reached when the will no longer has to do anything and abdicates its rôle in the meditation altogether. In this stage the garden is watered by the rain from on high. It is no longer necessary to make any effort of will in order to get the benefit of meditation, and, in addition, the benefit is far greater. The watering of the garden by the rain is far more effective and beneficial, and its results are far more creative than any of the other methods. And this is the real goal of the meditation practice.

The experience of every beginner in Yoga is that relaxation can only come, initially, by effort. And it is hard work to achieve such temporary relief from the constant tensions and anxieties of the everyday mental consciousness. But the relief grows with cultivation, just as St Teresa says it does, and the more the mind taps the inner source of peace and light, the stronger it will become. The more readily the mind returns to this state of inner equanimity and balance, the greater is the influence of this inner peace, which will gradually permeate the mind, not only at the time of the meditation, but during the whole of daily life.

But here we are still concerned with how to start the meditation—how to take the first steps in the practice. And relaxation, which is the first, can be induced (as already said) by concentrating on the breath, and by breathing in and out deeply a definite number of times—say, twenty-one. When that has been done, comes concentration—the focusing of the mind. Marjorie Waterhouse gives the illustration of the sun's rays which shine over the whole of the landscape on a sunny day but don't do anything obvious. The objects on which those rays fall are affected, but the changes are subtle and not apparent to the casual observer. But let those same rays be concentrated to a point by a simple lens, and they will at once start a conflagration. And that reveals the tremendous latent power of radiant energy which those rays contain.[1]

It is the same with the light of the mental consciousness which illumines, apparently indifferently, all the thoughts and ideas which arise in the mind—all the *vrittis*, to use the technical term employed in the Yoga classics. Let that light be focused by the mind through concentrated meditation and it will manifest its power of burning up error and falsehood, prejudice, and wrong ideas of many kinds, and reveal the light of truth. This second factor, concentration, can be practised after relaxing the tension of the mind through deep breathing, for example, by taking the symbol OM, and either pronouncing it or thinking of it and focusing the mind on it. And in this way the relaxed mind is emptied of all irrelevant thoughts. As they arise, they can be swept aside by thinking of this symbol, OM, and repeating it. In the course of the practice, the mind will put up resistance against tranquillity, concentration, and meditation. Do not give way to it; but do not try to wrestle with the mind; and do not quarrel with it, because, by doing so, you strengthen its resistance. Simply empty it. Empty it through the practice of OM, and rub out the impressions of egoity and desires. We have the feeling that we must fight with darkness, but this is wrong, say the yogis. The real way is to usher in the light.

There is a story of a spiritual man who went to live with a primitive community in Northern India. He was told that they were all afraid of a dragon which lived in a cave in the mountains, and that many of their ills were put down to the presence of this dragon. They asked him if he would get rid of it for them. He asked them: 'How long has it been here?' and they replied: 'It has been there for thousands of years. Our forefathers also knew of it.' He said: 'Alright, I'll do it'. He asked them to bring a lamp. He went to the cave, taking the lamp into the cave, and went to the end of the cave but he found nothing there. Then he came out and said: 'Well, now I have got rid of the dragon. You can come in and see'. And gradually he persuaded them, took them in and showed them that there was nothing there.

Many of our difficulties are phantom difficulties, due to the irrational fears and ideas which we have harboured in our minds. It is no good fighting with them, but they can be eradicated by ushering in the spiritual light. When the light is ushered in, they disappear, because in the presence of the light they can be seen to have no reason to exist. Shri Dadaji, the teacher of our teacher, said to his disciples: 'Let your love of truth, let your yearning for the good of all humanity, become a force able to strike into the darkest materialistic corners of the world'.

After relaxation and concentration, comes the third great factor involved in meditation—merging the mind in truth. To take a text for meditation and to merge the mind into the text—first into the words, and then into its meaning. This is one such text: I AM THE SPIRIT WHICH PERVADES ALL. These texts, given for meditation to the pupil yogis in this tradition, when fully understood, express deep insights into the spiritual truth. And they are capable of altering our whole outlook and understanding of our nature—not only of our own nature, but also of the nature of the world around us. They are designed to awaken the faculty of insight or spiritual vision. People may say: 'Oh yes, but meditation is simply auto-suggestion; it is simply imposing something on the mind from outside through long-continued imagination. It does not have any reality; it does not have any relevance to truth'. But it is not so. Meditation does use auto-suggestion initially and it *is* imaginative, but its aim is to prepare the mind for the inner enquiry and for knowledge. Imaginative meditation, which is called *dhyana* in Sanskrit, is not the same as knowledge. It does not produce knowledge, but it creates that state of one-pointedness in the mind in which concentrated enquiry can be carried out, and it is this enquiry (*vichara*) which can lead to knowledge. Yoga is not dogmatic. It aims at a spirit of inner enquiry leading to a knowledge of the spiritual truth about our nature. It is the enemy of dogma and prejudice. Again I quote Shri Dadaji: 'Do not become fixed and rigid in your ideas', he says, 'do not tarry; do not stagnate. Yoga is fluidity'. It means to have a free mind—a mind which can respond freely to truth from wherever it comes.

A pupil once went to a Zen teacher in the East, and asked for teaching about how to achieve spiritual enlightenment. The teacher was in the garden, and he had a sieve in his hand. He said to the pupil: 'Enlightening the mind is like filling this sieve with water. When you can find out how to do that then you will succeed'. The pupil went away very down-hearted, but something in the way that the teacher had spoken made him feel that there *was* a way. And he took it as a *koan*, as a riddle, that he had to solve. He thought about it for many days, and then he went to find the teacher again, and he found him with a sieve cleaning the gravel. He shovelled the gravel into the sieve, and then he went to the river and lowered the sieve into the water. And when he saw it, the pupil realized in a flash—this is how the sieve is filled with water. It was not a theoretical understanding; it was a practical demonstration. When the sieve was lowered into the water, then there was no question of effort—the sieve was filled with water. In the same way, say the yogis, if we merge the mind into that spiritual principle which is like an ocean of peace and light, in which the mind already lives, moves and has its being, then it will be filled with that reality. And all the impurities of error and ignorance which darken the empirical mental consciousness will be removed.

Remembering this principle, let us do the meditation for a few minutes together—trying to merge the mind in its source.

OM. I AM THE SPIRIT WHICH PERVADES ALL. OM.

Understanding or insight into truth, which is the goal of the inner enquiry, ultimately requires more than reason or intellect. It requires not only the discursive side of the mind, it also requires ultimately, love. Unless the mind is merged in identificative contemplation of the object of enquiry, the real knowledge does not come.

When the mathematician or philosopher is really absorbed in a problem, for the time being nothing else exists for him and he is unconscious of himself. He is like a lover, so to speak. Bertrand Russell gives descriptions of the intensity of his concentration, when he was engaged on trying to investigate mathematical or philosophical problems. He used to go into a trance-like state, in which he even forgot to breathe for minutes at times.[2]

Our teacher said: 'To think without being a thinker is to meditate constantly'. It is worth trying to understand this saying. To act without the consciousness of being an actor is the best way of acting. Effortless effort involves the negation of self-consciousness. The really expert action, the really expert thought, involves the negation of the individualistic consciousness—of the feeling 'I am doing it'. And he added that a lover who thinks: 'I am loving', has no idea what real love is.

The practice of meditation then, with its three stages of relaxation, concentration, and merging of the mind in truth, is to lead to inner enquiry (*vichara*). What is said about the truth by the competent experts is that it is first to be listened to (*shravana*), then it is to be thought about (*manana*), and then finally the mind is to be focused in one-pointed concentration on the enquiry into the truth (*nididhyasana*). And in this way, in the state of effortless effort, the enquiry becomes successful.

5

Attentive Silence*

At the end of each week *The Times* publishes a column by its radio critic reviewing the programmes broadcast in the previous seven days. A fortnight ago this critic, David Wade, began his column in the following way:

> I am in no doubt that the most arresting programmes to be heard in the past three weeks were scripted something over 2,300 years ago.

He was referring to the three broadcasts of dialogues from Plato's *Republic*, and he drew attention to the astonishingly life-like character of the conversation between Socrates and his companions. As he said: 'The listener constantly had the scene in his mind's eye' and then he went on to say something particularly interesting. He found that by being presented as spoken dialogue it had become more alive and more of a dialogue than it often appears to be from the printed page. To quote him again:

> Since Socrates does almost all the talking and, social chat apart, his audience's contribution is limited either to agreeing with him or asking the odd question, the reader can easily receive the impression that this audience is a pretty poor bunch and no match at all for an intellectual megalomaniac who has things so much his own way that, if he were to tell them day was night, they would

---

* A lecture given on 21st March 1975.

probably agree without demur. Socratic monologue seems a more exact description. And yet what we have been hearing will not bear that interpretation in the least; this has been a dialogue in the real sense that both principal speaker and audience are party to it... So what is going on? *The Republic* is a bit of teaching and perhaps our current notions of the teaching situation stand in the way of understanding this. If we polarize them, then either we have the teacher who does the telling and this we now regard with some disfavour as authoritarian, likely to create alienation, apathy and so on; or, at the other end of the scale, the teacher's rôle is that of the leader, referee even, in a kind of group discussion. This we now regard as 'right' and we associate with it argument and opposition, seeing these as necessary, productive, healthy.

It seems to me that in the light of this broadcast neither of these alternatives stand up; though Socrates holds the floor, he cannot be regarded as one who simply tells; on the other hand by no stretch of the imagination is *The Republic* a group discussion which he has managed to monopolize. *What we discover is this: that the audience's silence is an active one.* They have not come to dispute—not because they are unable, but because it is inappropriate: Thrasymachus, who tries it, very quickly finds himself out of tune and departs; he will get nothing. On the other hand they have not come to sit there like sacks of earth while Socrates lectures to them. They are there in a most energetic and attentive way to hear and understand him. They regard that as the correct approach. One might guess that, far from being more biddable than us, they have not had the ill-fortune to fall into the pit which we are either in or seem to be entering where neither teachers nor pupils any longer believe that—except in the most mundane sense—any man is wiser than the next.

And he goes on to describe the attitude of Socrates' pupils as one of 'attentive silence'.

It is not often nowadays that one reads such good sense in the newspaper! And the point that *The Times* critic is making here is one that needs to be made, because the current fashions of thought are particularly woolly-minded on this point. The sociologists have induced in people at large an exaggerated belief in group discussion, but that group discussion has to be of the kind that they prescribe. Its basic assumption is that no-one is wiser than anyone else, and that therefore no authority should be created or accepted. The didactic lecture is anathema, because it is authoritarian. We must be democratic, and the most ignorant or ill-informed shall have an equal voice with the greatest expert. If there is, for convenience, to be a group leader in the discussion, he is tolerated only because he can help to draw in all the individual members, or else because he can act as a focus for the critical sallies of the participants. An ineffective authority may be tolerated if it provides a suitable target for defiance and revolt.

This picture is deliberately exaggerated, but not greatly so, because it makes such an interesting contrast to the Socratic dialogue. There too there is a democratic spirit. Anyone is free to come and go; anyone is free to speak or raise questions. Their attitude is certainly not uncritical, but they have come with a desire, not to air their own opinions, but to participate in a common enquiry into truth, and the underlying bond which unites them all is a love of truth.

To take a musical analogy, it is a waste of time and opportunity, if you have the opportunity to invite Segovia with the guitar into your house, to allow him only to play one piece, and then to make him sit listening to the strummings of a beginner, simply on the ground that each and every player should be treated on equal terms. If you have a party of music-lovers there, none will want to play if they have the chance of listening to Segovia, unless you also have a Julian Bream there, in which case Segovia too will enjoy the alternative! This illustrates that we all recognize an authority in a field in which we are really interested, and that the most important thing is to be receptive, so that we have the chance of hearing such an authority when one turns up. The yogic view of the enquiry into truth, exemplified in the Socratic dialogues, is not that one should be uncritical, but that one should be open and receptive. This is not necessarily as easy to achieve as it looks! As our teacher, Dr Shastri, used to say, the most important qualification of a would-be learner is that he should be 'teachable'. This sounds a truism, but it is a qualification which is much rarer than might be supposed among students, and it implies something of the 'attentive silence' spoken of by *The Times*.

The fact is that argument and debate is not necessarily a very good way of arriving at truth. Over two thousand years ago Chuang Tzu, the Chinese follower of Lao Tzu, put it all very simply, and nobody has added very much to what he said about it then.

> Granting that you and I argue, if you beat me and not I you, are you necessarily right and I wrong? Or if I beat you, and not you me, am I necessarily right and you wrong? Or are we both partly right and partly wrong? Or are we both wholly right and wholly wrong? You and I cannot know this, and consequently the world will be in ignorance of the truth. Who shall I employ as an arbiter between us? If I employ someone who takes your view, he will side with you; how can such a one arbitrate between us? If I employ someone who takes my view he will side with me; how can such a one arbitrate between us? And if I employ someone who either differs from, or agrees with both of us, he will equally be unable to decide between us. Since, then, you and I, and man, cannot decide, must we not depend on another? Such dependence is as though it were not dependence. We are embraced in the obliterating unity of God. There is perfect adaptation to whatever may eventuate and so we complete our allotted span.[1]

There is another way of dealing with this problem than simply contentious argument or debate: and perhaps, as a first approximation, one can say that in the spirit of the Socratic dialogue—in which each of the participants obliterates himself, in the underlying unity of the search for truth—there is that perfect adaptation to whatever may eventuate, of which Chuang Tzu speaks. There is openness to whatever comes out of the discussion, and the willingness to accept truth because one genuinely loves it and wants it. It is the theme which runs through all the spiritual traditions: that if we truly seek, we shall find.

Attentive silence is not only a question of quietening down. Of course, if there is too much noise or disturbance, it is impossible to carry on an effective enquiry. The speaker well remembers some notoriously bad lecturers in his University days, whose efforts to talk to the students were rendered ineffective from the outset by the noisy disturbances which the more rowdy elements in their classes organized. A famous example of this in Glasgow (though somewhat before my time there) was Lord Kelvin, who was quite unable to keep order in his lectures, which became famous or infamous as a consequence. But, although it is obvious that one cannot really attend without peace and quiet, this is not the only meaning of silence. The most unteachable student is the one who is obstinately self-opinionated and doesn't really listen to what is being said to him, let alone consider it, because his mind is full of his own uncritically accepted views. In other words, he has prejudged the issue before he hears anything. He is certain that his view is right. This non-openness is precisely what is meant by the word prejudice. And someone who is prejudiced can't be a good pupil. He so much likes the sound of his own voice that he never stops talking, and never lowers it enough to listen to what anyone else may have to say. Therefore attentive silence means also silencing the uncritically held prejudices which prevent us from even considering any view other than our own.

In the Yoga philosophy, the first great means of approaching the enquiry into truth is listening, but even before this begins the spiritual teachers speak of the paramount need of purifying the mind. To the Japanese Zen masters, the image is that of 'emptying the cup'. The cup of the mind must be emptied, before it can be refilled by the teacher. To the Persian Sufis the image given is one of polishing the dust from the face of the mirror of the mind, so that it can accurately reflect the truth. But all traditions alike are unanimous on the need for purification of the mind and elimination from it of the *hubris* which supposes that our own opinions and prejudices are adequate guides to truth. To go back to the analogy of the musicians, it is foolhardy if you are a budding guitarist, not to recognize and grasp with both hands the chance to hear and learn from a Segovia, and, if by any chance you are already a great guitarist, you will welcome and enjoy the opportunity even more. If they are good teachers, skilled players can often be of immense help to beginners, because they bring an expert's insight into their difficulties and can show them how to overcome their mistakes. But, in any case, with regard to the enquiry into truth, few of us need to worry about being already masters of the art! And we shall certainly be wiser to put ourselves in the position of an earnest inquirer.

It is not only Nature that abhors a vacuum. According to the spiritual teachers God too is attracted to and fills the purified mind, emptied of all the dross of worldliness. Listen to these words of Eckhart:

> Where and when God finds you ready he *must* act and pour himself into you; just as the sun must pour itself into the air if it is clear and pure, and cannot help doing so. It would assuredly be a great lack in God if he would not accomplish great things in you, nor shower great blessings on you, if he finds you thus empty and stripped... When nature reaches its highest attainment, God gives his grace.[2]

The state of attentive silence may seem very passive, but it is, in fact, a state of the greatest activity. Most of our worldly activity on the other hand is sheer passivity. We are passively driven through most of our life by various neurotic drives which we allow to overpower us and to rule our lives. We don't enjoy these drives, nor do we choose them, but we are subject to them. It is the negation of the free and active state which man desires and which comes only from a truly loving attitude. It is these neurotic drives which lead to tension and anxiety, and through them to depression. One can say that it is almost endemic in modern life to encounter these tensions and anxieties, and it prevents anyone doing things in a truly relaxed and creative way.

If we analyze this state carefully, we shall find that it is always associated with undue ego involvement, in other words with a concern for the fruits of action. It is a desperate attempt to achieve some imagined object or objects, combined with a constant doubt in which the individual is tormented by the feeling 'Am I going to succeed or to fail?' One of the greatest lessons which the *Bhagavad Gita* can teach us, is that this is the root of most of our troubles in active life, and that it is only by doing actions for their own sake, because they are the right thing to do, and offering them to the Lord and to the common good, that we can escape this tension and anxiety which is associated with the ego-driven actions.

You will nowhere see a better example of the neurotic character of modern life than in the way people drive. The motor car is perhaps the most typical creation of our age, and it expresses a good deal of the character of its driver. We all know that it is essential to the efficient flow of traffic for cars to give way and yield at the appropriate time, but you will time and again see people neurotically and desperately trying to get ahead, so that the end product is that the whole of the traffic grinds to a halt in a great snarl-up. The ego's drive for supremacy is self-defeating in the long run. It is only by restraining these impulses that we can make the mental and physical traffic flow freely.

The Chinese philosopher, Lao Tzu, speaks of three jewels or precious things in human life. They are gentleness, economy and not taking precedence. The third of these is written with two Chinese characters which mean literally 'self after'. And the character for self was originally a picture of the cocoon which the silkworm spins. We have to learn not to give this unreal cocoon of the personality the first place in our life, because to do so prevents us from living wisely and happily. Individualism, if unbridled, becomes a kind of insanity.

One of the great spiritual symbols which one sees all over India is the figure of Shri Krishna as the divine flute player. Shri Krishna is the teacher, not only of Arjuna in the *Gita*, but of all who approach him in the traditional spirit. When they approach the Lord, having put aside their empirical individuality, and creating within their heart the attentive silence which constitutes true teachability, the Lord takes up his flute and plays to them the melody of the spiritual truth. The symbol of the flute is considered to have a deep meaning. The flute is enabled to kiss the lips of the Lord because it has emptied itself and become a hollow channel for his breath. This is what Eckhart means when he speaks about the Lord pouring himself into the one whom he finds ready, just as the sun pours itself into the air if it is clear and pure. According to the Yoga, we have to make the whole personality like the flute, and then our life will be inspired by the spiritual forces which rule the universe. This is what is meant by wooing the Lord.

There is a great and important connection, according to the Yoga, between sound on the one hand and thought on the other. All propositional thought depends on language—on the meanings which we derive from words and formulate in words. And words, in themselves, are sounds derived from the vowels and consonants (or, more strictly, phonemes) of which they are made up. There are, in simple terms, these two kinds of sounds: vowels which are (so to speak) continuous sounds, and consonants which, generally speaking, are mere transitional sounds, marking the beginnings or endings of vowels. For instance, we have the vowel O and we bring it to a stop with the dental D or we begin it with the explosive sound T making the words O-DE, T-OE or T-OA-D. All speech sounds come from vibrations in the larynx and the throat and the mouth. In the larynx the vocal cords vibrate and create waves of sound which pass upward through the resonating cavities of the pharynx, mouth and nose. There is a natural sequence of sounds which comes from these cavities. From the back of the throat comes the sound O, from the middle the sound OO, and as we come forward there is the sound MM which is half consonant and half vowel (a continuous sound with closed lips). This natural sequence of sound makes the word AUM or OM.

Swami Rama Tirtha points out how universal this sound is. It does not belong to any language. And it comes naturally untaught at birth, even in the child's cry. Even the mute can produce the sound OM. Joy finds natural expression in the prolonged O which is OM cut short. Sorrow too is expressed spontaneously in all languages by the sound OH! The sound is both one of the most natural and universal sounds and brings relief, either in joy or in sorrow. It is also found (albeit in an altered form) in the AMEN or the AMIN of the Jewish or Arab traditions.

Language, of course, only exists because there is the breath. The frogs were the first speakers in evolution, because they were the first breathers, and their breath allowed them to croak. The natural sound of the breath, according to the yogis, is SO HUM and this too is OM with the two consonants S and H added. It is the yogic tradition that the consonants, which are so to speak the transitions or boundaries of the words, cutting short and separating the continuous vowel sounds, represent the finite names and forms which cannot exist apart from the underlying reality. Consonants cannot in fact be pronounced on their own. They have to have a vowel underlying them in order to be pronounced. In the same way, the vowel represents the underlying reality in the world, the consonants the names and forms which cannot exist without that underlying reality. This is what the yogis teach traditionally concerning the syllable OM.

But beyond speech, there is the underlying reality. And that reality is realized by attentive silence.

> That from which the mind and speech turn back baffled is the silence accessible only to the yogis; that the wise become.[3]

6

The Meaning of Life*

In the first of his Reith Lectures, given in 1984, Professor Searle began with these words:

> For thousands of years, people have been trying to understand their relationship to the rest of the universe. For a variety of reasons many philosophers today are reluctant to tackle such big problems. Nonetheless, the problems remain, and in these lectures I am going to attack some of them.
>
> At the moment, the biggest problem is this: we have a certain common-sense picture of ourselves as human beings which is very hard to square with our overall 'scientific' conception of the physical world. We think of ourselves as conscious, free, mindful, rational agents in a world that science tells us consists entirely of mindless, meaningless physical particles. Now, how can we square these two conceptions? How, for example, can it be both the case that the world contains nothing but unconscious physical particles, and yet that it also contains consciousness? How can a mechanical universe contain intentionalistic human beings— human beings that can represent the world to themselves? How can an essentially meaningless world contain meanings?

It is certainly to be applauded that a contemporary professional philosopher is at last taking an interest in these problems again, after a period of rather dry concentration on linguistic analysis. And yet the theme of

---

* A lecture given on 7th December 1984.

meaning has continued to have a dominant importance. 'What do we mean by meaning?', is a question which sounds like a philosophical double somersault, or the equivalent of pulling oneself up by one's own bootstraps. The meaning of meaning and its dominant rôle in our thinking and our language is worth deeper thought, because it leads on to the even more fundamental questions: 'Has our life a meaning?' or, put in more general terms, 'Is there a meaning to life?' In this lecture some of the contemporary views will be considered in the light of the philosophy and teaching of Yoga.

The first thing to be said, perhaps, concerns the widespread view that the scientific picture of the world reduces the human mind to the level of an advanced digital computer. This topic is one which Professor Searle addresses in his second lecture, when he poses the question 'Can a digital computer think?' He answers the question with a clear 'No', because no matter how advanced the technology and how successfully the computer may simulate conscious behaviour, it does so by carrying out an elaborate set of pre-arranged instructions without any understanding of the meaning of the manipulations which it is doing. In other words, it may well be possible to create a robot to act in some respects like a conscious human being, but it will not have the conscious human being's understanding of the meaning of the words which it utters, even though it may combine them correctly in sentences. If you use the public telephone network in America, you will be astonished to hear, after dialling your number, a voice telling you the amount of money you have to put in the slot. If (as sometimes happens when one is fumbling in one's pocket for the desired coins) you put in only an insufficient amount, the same disembodied voice will tell you that you should 'put in another one dollar fifty cents', (or whatever the correct sum might be which is still outstanding). You could be forgiven for supposing that this was a charming operator at the other end, working out the sum as she went along, except that she speaks in a funny voice like an automaton. But if you attempt to speak to this voice, it is totally insensitive to your excuses or pleas for more time. It is entirely unsympathetic if you try to explain that you have just dropped the additional coins on the floor and you will put them in in a minute if she will only wait; because it is, in fact, a micro-computer chip programmed to carry out the necessary calculations and synthesize the necessary vocal message. The machine does not understand a word that either it or you are saying.

Understanding the meaning of something is therefore a key distinction between computers and minds. In technical terms the computer may be programmed to speak with absolutely correct syntax, but it is entirely innocent of semantic content. In Professor Searle's words 'the computer program is defined purely syntactically', that is to say, according to the rules governing how words are put together grammatically. But thinking is more than just a matter of manipulating meaningless symbols; it involves meaningful semantic concepts. These semantic concepts are what we mean by 'meaning'.

It is only with minds that meaning becomes important, because meaning involves the use of something to express something else. To put it at its simplest, words and ideas point to something outside themselves; they are symbols of something else. They are therefore not self-sufficient, in the sense that to fully comprehend them and their significance, one has to refer to something other than themselves. The word 'cat', for instance, refers to the animal which sits smugly on the mat in the external world, complacently manifesting its complete independence of our mind or our thoughts about it. In fact, all our mental life has this character; it consists of representations or symbols of things which exist outside the mind or are at least independent of its present state. Thus ideas seem to have a more abiding and enduring reality than their lightning-like progression through the mind might suggest, and mental images of the outer world, in the form of sensations, perceptions and memories, are recognized by all of us to be different from mere hallucinations or phantasies.

The two great characteristics of our mental life which distinguish it from the physical world of nature, are, on the one hand, the existence of consciousness which confers the subjectivity on our mental states, allowing them to constitute a kind of private experience, and, on the other hand, the character of referring to and representing something outside and apart from the mind. As Professor Searle says: 'The existence of consciousness ought to seem amazing to us. Consciousness is the central fact of specifically human existence, because without it all the other specifically human aspects of our existence—such as language, love, humour and so on—would be impossible'.

It may seem unnecessary to state something which is so obvious, but there is still quite an influential school of philosophers who regard consciousness as something which has no existence. This line of thought can be said to originate with William James. James wrote an essay entitled 'Does consciousness exist?' Having pointed out that, when analysed, it becomes 'only a name for the fact that the content of experience is known', he concludes that: 'It is the name of a non-entity, that has no right to a place among first principles. Those who still cling to it are clinging to a mere echo, the faint rumour left behind by the disappearing "soul" upon the air of philosophy'. A modern American philosopher, following this line of thought, has recently produced an article with the title: 'How to study human consciousness empirically or Nothing comes to Mind'! Clearly then, however obvious it may seem to us, the existence of consciousness as a fundamental feature of our mental life does need pointing out to some people.

Of course, James' view is really much subtler than it appears to be. What he actually believes is that the raw material out of which the world is built is not of two sorts, one matter and the other mind, but that it is arranged in different patterns by its interrelations, and that some arrangements may be called mental, while others may be called physical. 'My thesis is', he says, 'that if we start with the supposition that there is only one primal stuff or material in the world, the stuff of which everything is composed, and if we call that stuff "pure experience", then knowing can easily be explained as a particular sort of relation towards one another into which portions of pure experience may enter. The relation itself is a part of pure experience; one of its "terms" becomes the subject or bearer of the knowledge, the knower, the other becomes the object known'. James goes on in another essay to speak of 'a world of pure experience' and in this respect his conclusion could be said to be very close to that of the Vedanta philosophy itself. But James' thought was taken up by others with a much more purely materialistic and mechanistic bent of mind and led over the succeeding decades to Watson's behaviourism, which denied the existence of subjective states of consciousness or even thoughts, reducing them to the status of silent movements of the vocal cords. Thoughts were simply what you said to yourself in an inaudible voice, softer than even the softest whisper.

If the behaviourists were right, and man is simply an elaborate mechanical device in which all thought could be reduced to the level of the computer program, then indeed Macbeth's words would ring true that life is 'a tale told by an idiot, full of sound and fury, signifying nothing'. And it would be so because, for such a device, meaning has no existence. There are no meanings for a digital computer. There is no meaning in the life of a physico-chemical automaton.

Meaning, of course, implies purpose. The meaningless is *ipso facto* purposeless. Has life a meaning? And if so, what is it? It is interesting to look at the contemporary answers to this problem. Sir Karl Popper, for instance, took part in a series of broadcasts on the meaning of history in 1961. He identified himself with Immanuel Kant's view that the central idea of the Enlightenment was the idea of self-liberation through knowledge. He said that he did not himself believe that life or history had a meaning in the sense of something hidden and perhaps discoverable through a study of history, but he believed that man could make his life meaningful by his own efforts. 'The quest for the meaning of life (he said) turns into an ethical question—the question, "what tasks can I set myself in order to make my life meaningful?"' Or, as Kant put it: 'What should I do?'

Popper's view has interesting parallels if we compare it with the view of the teachers of Yoga. Swami Rama Tirtha, for instance, says that it is no use trying to find a meaning in the empirical world. To the question 'Why should this world exist at all?', Vedanta answers 'You have no right to ask that question... The Vedantic attitude is merely experimental and scientific. It establishes no hypothesis; it puts forth no theory. It does not claim to be able to explain the origin of the world; this is beyond the sphere of intellect or comprehension. This is called Maya.'[1]

One can say, in this sense, that the Vedanta philosophy agrees with Sir Karl Popper that the quest for a meaning of life by searching in the outer world is ultimately doomed to failure. But equally Vedanta has something to say on Popper's second thesis that one can give a meaning to the life of the individual by the way that one lives. Popper speaks of Kant's ideal of self-liberation through knowledge. Yoga adds a spiritual dimension to this ideal.

To quote Marjorie Waterhouse: 'Man comes into the

world in order to transcend himself and to know God'. But what does this mean? It is not enough to hear the words, we have to understand them, to know what they actually mean. Are we to know God as we know the ruler of the country? Miss Waterhouse answers the question in her book:

> To 'know' does not mean to grasp with the mind, it means 'to enter into—to be'. At first ignorant where this Lord Truth is to be found, man fashions symbols of His greatness, love and beauty and learns to worship Him through them. Slowly he accustoms himself to the rarefied atmosphere they create, and, at last, the symbol is discarded and the Reality behind it is intuitively recognized and known.[2]

There is a whole new dimension of meaning expressed here. The spiritual reality is not immediately accessible to man's empirical consciousness; it has to be known indirectly through parables and symbols. Encountering these in the teachings of the great spiritual traditions and in the writings of the saints and sages, we have to penetrate to the inner meaning of these symbols, just as we have to understand the meaning of the words and gestures used by our friends. In the case of the spiritual teaching, that meaning is not something arbitrarily imposed; it is the transcendent fact about ourselves and reality, which can only be fully grasped when we have passed beyond speech and idea and awakened to the reality within our own higher being.

In the little book *Vedanta Light* our teacher, Dr Shastri, has said:

> The only object of the ego of man, the seat of the I, is to realize its identity with God. It is in this school of the world to learn this one lesson: to forget its limitations and actively to realize its oneness with all.
>
> Love, beauty, and the sense of pleasure, are meant to open the eyes of man to the fact that within him is God, who is the seat of all love, all beauty and all bliss, and that indulgence in outer pleasures will not quench his thirst.

This, then, is the meaning of life according to the teachings of Yoga. The great question we have to ask about life—and it is a very contemporary question—is whether our empirical life in the world has any meaning. Does it point to something beyond itself? Or is it just as it is and there is an end to it? If man is merely an automaton, a beautifully constructed and advanced machine, due eventually perhaps to be overtaken by the future development of even better digital computers, then life is by definition meaningless.

But, in fact, all the characteristics of our life which make us peculiarly human demonstrate clearly that our life *does* have a meaning. We do understand the significance of symbols; we do learn how to use words to express meanings which are only subtly and distantly indicated by those words. We do have a mind with ideas and percepts which correspond to, and represent, things outside themselves and beyond the contents of the mind which contains them. In all these respects, man shows that he is a being whose life encompasses much wider dimensions than those of his physical environment or even his immediate mental environment. It is in this sense that we have to understand the ideal of Kant, espoused by Sir Karl Popper, that the meaning of our life is self-liberation through knowledge.

The true liberation can only come through self-transcendence, through the discovery of the freedom of the spirit. Man has an innate feeling that he is free; but if we examine the matter carefully we find that this idea is partly an illusion, if he imagines that his freedom is a characteristic of his empirical personality—the person that he is in everyday life. Our worldly life is hedged around with restrictions and limitations. But even if there were not outer restraints and regulations restricting our freedom, we should still not be free, empirically speaking.

Even if we could do exactly as we liked, without let or hindrance, we would not be entirely free agents. Indeed there is a degree of muddled thinking about our ideas on this subject. This was well known to the philosopher F H Bradley. In his *Ethical Studies* he examines the idea that we have that we are free to choose, and asks what exactly it means. And he suggests that we have an innate feeling that our will is identical with our self and that we are the uncaused cause of our particular willings. 'This I, in the act of "I will", is the self, as pure I, which is superior to all its contents, desires, etc., and descends into them only by its own arbitrary freedom of choice'. And he goes on to point out that this idea is precisely why we regard an individual as accountable for his actions. Since we have freedom to choose this or that, a man is accountable for what he does. If he did not have freedom, it would be most unfair to blame him for the actions which he takes. Yet, says Bradley, there is something paradoxical about this whole situation. '...you are free, because there is no reason which will account for your particular acts, because no-one in the world, not even yourself, can possibly say what you will or will not do next. You are "accountable", in short, because you are a wholly "unaccountable" creature'.

But Bradley goes on to point out that when one comes down to looking at how people behave in everyday life, we find that people are far from taking this point of view. As he says: 'What sayings in life are more common than, "you might have known me better", "I never could have done such a thing" or "it was impossible for me to act so, and you ought to have known that nothing could have made me"'.

So the man in the street wants to have it both ways, and his thinking is inconsistent. On the one hand, he recognizes that you can predict from knowledge of a man's character what he is going to do next and, on the other hand, he maintains that the individual has complete freedom of choice. The fact of the matter is, as the yogis tell us, that in regard to empirical life, man has a degree of freedom and a degree of freedom only. His real freedom comes through enlightenment and the realization of the freedom of the spirit. The English Prayer Book speaks of 'God, whose service is perfect freedom', and these words have a deeper meaning which we can easily miss. In fact, their full significance cannot be understood until we ourselves have awakened in our own mind the faculty of discrimination and grasped the significance of the teachings of the great spiritual traditions, which unanimously maintain that man, sunk in worldly life, is in bondage, and that it is only by knowing the truth that he can be set free.

In his lecture entitled 'The Goal of Religion', delivered eighty-two years ago yesterday, on December 6th 1902 in San Francisco, Swami Rama put the matter simply and directly:

> People suffer, not because they have not got the remedy, not because they do not possess the infinite joy in themselves, not because they do not have the priceless jewel within themselves, but because they do not know how to untie the knot which holds it, how to open the casket which contains it. In other words people do not know how to enter their own spirits and realize their own Self. All religion is simply an attempt to unveil ourselves and to explain our Self.[3]

What then is the meaning of life, the meaning of the world? A few words from Miss Waterhouse's lecture provide a clue: 'The universe itself may be said to be a huge symbol of divinity, and every now and then, if he is receptive enough, a searching man will receive a flash of the great Fact which it hides'.

7

No Time Like the Present*

In the first act of *The Tempest*, Shakespeare's last play, Prospero questions his daughter Miranda about whether she can remember anything of her past and how she has arrived on the island where she now is.

> Canst thou remember
> A time before we came unto this cell?
> I do not think thou canst, for then thou wast not
> Out three years old.

And Miranda answers:

> Certainly, Sir, I can.

Prospero presses her:

> By what? By any other house, or person?
> Of any thing the image, tell me, that
> Hath kept with thy remembrance.

Miranda: 'Tis far off...
And rather like a dream, than an assurance
That my remembrance warrants... Had I not
Four—or five—women once, that tended me?

Prospero: Thou hadst; and more, Miranda: But how is it,
That this lives in thy mind? What seest thou else
In the dark backward and abysm of time?
If thou remembrest aught ere thou cam'st here,
How thou cam'st here, thou mayst.

---

* A lecture given on 14th June 1985.

Our experience of time past, present and future is one of the most extraordinary and mysterious characteristics of our conscious life, although we take it for granted and hardly notice how extraordinary it is. The past has gone, and yet we can in a sense conjure it up here and now in the form of memory. What was immediate in our experience recedes into the past and we sense it only distantly; 'It is far off and rather like a dream, than an assurance' to use Miranda's phrase. Memory brings it back to us in some miraculous way from what Prospero calls 'the dark backward and abysm of time'.

What appears real and immediate in our present experience disappears into the past and becomes remote and distant, only half remembered and often inaccurately at that. In my youth, there used to be a hymn which we were given to sing at school:

> Time, like an ever-rolling stream,
> Bears all its sons away.
> They fly forgotten, as a dream
> Dies at the opening day.

Our life is apparently hemmed in or bounded by time. Behind us the past stretches out to unimaginable ages before we, as individuals, were born, and beyond that to the ages of prehistory and evolution measured in thousands of millions of years. Space too has the same dual character. 'Here', where I now am, is immediately known and familiar. It is directly perceptible to me at this instant. But space stretches out to the distant 'there' and to unknown regions beyond those accessible to my senses. And if we go to the astronomers, we are told of vast extensions of space, not only within our own galaxy but stretching out to a distance so vast and inconceivable that we can only measure it by the time which it takes light to reach the place where we are from those distances, and they are thousands of millions of light years away.

Space and time then, both have this dual quality of a 'here' and 'now', which is immediately accessible to us, and a 'then' and 'there', which is not directly accessible and which can only be sensed at all because of the messages which we receive indirectly from it in the form of sound waves or light waves or radio waves or, in the case of time, in the form of revived memories or (for that matter) tape recordings, old files, old films or photos, or history books. Just as the memory of a past event has to be experienced here and now in order to be known, even though we recognize it as applying to time past, so the distant galaxy that we see, is only seen when the light which carries its image to us reaches the spot where our eye is.

What we actually see now is the galaxy as it was thousands of millions of light years ago. Even the sun, which we think of as part of our nearby everyday world, is really the sun as it was eight minutes ago, because what we see is not the sun itself as it is now, but the light from the sun arriving at our eye after traversing the vast intervening space at an unimaginably fast velocity. One says 'unimaginably' legitimately, because although we can specify the speed of light in miles per second, as 186,300 miles per second, it is so much faster than anything else that we are used to dealing with, that we cannot actually conceive of something travelling at this speed. Even the speed of sound is relatively plodding compared with it, as we can tell when we experience a clap of thunder lagging many seconds behind the flash of lightning in a thunder-storm. The flash too takes time to reach us, but there is nothing faster than light which could demonstrate this delay to us, and so we are unaware of anything having happened until the light arrives.

Seen from this angle, there is an element of relativity about past and future, for it depends on where we are. What is past for the sun may be still a future experience for us, if the light which signals the event is still on the way. What is here and now depends on where the observer is standing. In this sense the feeling we have, that the future is what cannot be exactly foretold, while the past is what cannot now be altered, is only at best a half-truth. Some of our future is already some of somewhere else's past, and part of our 'now' is already 'then' there.

Bertrand Russell makes the point that:

> Space and time, however, as human beings know them, are not in reality so impersonal as science pretends. Theologians conceive God as viewing both space and time from without, impartially, and with a uniform awareness of the whole; science tries to imitate this impartiality with some apparent success, but the success is in part illusory. Human beings differ from the theologians' God in the fact that their space and time have a *here* and *now*. What is here and now is vivid, what is remote has a gradually increasing dimness. All our knowledge of events radiates from a space-time centre, which is the little region that we are occupying at the moment. 'Here' is a vague term: in astronomical cosmology the

Milky Way may count as 'here', in the study of the Milky Way 'here' is the solar system, in the study of the solar system 'here' is the earth, in geography it is the town or district in which we live, in physiological studies of sensation it is the brain as opposed to the rest of the body. Larger 'heres' always contain smaller ones as parts; all 'heres' contain the brain of the speaker, or part of it. Similar considerations apply to 'now'.[1]

Science professes to eliminate 'here' and 'now' but Russell points out that it is not wholly successful in doing so.

Individual percepts are the basis of all our knowledge, and no method exists by which we can begin with data which are public to many observers.[2]

Moreover, our knowledge of past and future is indirect. As Schrödinger puts it: 'There is really no before and after for the mind. There is only a now which includes memories and expectations'.[3] In regard to space and time, then, there is a region of experience which is immediately known to us which we call the present. It is present both in the spatial and temporal sense. It is the source of all our knowledge. But it also gives us indirect knowledge of the past and the future, of a spatial world extending in all directions from the point where we ourselves are established. This second kind of knowledge, the knowledge of the past through memory and of distant space through sensation and inference, is essentially indirect, as compared with what we can perceive directly in our present experience. It is (to use F H Bradley's phrase) an ideal construction. What we see brings us strong evidence of the existence of the external world and of the fact that we actually remember things which did happen in the past, but the evidence is not as strong as that for what we are at present experiencing. It is 'far off and rather like a dream', in Shakespeare's phrase. It is inference rather than direct perception. We remember things here and now and we anticipate and imagine things here and now. We experience the passing moment here and now. As Russell says in the passage already quoted: 'All our knowledge of events radiates from a space-time centre which is the little region that we are occupying at the moment'. For that is how it presents itself to us. It is the little region occupied by our bodies and minds which determines the perspective from which we experience the world.

In the eighth chapter of *Panchadashi*, Swami Vidyaranya, expounding the philosophy of Shri Shankara, points out that there are two aspects to the consciousness in the mind, which we can call, loosely, the relative consciousness and the absolute consciousness. The relative consciousness is the consciousness which (so to speak) takes on the form of the experience which it is viewing. As the perceptions and thoughts arise in the mind, so the relative consciousness becomes coloured by the qualities of the experience, like a crystal taking on the colour of a flower near which it is placed. Another simile used by Shri Shankara and the Vedantins to characterize this process is that of clay, or light. The impressions coming in through the senses mould the mind-stuff into the pictures (percepts) which are perceived as a stream of experiences by the consciousness in the mind. The mind-stuff itself is inert matter or energy, but like an iron ball taking on the heat and light of the fire in which it is placed, the mental image becomes conscious due to the proximity of the absolute consciousness to it. This relative individualized consciousness is called *chidabhasa* in the Advaita classics. It corresponds to the empirical consciousness of the individual soul or *jiva*, which is identified with, and submerged in, the stream of experience within the mind.

There is also a consciousness which is witness of the mind and untouched by the passing experiences of the mind. This is the consciousness which recognizes the state in which the mind is vacant and can detect the gap between one thought dying down and another one arising. If you can still your mind and become aware of this unchanging element of consciousness within the empirical experience, then (say the yogis) you are on the threshold of awakening to Self-realization, to a conscious awareness of the underlying reality which (like a thread) unifies and supports all empirical experience. It is this underlying consciousness which gives unity to the experience of past, present and future. And it is to be directly known. Indeed, there is no element of indirectness in it. This consciousness is what the yogis call *Atman*, the real Self of man.

In one of the incidents described in *The Heart of the Eastern Mystical Teaching*, when Shri Dadaji encountered a sceptical, Westernized young Bengali, he put the view of Yoga on this general topic in very simple and direct terms.

> Fundamentally, the conditions of the world's existence are time, space and the law of cause and effect. You assume time, you are yourselves in time, and yet you want to know the beginning of time. But the beginning of anything can only take place in already existing time and space and it is unreasonable of you to ask about the beginning of time when you know well that such 'beginning' implies the prior existence of time... In our philosophy the world is maya and this is, I think, the best explanation of it. Maya has its root in pure consciousness and is unexplainable and unaccountable... Wisdom consists in discovering the real purpose of life and the means to achieve it.[4]

This is not simply a matter of theory or philosophy. It has practical implications as well. On another occasion, Shri Dada enlarged on this when he said:

> Allow me to give you a few practical hints as to how to reach that state in which the bliss of Self may be experienced. The jiva [soul], when extrovertive, loses touch with Atman [the Self], the source of bliss. You must, therefore be introvertive, not necessarily in self-analysis, but in discouraging the whirl of sensations, thoughts and emotions. Anything that tires you is not of Atman and you should try to take your mind above the realm of the trio of thinker, thought and thinking. To let yourself be in any of these three categories is to slip into the realm of maya, the state of illusion and suffering, and as long as you have consciousness of time and space you will not be able to perceive the light of Atman. Maya is the realm of change, but to acquire the bliss of

Atman you must abide in the changeless witness state of Pure Consciousness, which is above both finite and infinite. If you still fail to achieve this, my children, meditate deeply morning and evening on the fact that the whole region of the senses and the mind consists of limitations and that all which is limited or limits is a source of suffering.[5]

The immediately known is characterized, empirically speaking, by being an experience of myself here and now. It is expressed in the conviction: 'I, here and now, am experiencing what I am experiencing'. As Swami Vidyaranya says in chapter six of *Panchadashi*, these three characteristics of the immediately known exclude the idea of the indirectly known.[6] The idea of 'I' excludes the idea of 'another', of you or he. Similarly the idea of 'here' excludes the idea of 'there', of something at a distance elsewhere; and the idea of 'now' excludes the idea of 'then', of an event distanced in time from the present, either in the past or the future. All three elements therefore are one of a pair of opposites or contraries and are essentially still within the realm of what the Vedanta calls the subject-object relationship—the sphere of the trio of thinker, thought and thinking. In other words, they are still coloured by the dimensions of time, space and causation, which is a characteristic of the relative consciousness. But that which reveals both subject and object, in one unchanging light, is the absolute consciousness called *kutastha*, the immutable, in the philosophy of Yoga.

Swami Vidyaranya sums up this aspect of the philosophy in the first chapter of *Panchadashi*.

Consciousness is distinct from the object, but is not different from itself. There is a unity of consciousness in the dreaming and the other states. It is therefore clear that one and the same consciousness abides in the three states. It is one and the same from day to day.

Through the many months, years, ages and world cycles, past and future, consciousness is the same and self-revealed. It persists and, unlike the sun, neither rises nor sets.

This ever-abiding consciousness is the Self (Atman). It is the highest bliss since it is the object of the greatest love. For love of the Self is seen in the universal feeling 'May I not cease to exist! May I continue to exist further!'[7]

Empirical life presupposes time, space and causation and the world of relativity. The events which make up the stream of our experience, whether external events or thoughts and feelings in the mind, are patterns of activity which begin and end. They are like the tunes in a symphony which emerge from the total mass of sound and have an identity and distinctness from each other, so that we recognize one or another as something we have experienced before. The same character can be said to typify our experience of objects and ideas in the external world. We recognize them when we meet them again even if they have changed greatly in the interim. The changing pattern is therefore an experience of something moving and transforming itself, appearing and disappearing, rising and falling, and it is inevitably limited to the world of time, space and causation experienced by the mind and the senses. In this sense we can all appreciate the words of the dying Hotspur in *Henry IV*, when he says:

> But thought's the slave of life, and life's time's fool
> And time, that takes survey of all the world,
> Must have a stop.[8]

If time stops, then there is no longer any past or future, and that leaves only the present. The consciousness of past and future is already something which we experience only in the present and, when we turn our back on the world of becoming and take our stand on the world of being, we re-establish our experience where it really is already established. Faust's compact with Mephistopheles in Goethe's great drama was that Mephistopheles would eternally amuse and divert him with the passing moment, but that if he became dissatisfied with this passing show and wanted to halt the process, Mephistopheles's power would be at an end. In the same way, Yoga tells us that it is only when we can overcome our preoccupation with the distracting stream of impressions which reach us from the sense world and the realm of memory, desire and imagination, that we can fully awaken to our own freedom as an independent spiritual being.

In January 1903, in the Golden Gate Hall in San Francisco, Swami Rama Tirtha gave his lecture on the topic of 'Maya or the when and why of the world'. He prefaced his remarks with the comment that Maya was a subject which superficial critics looked upon as the weakest point in the philosophy of Vedanta, and that many such critics say that, if it were not for the doctrine of Maya, then everything else in Vedanta would be acceptable, since it is so natural, plain, clear, beneficial and useful. The doctrine of Maya (he said) is often regarded as 'the one hitch, the one stumbling block in the way of the students of Vedanta'.[9] Vedanta holds that this universe of time, space and causation is unreal, is merely phenomenal. It is the world of becoming, which presents to us the tapestry of time, space and causation, with its finite objects, but in doing so distances us from these objects and conceals something of their nature from us. If we ask the question 'Why should this world exist at all?', says Swami Rama, Vedanta replies that the question is unanswerable and that we have no right to ask it. It plainly confesses its inability to explain the nature of the world or to penetrate and arrive at the ultimate reality behind this phenomenon intellectually. What it does say, however, is that it can 'prove to you experimentally and directly that this world, that you see, is in reality nothing else but God'. We can show to you conclusively through experiment (he says) that when you advance high enough in the realization of the truth, this world will be recognized to be unreal. Vedanta therefore does not propose any theory about the nature of the world. It says rather, 'see it, make an experiment, observe it; through direct realization you will see that the world is not what it appears to be... Similarly, Vedanta says, whether or not I am able to tell you why this Maya or ignorance is, it remains a fact. Why it came I may not be able to tell you. This is a fact, an experimental fact. The Vedantic attitude is merely experimental and scientific. It establishes no hypothesis, it puts forth no theory. It does not claim to be able to explain the origin of the world; this is beyond the sphere of intellect or comprehension.'[10]

The Swami says that there are many theories about how the world came into being but none of them is satisfactory. Those who say the world was created by a Creator are simply arguing by analogy. They see a house and they know that it was made by someone, so they say that the world was made by somebody. But if there is a Creator he must have existed, established somewhere, in order to create it and he must have begun to create it at some particular time. These questions imply the idea of when, where and why with regard to the world and these are the categories of time, space and causation. But time, space and causation are part of the world, not separate from it. This is the point also made by Kant and others. These are categories created by the mind and they are co-existent with empirical experience, not separate from it.

Bertrand Russell draws attention to the fact that the idea of a cause cannot apply to the whole of existence or reality. It is only applicable to an object among objects or a small part of the whole. This is because when we ask what the cause of something is, we ask by implication the question 'What *other* thing led to its existence?' But, *if there is no other thing*, then there can be no cause and the idea of causation is inapplicable. The same argument applies to the idea of seeking a purpose for the universe as a whole.[11]

Swami Rama Tirtha illustrates this point by a story

in which a school inspector came and tried to catch out a class of boys with a trick question. First he asked them: 'If I allow this piece of chalk to fall in air from this height, when will it reach the earth?' One of the boys answered correctly: 'In so many seconds'. Then the inspector said: 'If I drop a piece of stone from such and such a height, in what time will it fall?' And a boy answered correctly: 'In such and such a time'. Then the inspector said: 'If the earth falls from such and such height, what time will it take to fall?' And the boys were unable to answer the question, until one smart boy answered: 'First tell me where the earth will fall to?' The point is that the concept of falling applies only within the narrow confines of our everyday experience of gravity, the place where we are. As soon as we start trying to extend it, the paradoxes begin—like the simple-minded conclusion of an English child that things must fall upwards in Australia!

The conclusion is that the realm of time, space and causation is part of the framework in which the mind experiences the empirical world of everyday life. This is what Shri Shankara calls practical reality, but it is not the ultimate reality. It is the realm of phenomena or appearances.

Swami Rama Tirtha says:

Ma means 'not' and *Ya* means 'that', and hence *Maya* means 'not that'. The question is such as you cannot formulate. Not that. Now the question is, 'Is the world real?' Vedanta says, *neti*, Maya, not that, *nit*. You cannot call it real. Why not? Because reality means something which lasts for ever, which remains the same yesterday, today and for ever. That is reality. Now does the world last for ever? It does not last for ever, therefore it does not satisfy the definition of reality. In your deep sleep it disappears; in your state of realization, perfection or liberation, it disappears. So it does not last for ever, consequently you have no right to call it real.

Is the world unreal? Vedanta says *neti*, not that, Maya, *nit*. This is very strange, the world is not unreal. Vedanta says, 'No, it is not unreal, because unreal means something which never is, according to the definition of Vedanta, like the horns of a man. Did a man ever possess horns like a cow? Never. That is unreal, and the world is not unreal because it appears to you to be present just now. It appears to you to be present, therefore you have no right to call it unreal. Is the world real? Neti, nit. Is the world unreal? Neti, nit. Then is the world partly real and partly unreal? Vedanta says, 'Maya, neti, nit'. Not that even. Unreality and reality cannot subsist together. These answers to these questions are called the Maya theory of Vedanta. Such answers to these questions have another name, *mithya*, it is a word which is cognate with your word mythology. It means something which we cannot call real and which we cannot call unreal, and which we cannot call both real and unreal. Such is your world.[12]

Since the nature of the world is ultimately beyond the comprehension of the mind, the metaphysical questions have to be answered in a different way. As Swami Rama says:

Your intellect has work enough to do in this world;

let it work there. 'Render unto Caesar the things that are Caesar's, and render unto God what is God's.' Your intellect has work enough in the material plane, in the empirical realms, but in the realms of metaphysics you have to come only by one way, and one way only, and *that way is the way of realization, that way is the way of love, feeling, faith, or rather knowledge.* Strange kind of knowledge, strange kind of God-consciousness. When you come to this region through the proper channel, all questions cease, all problems are solved. In the *Kena Upanishad* of the Sama Veda, we have a passage which translated into English is something like this:

> I cannot say I know it:
> Nor can I say I do not know it;
> Beyond knowing and not knowing it is.[13]

And Swami Rama quotes Herbert Spencer in his *First Principles* as coming to the same conclusion, when he wrote:

> There must exist some principle which, being the basis of science, cannot be established by science. All reasoned-out conclusions, whatever, must rest on some postulate. There must be a place where we meet the region of the Unknowable, where intellect ought not to venture, cannot venture to go.[14]

8

Exchanging Complements*

This century has seen two major developments in the scientific view of the world which have radically modified the picture built up and accepted over the last three centuries that has come to be known as the classical physics of Isaac Newton. The seventeenth century was a time of great discovery, particularly in mechanics, and much of the philosophy of the time was coloured by the new recognition of what could be achieved mechanically. The development of watches, registering the exact time of day and doing so with such reliability that clockwork became proverbial for predictability and regularity, also influenced man's ideas about the universe in which he lived and about his own body. Newton's laws of motion explained and accurately predicted the movements of the moon and the planets and these too could be reproduced in a model driven by clockwork, as they were in the intricately constructed orreries and astronomical clocks of the period. For Descartes the body of man too was an exquisitely contrived machine, working like a well-wrought clock of infinitely superior design, controlled and inhabited by an immaterial mind which stood in relation to it somewhat like a skilled virtuoso player extemporising on a fine musical instrument. For the next three hundred years Western philosophy was dominated by the idea that there were two distinct and in some senses directly opposed principles, matter and mind.

* A lecture given on 21st March 1986.

The essence of Newton's view of the world was that it consisted of innumerable material objects existing within an absolute space and time. Matter was hard, solid and substantial in solid objects, although it could also exist in fluid and gaseous forms. This conception of the world as created from matter in an absolute time and space was virtually unquestioned until the twentieth century, except by the subjective idealists who believed that the material universe was only an experience in the mind of the experiencer. Leibniz and Berkeley saw the world as something mirrored or created in the inner experience either of the individual monad or of a cosmic spirit.

This matter/mind dualism of thought can be seen as an example of Hegel's doctrine that our understanding of truth develops through a dialectical process in which thought proceeds by any thesis being countered sooner or later by an opposite view, its antithesis, and that this contradiction is eventually reconciled in a synthesis which encompasses the elements of truth in both points of view.

Two major developments in physics in the twentieth century have shattered the Newtonian world view: Einstein's Theory of Relativity and the Quantum Theory developed by Planck, Bohr, Heisenberg, Schrödinger and others. The Theory of Relativity has shown us that Newton's Laws of Motion only apply to solid objects moving very much more slowly than the speed of light and that the whole idea of solid objects in a world made up of a substance called matter is erroneous. What we find at the basis of material things is the play of electromagnetic force, and the hallowed principle of the conservation of matter has been replaced by the more fundamental principle of the conservation of energy. Matter as we know it is interchangeable with energy, as Einstein proclaimed in the famous equation $E=mc^2$, and its substance or mass can be transmuted into pure energy, as we can all now appreciate in the case of the nuclear explosion or the nuclear power station. Such transmutation is indeed going on all around us and is the basis of the sun's heat and the light of the stars and galaxies.

But the new picture of the world is not as straightforward as it looks at first sight. We think of electromagnetic energy in terms of waves of different frequencies, radio waves, infra-red waves, the visible colours of the spectrum, the ultra-violet rays, X-rays, gamma rays, cosmic rays and so on. Paradoxically, however, we find that light and other rays have a curious and puzzling dual character; in some respects they behave as if they were waves and in other respects as if they were made up of discrete particles or packets of energy indivisible and discontinuous. Light can produce interference patterns, for instance, like the ripples on a lake; in this respect it behaves like waves, yet in its photo-electric effects and its emission or absorption by atoms, light can only be absorbed or emitted in discrete amounts or quanta, called photons.

There is therefore something extremely paradoxical and mysterious about the nature of the world as it is presented to us by the profound scientific investigations of modern physics. It is not simply a question of an unfinished enterprise. The paradoxical and apparently contradictory properties of subatomic matter are now so well established and recognized, that it is clear that they represent a fundamental and important feature of the nature of the world as it is revealed to the mind through scientific enquiry. This point has been well made by Niels Bohr:

> The great extension of our experience in recent years has brought to light the insufficiency of our simple mechanical conceptions and as a consequence, has shaken the foundations on which the customary interpretation of observation was based.[1]

Werner Heisenberg, one of the co-founders of modern physics, speaks eloquently of the impact of this new view of the world on its discoverers:

> I remember discussions with Bohr which went through many hours till very late at night and ending almost in despair; and when at the end of the discussion I went alone for a walk in the neighbouring park I repeated to myself again and again the question: 'Can nature possibly be so absurd as it seemed to us in these atomic experiments?'[2]

Einstein commented in similar terms:

> All my attempts to adapt the theoretical foundation of physics to this [new type of] knowledge failed completely. It was as if the ground had been pulled from under one, with no firm foundation to be seen anywhere, upon which one could have built.[3]

Capra, who quotes these and many other examples

in his book *The Tao of Physics*, published in 1975, points out that these developments in scientific knowledge have brought it into close agreement with what the mystics of the great spiritual traditions of India and China have said about the nature of the world: that it is fundamentally mysterious and that the deeper one tries to plumb its depths, the more surely is one faced with paradoxical conclusions. It is interesting to find that many of the great scientists personally concerned with these developments like Bohr, Heisenberg, Schrödinger and, later, Oppenheimer have recognized this convergence and have themselves expressed the view that modern science was being more and more clearly led to a unity of views with these mystical traditions on the nature of the world.

Niels Bohr adopted as his motto the Latin *Contraria sunt Complementa*, 'Contraries (or, as we might say, contradictions) are complementary'. This implies that for a full understanding of truth in the empirical sense one has to envisage more than one mental framework, no one of which may be wholly true or untrue. The mathematical models which treat electrons as waves or as particles are each valid in their own context even though they are irreconcilable, because they each enable one to explain and predict certain behaviour. What 'the thing-in-itself' is, is another matter. And Niels Bohr's coat of arms was completed with the Chinese symbol for the two principles Yin and Yang which together make up a perfect circle. These two elements of the Chinese symbol T'ai-chi represent the harmony of the combination of the pairs of opposites which are complementary. The wave and the particle are simply an example of the same principle. Complementarity in Bohr's sense—and the associated appearance of irreconcilable contradictoriness—is characteristic of the nature of the world.

In fact, this puzzling and contradictory character of things is universal and soon reveals itself to us when we seriously attempt to investigate them. It is a fundamental characteristic of the nature of all objects in the world and not only of the behaviour of the subatomic particles studied by the physicists. This is well established by the conclusions to which the greatest of the philosophers have come. Take, for instance, the paradox at the heart of our idea of any ordinary object, such as a table or a chair. We recognize it as having a particular colour, shape, hardness and position, as being of such-and-such a size and constructed of a particular kind of wood. But all these are in the end simply descriptions of incidental qualities of the table. Its colour may change if we paint it or view it in a different light, its composition may change if we repair it or replace its top with plastic, yet we think of these things as incidental changes which we have made to the table and we recognize the table as the same table before and after these changes. In other words our whole way of thinking of things suggests that the thing itself exists independently of the incidental qualities which we associate with it. It is as if the table owned these qualities but existed apart from them. Yet if we ask what is the thing-in-itself, we find that any description we could give of it amounts to a collection of qualities or relations, and there does not seem to be anything left over when we have eliminated all these changeable properties to constitute the real core of the table itself.

It is not different with persons. We may think of a person as a man who lives at a particular house or as someone we see at the same time each morning travelling in the train; but we recognize these descriptions as purely incidental and would not think the individual any less the same person if he moved house or started using his car instead. Even if we say that what identifies someone is a particular body or mind, we find ourselves in similar difficulties, because the body changes radically throughout life and the mind is even more changeable than the body. Both can be regarded as an elaborate bundle of characteristic qualities; but there is nothing in such a bundle to justify our feeling of the real person existing as the core of the personality independently of all the passing features. The philosopher John Locke said that when he experienced objects he found the real object to be 'a something I know not what', because, when it was divested of all incidental qualities and relationships, there appeared to be nothing else left which the mind and senses could grasp. Kant echoed this verdict when he distinguished between the unknown and unknowable thing-in-itself which he called the *noumenon*, and the phenomenal characteristics with which the mind associates it in the realm of time and space and causation. The nineteenth century philosopher, F H Bradley, held that the puzzling and contradictory character of our way of thinking in terms of substances and qualities showed it to rest on the acceptance of what was only an appearance as if it were reality.

Hence Shri Shankara is not making a point which is totally alien to Western science or to Western thought when he points out the paradoxical and contradictory nature of our ideas about the Self and the not-self. On the one hand, we think of the Self as continuous, indivisible and undivided, and as the owner of all the states of mind. But, as David Hume and others have shown, when we look for this real abiding Self—in which we implicitly believe—within the mind and the personality, we find nothing but an ever-changing stream of thoughts, perceptions, feelings, moods and energies.

But there is an even more fundamental contradiction between two complementary pictures which we have of ourselves. On the one hand we feel that we are in some sense the spectator who experiences as a witness the sequence of events both in the mind and in the external world. But in another sense we think of ourselves as the participant in these events, as both the doer of the deeds and the enjoyer of the experiences. As an enjoyer we are not an empirical witness; rather we are like the man who partakes of the meal which is put in front of him and subsequently suffers the consequences in the form of toothache or indigestion or simply the self-satisfied feeling of having supped our fill or the unsatisfied feeling of not having had enough and being still hungry. This dual character of the Self which appears as the ego to be the chief actor in the drama of our life and as the abiding and unaltered witness of the events is (so to speak) a *koan* (or riddle) which has to be solved if we are to discover our true identity. Niels Bohr recognized this parallelism between the paradoxical complementarity of nature revealed by modern physics and the mystery of the nature of the Self which the yogis speak of as 'the knot of the heart' when he wrote:

> For a parallel to the lesson of atomic theory... (we must turn) to those kinds of epistemological problems with which already thinkers like the Buddha and Lao-Tzu have been confronted, when trying to harmonize our position as spectators and actors in the great drama of existence.[4]

According to the yogis the inadequacy of the human mind in comprehending the nature of reality is an inevitable consequence of the fact that it is a finite and limited instrument, working within the framework of time, space and causation. Whatever it conceives or perceives has, as Bradley emphasized, an element of unreality about it because it deals with the realm of appearances, and appearances, no matter how deeply we probe them, always leave something out of account in their view of reality; moreover they are in many cases frankly misleading.

We can see these characteristics even in our attempts to make images of things in everyday life. In map-making, for instance, we have to choose the co-ordinates we are going to use in projecting the surface of the spherical world onto a flat sheet of paper. There are various ways of doing it and each has its own particular merits, but each equally distorts the picture in one way or another.

It is no different with linguistic models. When we try and describe something in language—even in the sophisticated language of mathematics—what we end up with is an exhaustive but obviously inadequate account of the things we are describing, which concentrates on certain details and may convey important information, but is invariably an incomplete description of the thing itself. How can we adequately describe in words the facial appearance of a friend or the taste of a well-cooked meal?

But the mind deals only in such descriptions, either linguistic or non-linguistic. Either it has to resort to words which, however long the description, fall far short of completely describing what we see, or it must rely on images which are equally inadequate, as any painter or photographer knows. If, then, it is beyond the competence of the mind to give a full and exhaustive account of even the empirical reality, how much more so must this apply to the fundamental reality of the Self within the personality!

The yogis say that we have to rely on a different faculty, and that it is only when we go beyond the empirical mind with its powers of imagination and sensation and seek to know the real nature of our being, that what Shri Shankara calls *anubhava* or direct experience of reality is achieved, that the knot of the heart is untied and the *koan* is solved. One of the traditional *koans* given to the Zen students by the teacher is: 'Seek to know your original face, the face that you had before you were born'. The empirical personality is like a series of masks worn by the individual on his way through life. They may express the appearance which he presents to various groups of his friends and acquaintances, but they are not the real 'I'.

If we accept that the reality behind our own

experience of the world is beyond the grasp of the mind with its finite categories of wave and particle, substance and quality, subject and object, then it follows that the attempts to know this reality by the ordinary processes of intellectual enquiry are doomed to failure. As Swami Rama Tirtha says, if we try to use the local consciousness to know the infinite reality we are plainly going to fail entirely in our enterprise. We may by reason be able to reach up to the infinite by inference and know that there is an infinite, but what it is we can never know directly by means of the mental categories. This is not a dogma; it is an obvious truth. If the nature of the infinite could be fully known by the mind, we would immediately have established duality, because there would have been something other than the infinite able to handle it and objectify it and examine it. But, like the Western philosopher Bradley, the Vedanta maintains that the reality behind each and every one of our experiences is the underlying Absolute, which is of the nature of existence, consciousness and bliss. Since empirical knowing will tell us only of the finite world of relativity, with its qualities and relationships, and its network of objects linked by the laws of time, space and causation, we have to rely on another means of knowing.

The Anglo-Indian judge, Sir John Woodroffe, who made a deep study of the Vedanta, puts the matter thus:

> The only certitude is in direct experience itself. Nothing useful is gained in attempting to prove that that experience is in itself not real, or is an appearance of something unperceived. If we would

> know what some other than ordinary experience is, we must actually shift, not our speculative thought on to it, but our being into it. In other words we must have that experience directly... We must experience reality, whatever be its aspect—and not merely discuss it.[5]

And he goes on to point out that when we do so, our present experience will appear to us, not as totally false, but as a relative truth, characteristic of the stage at which it is experienced, but corrected or revised in the light of the deeper insights gained from a more adequate view of the real. As the seventeenth-century English Quaker mystic, Isaac Pennington, says, there is no truth except the last, yet everything is true in its own part. Each is a shadow, cast by an intenser substance. This is the view of Bradley, who holds that in our quest for truth we penetrate into deeper levels of reality, which still retain an element of deceptive appearance in their make-up, but correspond more and more closely to the truth of the Absolute as we more nearly approach it. This idea also has some kinship with Hegel's doctrine of the dialectical process in which the contradictory thesis and antithesis are transcended in a more fundamental synthesis. The progress in science in this century has led us to a similar situation in which the paradoxes emerging from the view of the world which it has produced have led us towards a reconciliation with the teachings of the great spiritual traditions.

Swami Rama Tirtha puts the matter in much simpler terms:

The agnostic and the free thinker each says 'I will investigate for myself', and we see how far he gets on. He says that light is in this match. Now where shall we discover it? So he cuts the match into little pieces, and cannot find the light. Then he pulverizes it, still he cannot find the light. Then he says that life is in this body. He takes the body and pulls it to pieces; life cannot be found. He crushes the bones, but life is not there. He says: 'If there is a Reality, I must be That, but it is unknowable'. That is true so far as he has gone, but he has not yet developed the cosmic consciousness; he has used the local consciousness entirely to know the infinite, but that he can never know it in this way is plain.[6]

Swami Rama points out that the word 'Vedanta' literally means 'the end or goal of knowledge'. It signifies the ultimate truth and thus it has nothing sectarian or narrow about it. It is universal. His claim is that whoever throws aside his prejudices and frees himself from them, will concur with the conclusion of Vedanta.[7]

This does not mean that Vedanta is trying to compete with science to explain the nature of the world. On the contrary: Vedanta does not propose any theory of the kind that science makes about the nature of the world. It does not pretend to be able to explain the world. What it does is to make a direct appeal to experience in saying that the empirical world turns out to be an experience without a substantial basis. If we actually look to see by making the experiment and observing it, we will find by direct realization that the world is not what it appears to be, and that it is ultimately mysterious (*mithya*).[8]

> The Vedantic attitude is merely experimental and scientific. It establishes no hypothesis, it puts forward no theory. It does not claim to be able to explain the origin of the world; this is beyond the sphere of intellect or comprehension.

Swami Rama points out that when you begin to examine questions such as when the world began, you are trying to separate two ideas—the idea when, where and why, on one side, and the idea of the world, on the other—but the ideas of time, space and causation are themselves a part of the world, since they are categories conceived and used by the finite mind in its activity as the organ of empirical experience. If the ultimate reality is beyond time, space and causation (as it must be if it is infinite), if the absolute exists as the real background of the world of relativity and it is possible to penetrate beyond the world of deceptive appearances to the underlying reality, then that experience must transcend these categories. When we think of God and try and impose our mental ideas and concepts on him, attributing purpose or personality to the Absolute, then we are (so to speak) attempting to bring God down into the dock of the tribunal of our mental consciousness. It is like trying to reduce the world of thought to a microscope slide which we can examine by the eye.

In the *Brihadaranyaka Upanishad,* the sage Yajnavalkya teaches his pupil Ushasta Chakrayana about the spiritual reality, but the pupil complains:

> You have explained this to me just as one might say 'This is a cow' or 'This is a horse', but explain to me

properly the nature of the Absolute, which is immediately present and directly perceived, that is the Self of all things.

And his teacher replies:

> You cannot see the seer of seeing,
> You cannot hear the hearer of hearing,
> You cannot think the thinker of thinking,
> You cannot understand the understander
>   of understanding.
> He is your Self which is in all things.[9]

9

A Good Koan*

First, in case there are some of you who do not already know the word, let me try and clarify what is meant by the word *koan*. In the Zen Buddhist tradition in Japan, the spiritual teacher (often the Abbot of a monastery), as well as training his pupils in the practice of daily meditation—and Zen comes from the Sanskrit word *dhyana* meaning meditation—also sometimes presents his pupil with a challenging puzzle, a kind of riddle which contains within itself the clue to a profound spiritual truth, but which he has to wrestle with in his mind before an awakening to the truth it contains becomes possible. Often, the awakening leads to an expansion of the pupil's consciousness (called *satori*), because it involves getting over some of his most cherished prejudices and arriving at an entirely new view of the world and of truth. The *koan* then is a seed thought which is initially baffling and challenging, but has a profound meaning buried within it. Although there are said to be over 1500 traditional *koans* which have been handed down in the Zen tradition, *koans* are not limited to the formal type. Indeed the Zen Masters themselves say that the Universe itself is a great, living, challenging *koan*, which we have to try and solve.

This lecture takes as its starting point a statement which has the character of a *koan*, although it is not one of those traditional *koans* given by the Zen Masters in the

---

* A lecture given on 5th June 1987.

Japanese tradition. On the contrary it is a statement by one of the great figures in modern Western philosophy, Ludwig Wittgenstein.

Wittgenstein came from a rich Jewish family in Vienna, which, until Ludwig came along, was more renowned for its interest in music than in philosophy. Brahms had been a close friend of the family and the Wittgensteins had supported his friend, the great violinist Joachim, in his youth, putting him up in the family house and arranging to send him to Mendelssohn for his studies. Ludwig Wittgenstein's brother, Paul, who was head of the family in his day, embarked on a career as a concert pianist, but lost his right arm on active service in the First World War. He continued to play with his left hand and commissioned works from Ravel, Richard Strauss, Prokofiev and Benjamin Britten among others, all of them written for the unusual combination of a left-handed pianist and orchestra. Paul's brother, Ludwig, was equally gifted in another sphere, being an outstanding mathematician who started out to train in aeronautical engineering. He came to Manchester in 1908, but became so interested in the fundamental logical basis of mathematics that he went to study with Bertrand Russell in Cambridge before the First World War (in 1912) and became a philosopher. Called up for service in the Austrian army in the 1914-18 war, he ended up in a prisoner-of-war camp in Italy, where Russell went to visit him. He discovered that Wittgenstein had in his rucksack the manuscript of a work he had written down in notebooks during his army career, the *Tractatus Logico-Philosophicus*, which is now regarded as one of the great philosophical classics of the twentieth century. During his war service, in the course of which he was awarded a number of medals for bravery, he used to be called by the soldiers 'the one with the Gospel' because he always carried with him Tolstoy's edition of the Gospels.[1] When he got home to Vienna, almost the first thing he did was to give away all his considerable wealth to his brothers and sisters (he was the youngest of eight children). He then spent six years (from 1920 to 1926) as an elementary school-teacher in several small villages in Lower Austria. After this he gave that up to spend two years building a house for one of his sisters in Vienna, incidentally proving himself to be a brilliant architect in the process. People still visit the house on account of its striking and unusual design.

In 1929 Wittgenstein returned to Cambridge and was proposed for a Lectureship in Philosophy there, although he did not qualify under the University statutes because he had not got his Ph.D. degree. In order to satisfy this requirement, it was arranged that he should be examined for this degree, with the *Tractatus* as the thesis. Russell and Moore were appointed as the examiners, and spent the time discussing with him a few of the questions raised in his book. Russell is reported to have said as Wittgenstein came into the room for the examination: 'I have never known anything so absurd in my life'. Later, in 1938, Wittgenstein succeeded Moore in the Chair of Philosophy at Cambridge. Before his appointment, when the issue was still in doubt, Professor Broad, who was himself a Cambridge philosopher of world renown, said that to refuse to give Wittgenstein the Chair of

Philosophy would be like refusing Einstein a Chair of Physics! Clearly then Wittgenstein was one of the most brilliant and unusual thinkers of his generation.

Wittgenstein was particularly interested in the relationship between language and thought, and in the basis of logic. He once said that all the sciences and what is known as common sense attempt to say more than we really know and that 'the difficulty in philosophy is to say no more than we know'.

Wittgenstein's friend, Dr M O'C Drury, describes how Wittgenstein was once invited to give a lecture to a general audience who had no particular interest or training in philosophy. He chose to give a lecture on Ethics and he started by explaining to his audience the reason for choosing the subject:

> When your former secretary honoured me by asking me to read a paper to your Society, my first thought was that I would certainly do it, and my second thought was that if I was to have the opportunity to speak to you I should speak about something which I am keen on communicating to you and that I should not misuse this opportunity by giving you a lecture about, say, logic.

What he then gave them, in the course of his lecture on Ethics, was what one can only describe as a *koan* on the subject of Ethics, one of the most challenging and astonishing *koans* imaginable. Comparing statements about science with those about ethics, he said:

> We cannot write a scientific book, the subject matter of which could be intrinsically sublime and above all other subject matters. I can only describe my feeling

by the metaphor, that, if a man could write a book on Ethics which really was a book on Ethics, this book would, with an explosion, destroy all the other books in the world. Our words used as we use them in science, are vessels capable only of containing and conveying meaning and sense, *natural* meaning and sense. Ethics, if it is anything, is supernatural and our words will only express facts; as a teacup will only hold a teacup full of water even if I were to pour out a gallon over it.[2]

This then is the first statement of the *koan*:

Ethics, if it is anything, is supernatural and our words will only express facts; as a teacup will only hold a teacup full of water even if I were to pour out a gallon over it.

What makes this statement like a *koan* is that it is at first sight puzzling and that it is made by someone of great authority in the field of philosophy who was clearly trying to convey something very serious and important to his audience about ethics.

Ethics is generally considered a pretty dull subject nowadays and one in which many philosophers have lost interest. Many would say that it does not deserve to be part of philosophy, that it is not quite respectable, because it is concerned with value judgements. These are arbitrary (it is said) and determined by man's feelings. They are therefore irrational and, by implication, unreliable, if not downright capricious. Just as beauty is popularly held to be in the eye of the beholder, so there are those who would maintain that one man's good is another man's poison. In other words, there is no such thing as 'the good' and certainly no such thing as the highest good or *summum bonum* of which many of the classical philosophers have spoken. On this currently fashionable view, the idea of an absolute value is a myth; everything is relative and comes down in the end to a matter of opinion or preference—of an individual's value judgements.

It is not surprising that, in this intellectual climate, *goodness* is not a very fashionable topic nowadays and that you do not find many people wanting to talk about ethics or morality. Yet, even in this age of permissiveness, we all have a clear idea about what we think is not good and we all have the still small voice of conscience within us, giving us the feeling that we are not entirely what we ought to be in our everyday behaviour and dealings. What then are we to make of this *koan* of Wittgenstein's which appears to give such a transcendent rôle to ethics—and could induce him to say that '*If a man could write a book on ethics which really was a book on ethics, this book would, with an explosion, destroy all other books in the world*'.

Let us see if we can find any clues which may make these astonishing statements of Wittgenstein's about ethics a little more understandable.

Perhaps one of the earliest texts on ethics can be found in the yogic literature, in the *Katha Upanishad*, which has the verse:

> Both the good and the pleasant approach a man. The wise man, pondering over them, discriminates between them. The wise chooses the good in

preference to the pleasant. The simple-minded, for the sake of worldly well-being, prefers the pleasant.³

We can all understand the distinction being made here, but it is more difficult to say precisely what we mean by the good.

What is the good and how can we recognize it when it approaches us? This is the theme of much philosophy. The nineteenth century English philosopher, F H Bradley, devoted the whole of his book *Ethical Studies* to this one topic, and there are also classical philosophical works on ethics by Spinoza and Aristotle among others. Many other thinkers have discussed what constitutes the highest good which man can aspire to, among them St Augustine and St Thomas Aquinas. Bertrand Russell in his *Human Knowledge: Its Scope and Limits* holds that most ethical theories are of two kinds. According to the first kind, good conduct is conduct obeying certain rules (and he instances the Ten Commandments of the Old Testament and the principles proposed by Kant as being of this type). The second type holds that good conduct is conduct designed to realize certain ends (for instance, the greatest possible excess of pleasure over pain for the greatest number of people). But Russell admits that there are theories which are of neither of these two kinds.⁴ This is certainly true of the conclusions reached by F H Bradley. Bradley considers every possible view of what the basis of ethics might be, from the simple view that it aims at maximizing pleasure, which he easily shows to be false, to the view of ethics as conforming to the rules laid down by society. But it is convincingly shown that this is not what we mean by good in the deeper sense.

It is undoubtedly true that the child first comes

across the concept of right and wrong through getting to know what it is which incurs the approval or disapproval of his parents. As Freud has pointed out in his theory of the development of the super-ego, the mind of the child through its love of the parents begins to create an ideal picture of what it should be—i.e., of its own better self—which it feels to be all too often contradicted by its lower self as it is. The good and bad selves in this way come to exist within the mind of the growing individual. Later in life the rôle of the parents comes to be taken over, to a great extent, by the ideals inculcated by the society in which the individual lives.

But these rules are relative and changing. What is approved of or disapproved of in one society is not so in another. And historically the rules of good behaviour have changed radically even in the same society over a very short space of years. Consider, for instance, the difference between the social conventions accepted in Victorian England and in our own age of permissiveness.

The idea of good, however, is not dependent simply on these temporary conventions. In fact, the human mind recognizes a good which is higher than any social conventions. Just think of the great figures who have defied the conventions of the society in which they lived for the sake of their own higher principles. The Jewish philosopher Spinoza was excommunicated by the Jewish community in which he lived in seventeenth century Amsterdam, because his love of truth and philosophy made him no longer able to conform to their code of what was considered right and good. He preferred to cut himself off, so that he could follow the path which he had chosen, to seek truth through philosophy wherever it might lead.

In our own day Sakharov has defied the rules of conduct acceptable to the Marxist government of his own Soviet society in order to speak out for the truth as he sees it, and the same is true of Solzhenitsyn and others. Therefore we cannot accept as valid any theory of ethics which suggests that it depends simply on the conventions which society accepts or approves.

What then is the essence of morality according to Bradley? He argues that the common feature in our urge to admire and follow the good in our lives is an expression of the urge to realize the ideal self and to negate the bad self. There is this felt contradiction within us; we are divided against ourselves, so to speak, by this feeling of what we ought to be, which conflicts with what we feel we are. But what is this ideal self? And how does it come to have the power over us that it has?

At the level of empirical life, considered just in terms of morality, the ideal self is simply an idea, a conception that we have of what we would like ourselves really to be like. And in this sense, says Bradley, morality is something which points beyond itself to religion, because it is only when one considers the teachings of the spiritual traditions that we find that the ideal self is something which is really existing and which is already within man. It is, indeed, the bad self which (in the spiritual teachings) turns out to be the unreal and negative element. It is simply those elements in the raw and unregenerate mind which oppose the realization of the good self.

In this sense we can begin to understand how Wittgenstein can speak in such astounding terms about ethics, for to fully unveil the underlying basis of ethics is to unveil the existence of the real self of man, which is not only perfectible, but already perfect in its real essence. When Christ commanded his followers: 'Be ye perfect even as your Father in heaven is perfect', he was certainly insisting on the demand of ethics—that we should aim for and strive to reach the highest good. But the demand has a deeper, spiritual dimension, namely, the recognition that the highest good is already present as the good self, the real Self, hidden within the innermost heart of each and everyone. The Kingdom of Heaven is within you, and is not to be sought somewhere outside.

Bradley makes a very important point about the ethical sense in man. He says that, from the empirical or worldly point of view, the moral sense is a self-contradiction and a demand for what cannot be.[5]

> Neither in me, nor in the world, is what ought to be what is, and what is what ought to be.

And he further says:

> The reason of the contradiction is that man (himself) is a contradiction. But man is more; he feels or knows himself as such, and this makes a vital difference; for to feel a contradiction is *ipso facto* to be above it. Otherwise, how would it be possible to feel it? A felt contradiction which does not imply, besides its two poles, a unity which includes and is above them, will, the more it is reflected upon, the more be seen to be altogether unmeaning. Unless man was and divined himself to be a whole, he

could not feel the contradiction, still less feel pain in it, and reject it as foreign to his nature.

This is a very profound point which Bradley makes and one which is well worth meditating upon. Man is a contradiction because he knows himself at one and the same time to be both the bad self and the good self. He may sometimes be identified more with one and at other times more with the other, but they are both aspects of himself, empirically speaking, and he feels the conflict between them as the discrepancy between what is and what ought to be.

> If we can know the whole, it can only be because the whole knows itself in us, because the whole is self or mind, which is and knows, knows and is, the identity and correlation of subject and object.[6]

But to fully grasp this point we are stretching language to its limits and beyond. As Wittgenstein says:

> I at once see clearly, as it were a flash of light, not only that no description I can think of would do to describe what I mean by absolute value, but that I would reject every significant description that anybody could possibly suggest, *ab initio*, on the ground of its significance... My whole tendency and I believe the tendency of all men who ever tried to write or talk Ethics or Religion was to run against the boundaries of language. This running against the walls of our cage is perfectly, absolutely hopeless.[7]

What Wittgenstein is saying here is that there can be no adequate definition in words of what we mean by the highest good, of absolute value, *not because it does not exist*, but because it is beyond the sphere of Nature. It is supernatural, and hence finite language is inadequate to describe it. No wonder then that present-day professional philosophers are not keen on producing ethical theories. From their point of view, it is no good waffling on about something you cannot adequately describe and expressing mere opinions, however dogmatically. This is what Wittgenstein stressed when he said that 'the difficulty in philosophy is to say no more than we know'.

But there may be a value, if you do know, in providing hints and clues—in a good *koan*, for instance—if, like the pointing finger which leads us to look for ourselves and discover the new moon in the sky, it awakens the faculty of direct experience in us and provides us with the means to intuitively verify the truth. Wittgenstein's friend, Dr Drury, who quotes the words from his lecture on ethics, comments that:

> This drawing of a firm and unbreakable boundary round the sphere of what can be said significantly is not done to condemn or ridicule those who have tried to overleap this boundary; on the contrary, it is done to intensify the very impetus and desire to break out of our cage.[7]

He goes on to quote from Simone Weil:

> There is a reality outside the world, that is to say outside space and time, outside man's mental universe, outside any sphere whatsoever that is accessible to human faculties. Corresponding to this reality, at the centre of the human heart is the longing for an absolute good, a longing which is always there and is never appeased by any object in the world.[7]

This is another statement which can serve as a clue to Wittgenstein's *koan*.

In the contemporary world, dominated by the successful rise of scientific knowledge and technology, the rôle of ethics has been devalued and truth is considered to be entirely independent of value judgements. But this is a one-sided view which is not shared by those who have thought most deeply and profoundly about this matter. The philosopher Whitehead, for instance, who was also a brilliant mathematician and co-author with Bertrand Russell of *Principia Mathematica*, the great modern classic on the basis of logic and mathematics, says in his book, *Adventures of Ideas*:

> Beauty is a wider, and more fundamental, notion than Truth... Beauty...concerns the inter-relations of the various components of Reality, and also the inter-relations of the various components of Appearance, and also the relations of Appearance to Reality. Thus any part of experience can be beautiful. The teleology of the Universe is directed to the production of Beauty. Thus any system of things which in any wide sense is beautiful is to that extent justified in its existence. It may however fail in another sense, by inhibiting more Beauty than it creates. Thus the system, though in a sense beautiful, is on the whole evil in that environment. But Truth has a narrower meaning in two ways. First, Truth, in any important sense, merely concerns the relations of Appearance to Reality. It is the conformation of Appearance to Reality. But in the second place the notion of 'conformation' in the case of Truth is narrower than that in the case of Beauty.

For the truth-relation requires that the two relata have some factor in common.[8]

Notwithstanding the possible unseasonableness of the truth-relation, the general importance of Truth for the promotion of Beauty is overwhelming. After all has been said, yet the truth-relation remains the simple, direct mode of realizing Harmony. Other ways are indirect, and indirectness is at the mercy of the environment. There is a blunt force about Truth, which in the subjective form of its prehension is akin to cleanliness—namely, the removal of dirt, which is an unwanted irrelevance. The sense of directness which it carries with it, sustains the upstanding individualities so necessary for the beauty of a complex. Falsehood is corrosive…[9]

From these functions of Truth in the service of Beauty, the realization of Truth becomes in itself an element promoting Beauty of feeling… Thus Truth, in itself and apart from special reasons to the contrary, becomes self-justifying. It is accompanied by a sense of rightness in the deepest Harmony. But Truth derives this self-justifying power from its services in the promotion of Beauty. Apart from Beauty, Truth is neither good nor bad.[10]

The essential implication of what Whitehead seems to be saying here is that, when fully realized—that is to say, when the appearance fully conforms to the reality and reality is therefore seen as it really is—the truth is discovered to be beautiful. It is a point which reminds one of Einstein's conviction that the fundamental truth which he sought in Nature could be recognized by its beauty—in other words that the main criterion of even scientific truth lay in its aesthetic perfection.[11]

Of course, this does not apply to the appearances which the world presents to us in ordinary life, which often appear far from beautiful, if not downright ugly in some respects. But—if we are to believe the mystics and the saints—even these apparent uglinesses and distortions will be seen at a deeper level to be unreal elements in a harmony underlying all creation.

Whitehead indeed says:

> The attainment of Truth belongs to the essence of Peace. By this it is meant, that the intuition constituting the realization of Peace has as its objective that Harmony whose interconnections involve Truth. A defect in Truth is a limitation to Harmony. There can be no secure efficacy in the Beauty which hides within itself the dislocations of falsehood.[12]

It is in this sense that Whitehead can say that beauty is a wider and more fundamental notion than truth. As he says:

> The truth or falsehood of propositions is not directly to the point in the demand for Truth... This bare 'truth or falsehood' of propositions is a comparatively superficial factor affecting the discursive interests of the intellect. The essential truth that Peace demands is the conformation of Appearance to Reality.[12]

It is 'the feeling of dislocation of appearance from reality' which gives rise to dissatisfaction with things as they are in empirical life and leads both to the birth of the desire to find that which will assuage the dissatisfaction and, at a higher level, to the moral drive to become what we feel we ought to be. As Whitehead says:

> Sense-perception, which dominates the appearance of things, in its own nature re-arranges, and thus in a way distorts... In its own nature Sense-perception is an interpretation, and this interpretation may be completely misleading.[13]

It is this deluding power of the sense appearances which leads to the dislocation of appearance from reality, which the yogis call nescience (*avidya*). And in its turn this leads to the dissatisfaction which is at the basis of the moral imperatives. As Whitehead says:

> If there were a necessary conformation of Appearance to Reality then Morality would vanish. There is no morality about the multiplication table, whose items are necessarily linked.[13]

If we accept what Whitehead says, it is a mistake to separate the ethical questions from the quest for truth, because they are in fact inseparable. Beauty is that which gives bliss to us when we contemplate it. When the nature of the supreme reality or Truth is directly realized, according to Vedanta, it is found to be *sat-chit-ananda*, the ultimate truth, consciousness absolute and supreme bliss. In Keats's words:

> Beauty is truth, truth beauty,—that is all
> Ye know on earth, and all ye need to know.

10

Reconciling the Contradictions*

We all know the great speeches from Hamlet. They are part of our national heritage, and lines from them have become proverbial, so that they are part of the common currency of speech. The reason for their power over us is that they awaken echoes of our own experience and have a universal validity. Hamlet expresses, far more nobly and far more eloquently than we could, that negative mood which assails each and every man at some time in his life. You remember the words:

> I have of late, but wherefore I know not, lost all my mirth, foregone all custom of exercises: and indeed it goes so heavily with my disposition, that this goodly frame the earth, seems to me a sterile promontory, this most excellent canopy the air, look you, this brave o'erhanging firmament, this majestical roof fretted with golden fire, why it appearest nothing to me but a foul and pestilent congregation of vapours...
>
> What a piece of work is a man! how noble in reason! how infinite in faculties! in form and moving, how express and admirable! in action, how like an angel! in apprehension, how like a god! the beauty of the world! the paragon of animals! and yet to me, what is this quintessence of dust? Man delights not me, no, nor woman neither...[1]

Hamlet is presented to us as a heroic character, but

---

* A lecture given on 11th November 1987.

the same mood of disillusionment is met with elsewhere in Shakespeare in less admirable characters, as when the ambitious Macbeth speaks of man's life and aspirations as 'a tale told by an idiot, full of sound and fury, signifying nothing'.

As spectators of the plays, we are moved by the grandeur of these speeches and have a sense, half-grasped rather than fully understood, that they somehow express another dimension of the human spirit, which takes it far above the currently nihilistic view of the world which the words seem to be expressing. And we are not wrong about this, for the great paradox of these speeches is that Hamlet and Macbeth are speaking and behaving as if they were, not man, but man's Creator, looking on his work and seeing that it was *not* good.

Tolstoi, who reached a similar mood of disillusionment and despair in his own life, describes how he suddenly saw, with a blinding flash of insight, that his rejection of the world as bad was in fact a rejection of his own life. This was one of the turning points of Tolstoi's career, and it marked the point at which he turned away from the life of self-indulgence which he had led hitherto and set out to follow the teachings of Christ. His real life experience echoes the same potential situation which is portrayed in dramatic terms by Hamlet and Macbeth. What is remarkable about it is that it demonstrates the individual as, at one and the same time, judge and prisoner in the dock. Hamlet rejects mankind, but he himself is a man; Macbeth rejects man's life, but (like Tolstoi) it is really his own life which he is rejecting as meaningless. When we remember the point made by Spinoza that one of the most fundamental drives within every living thing is the urge to self-preservation and self-transcendence or self-perfection, which he calls '*conatus*', this is all the more remarkable. As he says 'No one forgoes a good except in hope of a greater good'. What greater good is it that man senses which brings him to the point of rejecting his empirical life and personality?

How is it that man can apparently come to reject himself? It can only be because that element in man's personality which sits as judge and jury on his empirical personality and its failings, is different from the empirical personality which stands in the dock before him. There is therefore an apparent contradiction which faces man when he begins to ask himself the question 'Who am I?' And in this context he is faced with the question 'Which is the real I?', the 'I' which is rejected or the 'I' which does the rejecting?

According to Hegel the whole process of history and the advance of knowledge takes place through a dialectical process, in which contradictions arise between two apparent truths, the thesis and the antithesis, which seem to lead to opposite conclusions and are then reconciled by a leap forward in an insight which recognizes both half-truths as aspects of a higher truth, which embraces and encompasses them in a wider synthesis of knowledge. In the case of self-knowledge, this represents a process of becoming more conscious of what we really are. Much of what we believe about ourselves is unconsciously and uncritically accepted on the basis of appearances, and we do not bother to think it out at all. But as we grow and become more aware of ourselves, the apparent paradoxes and contradictions of human nature present themselves ever more vividly before us, and we can only solve these paradoxes by deepening our understanding of our own nature.

There are many such paradoxes, like the question of freedom and responsibility, guilt and innocence, which face us in ordinary life. Even the common law has to face and deal with these problems, but it does so in a makeshift fashion employing many compromises and approximations, relying on the good sense of the judges and juries to administer the law with wisdom. We speak about 'extenuating circumstances' and 'letting people off for diminished responsibility', and most people would accept that the law is only the best that we have been able to do so far in dealing with an urgent empirical problem. Few would regard it as perfect, nor can we maintain that justice is always done.

Samuel Butler highlights the problem of responsibility, when he describes a mythical country called 'Erewhon' in which anyone who is sick is sent to prison, while those who commit what we would call crimes are sent to hospital. Things are not yet quite like that in our society, but we have moved much nearer towards it since Butler's day, and every time psychiatrists are called on to defend an accused person on the grounds that he was suffering from mental illness, we are in a sense invoking the principles of the state of Erewhon. And there are examples of epileptics, for instance, who have been successfully defended for quite serious crimes committed by them, on the grounds that they were committed automatically without their knowledge while they were having a fit. One aspect of the question, 'Who am I?' is therefore the problem of responsibility, a sort of cosmic 'whodunnit'. But the fact that each and every individual can stand back in his mind and judge himself, even to the point of rejecting his own life and behaviour, shows that there is an element in the human personality which transcends the ordinary empirical ego with its narrow self-interests, and that this higher self is able to recognize with more wisdom and far-sightedness the self-defeating and evil character of Macbeth's ruthless rise to power through treachery and murder, even when it is cloaked with deception, as in the case of Hamlet's uncle, King Claudius of Denmark.

The nature of the self has not only interested the Eastern philosophers of the Yoga. It is a recurrent theme which runs through much of Western philosophy too, since it is a central question facing mankind. Schrödinger has said that it is *the* central question and that the ultimate aim, not merely of philosophy, but of modern science as well, is to answer it. It is also the central question of the Yoga of Self-knowledge. As Shri Shankaracharya says in his *Upadesha Sahasri*:

> To know the real Self to be one's own is the greatest achievement according to the scriptures and to reasoning. To know wrongly the non-self, such as the ego, etc., to be the Self is no attainment at all. One should therefore give up this misconception of taking the non-self for the Self.[2]

The problem then, with regard to our self, is to distinguish between appearance and reality. Our ordinary ideas are unthought out and muddled, and we don't take the trouble to examine them critically. In our Western tradition, it was Locke in the seventeenth century who first pointed out that all our knowledge of objects comes to us indirectly, either through the sense impressions which we receive from the outer world or from the ideas in our mind. But, as Locke points out, the picture that we derive of objects through the sense impressions entering the mind is indirect. We know the table through its colour, its shape and its feel, but the picture which we get of the table is of an object which happens to possess these qualities as attributes. What the actual table is in itself, is, as Locke put it, 'a something I know not what'. All the objects of the world are known to us only as they appear to us through the senses and the mind, but these appearances are often misleading and, in any case, do not fully reveal to us the nature of the object itself.

Even scientific investigation, which extends the scope and subtlety of our analysis of these appearances, depends in the end on the sense data. And the scientific investigation leads us to apparently impenetrable contradictions in the appearances presented by the world. We are told by the scientists of electrons being neither waves nor particles, but sometimes behaving as if they were one, and sometimes as the other. We are told of a world of electromagnetic energy, in which there is no substance and no medium, such as the ether, for it to exist in. Our common-sense view that we know where we stand is very soon exploded and our basic assumptions and certainties dissipated into thin air. Some philosophers, like Berkeley, question the very existence of the external world.

It seems, at first sight, that when we come to the mind itself we are on much firmer ground. Descartes first enunciated the axiom, *Cogito ergo sum*, 'I think therefore I am', asserting that we knew with certainty the existence of our ego and that this was the element in experience which owned and linked all the elements in our mental life. But David Hume in the eighteenth century pointed out that if there was such a self in the mind, as distinct from the stream of impressions, it would have to persist as a permanent element of self-identity and that when you came to look at it there was no such impression, constant and invariable, in the mind. As he said:

> For my part, when I enter most intimately into what I call *myself*, I always stumble on some particular perception or other, of heat or cold, light or shade, love or hatred, pain or pleasure. I never catch myself at any time without a perception, and never can observe anything but the perception... If anyone upon serious and unprejudiced reflection thinks he has a different notion of *himself*, I must confess that I can reason no longer with him. All I can allow him is that he may be in the right as well as I, and that we are essentially different in this particular. He may perhaps perceive something simple and continued, which he calls *himself*; although I am certain there is no such principle in me.[3]

Hume concludes:

> The mind is a kind of theatre, where several perceptions successively make their appearance; pass, re-pass, glide away, and mingle in an infinite variety of postures and situations. There is properly no *simplicity* in it at one time, nor *identity* in different; whatever natural propension we have to imagine that simplicity and identity. The comparison of the theatre must not mislead us. They are the successive perceptions only, that constitute the mind; nor have we the most distant notion of the place, where these scenes are represented, or of the materials, of which it is composed.[4]

But Hume was honest enough in the Appendix to his treatise to admit that he could not give any really satisfactory account of the unity and identity which unites all the experiences of an individual. As he said there:

> I am sensible that my account is very defective, and that nothing but the seeming evidence of the precedent reasonings could have induced me to receive it. If perceptions are distinct existences, they form a whole only by being connected together... But all my hopes vanish when I come to explain the principles that unite our successive perceptions in our thought or consciousness. I cannot discover any theory which gives me satisfaction on this head. In short, there are two principles which I cannot render consistent; nor is it in my power to renounce either of them, namely, *that all our distinct perceptions are distinct existences,* and *that the mind never perceives any real connection among distinct existences...* For my

part, I must plead the privilege of a sceptic and confess that this difficulty is too hard for my understanding.[5]

Immanuel Kant was 'woken from his dogmatic slumbers' by reading Hume and went on to point out that the unknowability of the external object as it really is, which Locke had originally drawn attention to, applied equally to the objects of knowledge in the mind, which also appeared to us only in the form of qualities and relationships existing in things which were themselves inaccessible to knowledge. Just as with regard to the objects of the external world, the thing in itself was unknown and unknowable, except through the appearances which it presented to us phenomenally through sense perceptions, so the 'I' which we inferred to exist as the owner and unifier of all the thoughts in the mind was a transcendental ego which could never become an object of our knowledge, except indirectly through an idea, and any idea is a bundle of qualities and relationships, an appearance presented by the thing represented and not the thing-in-itself.

This accepted the point that Hume himself had been making, but not his conclusion. As Hume had said: 'If colours, sounds, tastes and smells be merely perceptions, nothing that we conceive is possessed of a real, continued and independent existence, not even motion, extension and solidity, which are the primary qualities chiefly insisted on (by Locke)... When we exclude these sensible qualities, there remains nothing in the universe which has such an existence'.

Kant replied to this that, while this was true of our knowledge of the objective world, we have to look elsewhere for the real and abiding element in the world or ourselves. The *noumenon*, said Kant, the thing itself, was unknown and unknowable by the instruments of knowledge provided by the mind and the senses. The self was something, the existence of which had to be inferred by reason, from what Kant called *the transcendental unity of apperception*, the fact that in experience we *did* have presented to us a unified stream of consciousness. But what this self is which unifies experience remains a mysterious element in Western philosophy. It is certainly not the ego which we know in the mind, because this arises, not as a primary element in experience, but along with the other objects of experience as part of the mental stream of ideas.

Kant agrees with Hume that the permanent self is not given as an element in this stream of experience in the mind, but he holds that all the elements in the mind are related to what he calls *the transcendental unity of apperception* and this points to, although it cannot prove, the existence of a transcendental ego, of a real self which is the thing-in-itself and not a mere appearance of that thing. Shankara puts the matter much more simply:

> That one's self exists is undoubted. You may call it knowledge, self or whatever you like. But its non-existence cannot be admitted, as it is the witness of all things existing and non-existing.[6]

Vedanta says that this muddled perception of what we really are in ordinary life lies at the basis of many of the apparent contradictions in our nature. There is in us an instinctive recognition of our transcendent nature. It is this that makes us dissatisfied with anything less than the best for ourselves, that gives us the feeling that we want to be immortal, and that we therefore reject the idea of death for ourselves. It is the same impulse which makes us wish to find real and lasting happiness and to escape the pain and suffering of empirical life. While we are identifying our interests with the empirical ego, with the body and the mind, we are, in Shankara's words, 'sunk in the misconception of taking the non-self for the self'. We therefore make a laughing stock of ourselves by grossly overvaluing our empirical personalities, a fact which is all too glaringly obvious to our friends. We are not even conscious of our own egocentricity. We mistake our ego for God almighty, which is all the more astonishing when you think of what a poor player it is, for all its strutting and fretting.

Ernest Newman tells the delightful story of a well-known violinist who met a friend in the street, and kept him standing for half-an-hour, talking about himself and his achievements. He was obviously an accomplished soloist for whom anyone else was destined to play a supporting rôle. Suddenly the violinist turned to his friend and said: 'Now that's enough about me! Let's talk about you. How did you enjoy my concert last night?'

We all laugh at Bottom in *A Midsummer Night's Dream* having been given the chief part in the play of Pyramus and Thisbe, also wanting at the first rehearsal to play all the other parts as well. It strikes an uncomfortable chord of familiarity, because every man in his time has the desire, secret or open, to play the leading part. But as Shakespeare says, in the mouth of the disillusioned Richard II at the end of his career:

> Thus play I in one person many people,
> And none contented: sometimes am I king,
> Then treasons make me wish myself a beggar,
> And so I am: then crushing penury
> Persuades me I was better when a king;
> Then am I kinged again, and by and by
> Think that I am unkinged by Bolingbroke,
> And straight am nothing...
> But whate'er I be,
> Nor I, nor any man that but man is,
> With nothing shall be pleased, till he be eased
> With being nothing.[7]

At the end of his great epic, Ibsen pictures Peer Gynt looking back on his life and likening himself to an onion, in which he peels off layer after layer, each corresponding to one of the many different parts he has played in his life, only to find nothing inside the core.

According to the yogis, man, like Joseph, spends his spiritual youth in exile, dressed in his coat of many colours, but it is only when, through suffering and experience, he becomes alive to the need to answer the question 'What am I?', that his spiritual odyssey really begins. The aim of that odyssey is to know the real self to be one's own, which, as Shri Shankara says, is the greatest achievement that man can aspire to.

Swami Rama Tirtha gives a clear exposition of the

Vedantic position with regard to the 'I' of 'I think therefore I am' in one of his lectures. He says there that anything that can be perceived, has become an object, and that, in so far as you can perceive the intellect and think about it, the intellect is an object and not a subject. The real subject cannot be either perceived or conceived. How can the knower be known?

Thus Vedanta is in agreement with Hume in his criticism of those earlier philosophers, like Descartes and Berkeley, who maintained that the 'I' which gave unity and continuity to all experience and owned the thoughts and perceptions in the mind, was known directly to us in mental experience. The Vedanta agrees that it is not known directly to us in mental experience, since it cannot be an object and hence is unknowable by the mind. It was indeed one of the main teachings of the earliest classics on Yoga, the Upanishads, that the Self was 'that from which the mind turns baffled back again'. It can never become an object among objects.

But the self *is* known to us, say the yogis, as the light of consciousness which reveals the mental experience. It is the witness consciousness which provides what Kant calls the transcendental unity of apperception. As Swami Rama Tirtha says, the real subject is the true Self (*Atman*), although the practical subject is the light of the *Atman* reflected, or shining, within the intellect (*chidabhasa*). What is commonly called the subject is the real *Atman*, in association with the intellect as an *agent*.

This is the subtle doctrine of the Vedanta. The real light of consciousness which reveals the mental stream of perceptions and ideas is the Absolute, the thing-in-itself, but this consciousness is also reflected in the mind and appears as the ego, the acting, owning, self-regarding 'I' of everyday experience. This complex is what the yogis call 'the knot of the heart'. It is a knot because the experience of 'I' presents us with what Shri Shankara calls a misapprehension, a confusion between what is peculiar to the mind and its contents and the transcendent consciousness behind the mind.

The idealists were not wrong in thinking that the Self has sometning unique about it which enables it to confer unity and identity on the experiences within the mental stream of consciousness, but they were wrong in identifying this 'I' with the empirical 'I' in the mind. As the Upanishads say: 'The Self is the clue to this all, for by it one knows this all'. The realists were equally right in rejecting Berkeley's idea that the whole world was in some way a creation of the little 'I' in the mind. But Vedanta reconciles this contradiction by saying that the thing-in-itself within the intellect is *Atman*, the real Self, but that the same reality is also in each and every object.

Empirical experience is made up of names and forms, of bundles of qualities, properties and relationships, but this is not to say that there is nothing outside the mind to produce them. On the contrary, the Vedantic doctrine of perception is that the mind takes on the forms or qualities of the external objects, like copper taking on the form of a mould into which it is poured, or light taking on the form of the things it illuminates. Perception of the external world is, says Rama Tirtha, an example of the principle of action and reaction being equal and opposite, like the clapping of the two hands or the collision of two waves in water. Both the action and reaction take place not in reality in the *Atman*, the thing-in-itself, but in the empirical sphere, which is *Atman* as defined by the limited consciousness reflected in the phenomenal matter and mind. In this conclusion, the Western philosopher who is nearest to the Vedantic view is probably F H Bradley, who regarded the whole of the universe as made up of appearances presented by the absolute reality.

Vedanta is thus able to comprehend the truth grasped by Descartes and Berkeley and also the truth of its refutation by Hume and also the truth of the answer to Hume given by Kant. It also recognized, long before Bradley, that the empirical 'I' in the mind was not a primary element in the mind, but arose secondarily, with the division of conscious experience into the dualism of the seer and the seen, like the appearance of the hero in a drama, distinct from the villain and the rest of the supporting cast, after the curtain has risen. The triad of the knower and the known and the act of knowing is already within duality, and the real thing-in-itself, *Atman*, transcends the sphere of duality, and is non-dual. The empirical hero appears only when the play has already begun and he is an essential part of it, but the author never appears on the stage at all, although it is his story which is being told.

As Shri Shankara puts it:

To know the real Self to be one's own is the greatest achievement according to the scriptures and to reasoning. To know wrongly the non-self, such as the ego, etc., to be the Self is no attainment at all. One should therefore give up this misconception of taking the non-self for the Self.

11

An Example of Greatness*

In the third chapter of the *Bhagavad Gita* there is a verse which proclaims:

> Whatsoever a great man does, the same is done by others as well. Whatsoever standard he sets, the world follows.

Something of the same sentiment is echoed in the lines of Longfellow:

> Lives of great men all remind us
> We can make our lives sublime,
> And, departing, leave behind us
> Footprints on the sands of time.
>
> Footprints, that perhaps another,
> Sailing o'er life's solemn main,
> A forlorn and shipwrecked brother,
> Seeing, shall take heart again.

These lines come from Longfellow's *A Psalm of Life*, and some other lines from this poet equally remind us that there is truth also in Shri Shankara's saying that the achievement of truth does not come without effort like a ripe fruit falling into the palm of the outstretched hand.

> The heights by great men reached and kept
> Were not attained by sudden flight,
> But they, while their companions slept,
> Were toiling upward in the night.

* A lecture given on 9th December 1988.

Yoga tells us that the potentiality for greatness is hidden in each and every man. But in practice we don't really believe it. We have to remember that Yoga is important, not because it is some very unusual and exotic teaching introduced from the Far East, but because it deals with the human personality and the nature and significance of the human experience which is common to all of us. Swami Rama Tirtha says clearly that where individuals are successful and inspired, they are putting into practice the principles enunciated by the Vedanta, whether they know it or not.

Let us take a specific example, a man who has been described as 'the greatest of all experimental investigators of physical nature' and 'a member of the small class of supreme scientists, which includes Archimedes, Galileo, Newton, and Darwin'. Perhaps you can guess who it was. If not, let me tell you some more about him. He was the son of a blacksmith who came from a small village in Yorkshire and his mother was the daughter of a local farmer. The family moved to London before he was born and he went to school only between the ages of five and twelve. He himself later said: 'My education was of the most ordinary description, consisting of little more than the rudiments of reading, writing and arithmetic at a common day school. My hours out of school were passed at home and in the streets', (where he used, incidentally, to play marbles). When he was nine years old, the family was so poor that it was on public relief and the boy was receiving an allowance of one loaf of bread to last him a week.

At the age of twelve he left school to become an

errand boy to a bookseller and newsagent called Riebau, who had a shop in Blandford Street, close to Manchester Square. His duties included the early morning paper round. He also had to dust the room and black the boots of a lodger to whom the bookseller rented a room above his shop. The lodger was a French refugee who was a good professional artist (he had earlier painted Napoleon's portrait) and he took a liking to the boy and gave him lessons in drawing. After a year's probation, the boy was apprenticed to the bookseller and, as well as working in the shop, was set to learn the art of book-binding. He used to read as much as he could of the books given to him to work on. He first became interested in science at this time by reading an article on electricity in an encyclopaedia that he had to bind. He also particularly liked a book called *Conversations in Chemistry* by a Mrs Marcet.

After some years the bookseller allowed him to go occasionally in the evening to hear some lectures on Natural Philosophy delivered in a house near Fleet Street. The fee for each lecture was one shilling, which was a lot of money then, but the boy's elder brother, who was now himself a blacksmith, paid the entrance fee for him. The lectures were in fact the beginnings of what later became Birkbeck College. The boy's father had died seven years after he started in the shop, when he was nineteen, and his mother at that time kept herself by taking in lodgers until her sons could support themselves and her. The boy went on working as a book-binder for eight years in all (that is, until he was twenty-one). One could hardly have a more unpromising start to a career of greatness.

The man's name was Michael Faraday. At the age of twenty-one he had done virtually nothing of any importance, but—if more evidence of what he was to go on to achieve were needed—one can quote the remark by Einstein that the history of physical science contains two couples of equal magnitude: Galileo and Newton, and Faraday and Clerk Maxwell. The first two transformed our idea of the nature of the physical world in the sixteenth and seventeenth centuries by recognizing the laws of motion governing gravity and the movement of the stars, as well as the movement of all physical objects. Faraday and Clerk Maxwell were the two people who successively brought about an equally momentous scientific revolution by recognizing and clarifying the nature of electromagnetic forces and their fundamental rôle in the constitution of the physical world. As such they were the true fathers of the Theory of Relativity and of a large part of modern technology.

How did this ill-educated errand boy and bookbinder of twenty-one come to bring this about? His first, not very important, scientific research was not published until he was twenty-five and he made no important discovery until he was over thirty. His major contributions to changing the conceptual basis of science did not begin until he was about forty-five.

One major factor in the formation of Michael Faraday's character and the shaping of his life lay in his spiritual life. His father was a member of a very small sect called the Sandemanians, which had been founded by a Scottish Presbyterian minister, who left the Church because he believed that it should not be subject to any worldly covenant, but should be governed only by the doctrines of Christ and his Apostles. He held that Christ had come to teach the existence of eternal life and not to establish any worldly power, and that no church could become the established religion of any nation without being perverted. The Sandemanians did not try and convert anyone and the congregations were small. They simply tried to follow the teachings of Christ. They used to try and follow the practice of the Apostles, breaking bread together on the Sabbath and eating a common meal in the room next to the chapel after the Sunday service. They had no priests; they were led by a number of elders, who were elected unanimously by the congregation and who presided in turn at the services. They considered the saving of money sinful and Faraday was scrupulous about this throughout his life. He never discussed religion without invitation and considered that it was concerned with an order of truth different and higher than natural truth. He continued to attend these services all his life. He was elected an elder at the age of forty-nine, by which time he was world-famous as a scientist. It was said of his readings from the Bible:

> The perfection of the reading, with its clearness of pronunciation, its judicious emphasis, the rich musical voice, and the perfect charm of the reader, with his natural reverence, made it a delight to listen.

Elders were expected to attend every Sunday without fail and on one occasion Faraday absented himself in order to obey the command from Queen

Victoria to dine with her at Windsor. The congregation would not accept that this excuse was reasonable and his eldership and membership were temporarily suspended, although he continued to attend the services regularly.[1] Faraday was soon re-admitted to his Church, but was not re-elected as an elder for many years.

While still employed by the bookseller and attending the evening lectures on Natural Philosophy, Michael Faraday became acquainted with a well-educated Quaker youth, called Benjamin Abbott, who was younger than he was, and started a correspondence with him. In it he explains that he is lacking in a knowledge of grammar and in the art of composition, but would like to improve his knowledge by correspondence with Abbott. He tells Abbott that he has made already a few simple experiments into the principles of electricity, himself making a voltaic battery and studying the electrolytic decomposition of magnesia. In another letter he replies to Abbott who has complained of his own shortage of philosophical ideas, that a philosopher cannot fail to abound in subjects for investigation, and that his main problem is that he is short of time.

> O, that I could purchase at a cheap rate some of our modern gents' spare hours, nay, days; I think it would be a good bargain both for them and me.

One of the great principles enunciated by the spiritual teachers is 'Seek and ye shall find'. As the Lord says in the *Bhagavad Gita*: 'By whatever path men approach Me, so do I reward them'. So it was with Faraday.

It happened that a Mr Dance who was a member of the Royal Institution, was a customer of the shop where Faraday worked, and the young bookbinder impressed him so favourably that he gave him tickets for the last four lectures to be delivered by Humphry Davy in the Royal Institution between February and April 1812. Faraday went and took notes at these lectures, and copied them out fully afterwards in a quarto volume, adding some beautiful illustrations, and sent them to Davy, asking to be enabled to quit trade, which he found vicious and selfish, and to devote himself to science. The notes covered 386 pages of manuscript and this famous book still exists in the library of the Royal Institution. In his letter Faraday said that he wished to serve science which he imagined made its pursuers amiable and liberal. He therefore asked for any laboratory appointment that might be available. Davy wrote back as follows:

December 24th 1812

Sir

I am far from displeased with the proof you have given me of your confidence, and which displays great zeal, power of memory and attention. I am obliged to go out of town, and shall not be settled in town till the end of January. I will then see you at any time you wish. It would gratify me to be of any service to you. I wish it may be in my power.

I am, Sir, your obedient humble servant

H. Davy

Early in the following year Davy sent for Faraday and talked to him about the job of an assistant in the laboratory. However, he advised him not to give up his prospects as a bookseller's apprentice, telling him that science was a harsh mistress. He smiled at Faraday's notion about the superior moral feelings of the followers of science, saying that he would leave it to the experience of a few years to set him right on that matter. Having recommended him to stick to book-binding, he promised to send all the Royal Institution's book-binding orders to him, and to recommend him as a book-binder to his friends. But he engaged Faraday for some days as an amanuensis, to take down dictation from him, after he had injured his eye during experiments with nitrogen chloride. So Faraday soon went back to the shop.

In his lectures Swami Rama Tirtha makes the point that as soon as you have truly renounced a strong desire, it is almost automatically achieved. The principle 'Seek and ye shall find' (he says) is only half the truth; we also have to remember that other great spiritual principle enunciated by Christ: 'Seek ye first the kingdom of heaven and all these other things shall be added unto you'.[2]

One evening some weeks later, while Faraday was undressing upstairs, he was startled to hear a loud knock at the front door. A carriage had drawn up outside the house, and Davy's footman left a note requesting him to call next day at the Royal Institution. Davy asked him whether he still desired to be engaged in scientific work. It turned out that Davy had had to sack his laboratory assistant, and thought of offering the position to Faraday. He would get two rooms at the top of the Royal Institution to live in, and 25 shillings a week. Faraday was twenty-one years old.

An Example of Greatness

Shortly after moving into the Royal Institution, Faraday wrote a long letter to his friend Abbott about what makes a good lecture, preceding his remarks with a passage which gives a delightful flavour of his personality at this time:

> As when on some secluded branch in forest far and wide sits perched an owl, who, full of self-conceit and self-created wisdom, explains, comments, condemns, ordains and orders things not understood, yet full of his importance still holds forth to stocks and stones around—so sits and scribbles Mike.

At twenty-one Michael Faraday's *curriculum vitae* was not impressive. He had had no proper education and his work experience was of nine years, first as a newspaper boy and general factotum in a bookseller's and later as a book-binder. His only knowledge of science was what he had picked up from reading one or two popular books and what he learned by occasionally going to hear the evening lectures on natural philosophy delivered by a Mr Tatum. It was a fairly unpromising start to his career. But an opening to science, which he was already beginning to love, had been offered to him in the shape of the tickets to Humphry Davy's four lectures at the Royal Institution and he had grasped it with both hands, as evidenced by his producing the notes and illustrations to send to Davy.

Being appointed Davy's lab boy was the turning point in Faraday's career, but events still took a totally unforeseen, and not necessarily favourable, turn. Davy, who had been a great chemist with a lot of discoveries to his credit, was beginning to settle down to enjoying the fruits of fame and success and spent more and more of his time hob-nobbing with the aristocracy. He had recently been knighted and, shortly after appointing Faraday, he decided to resign from the Royal Institution and to marry, unwisely choosing someone who was rather a snob herself. He then decided that he would travel abroad in Europe and the Near East, visiting notable scientists, and he invited Faraday to accompany him and to assist him. He took with him a small case of chemicals with which he proposed to do experiments *en route* and he wanted Faraday to assist him in these and in taking down his writings to dictation.

Sir Humphry and Lady Davy set out, with Faraday accompanying them, in October 1813, travelling to France, Italy, Switzerland and the Tyrol, keeping a journal of all the eminent men of science whom they visited. Faraday had never before been more than twelve miles from London and he was first impressed by the scenery in Devonshire which they passed through on their way to Plymouth, where they were taking ship for France. France was at war with England at the time—it was only two years before the battle of Waterloo—but such was Davy's reputation as one of the foremost chemists of the time that he had special permission for his party to enter France. While they were there, they met many of the most eminent men of science, including Ampère and Gay-Lussac. Faraday saw Napoleon in his carriage on the way to a State Visit to the Senate. While in France, Davy also carried out experiments on the newly discovered element, Iodine.

Then they travelled on to Italy, where, during a stay in Florence, they burned diamonds in oxygen, using the Grand Duke of Tuscany's great lens. They also met the elderly Volta, who had invented the battery in 1800, some 15 years before, and saw Vesuvius in eruption, picnicking on its slopes, before going on to Switzerland and Germany.

On this journey Faraday had the great good fortune to meet many of the foremost scientific minds of the day, which widened and deepened his love and knowledge of science; but the experience was by no means an unmitigated joy for him. Davy had been unable to engage a valet and gradually called on Faraday more and more to act as his valet as well as carrying out all his other duties. Davy treated Faraday quite well, but Lady Davy treated him as a menial and continually scolded him. Faraday wrote home to his friend Abbott that he had seriously considered ending his appointment, but that he had decided to complete it. The opportunity of working with Davy was not to be missed. He comments wryly in the letter: 'I should have but little to complain of were I travelling with Sir Humphry Davy alone, or were Lady Davy like him...' He adds that he will probably return to book-binding when he gets home.

In Switzerland, they stayed in Geneva with Davy's friend, the scientist De La Rive. At first Faraday was sent to have his meals with the servants, but when De La Rive got to know him, and found out that he was not a valet, but Davy's lab assistant, he was shocked, and proposed that Faraday should dine with the family. Lady Davy would not agree, however, and De La Rive reacted by arranging for Faraday to have his meals served in his own room. Faraday used to speak appreciatively in later life of the way that De La Rive treated him at this time. In one of his letters to Abbott he speaks of the ills and trials of life, comparing them to 'clouds which intervened between me and the sun of prosperity, but which I found were refreshing, reserving to me that tone and vigour of mind which prosperity alone could enervate and ultimately destroy'. His letters to his mother are full of affection.

When the party got back to London in 1815 Faraday was re-engaged by the Royal Institution as a laboratory assistant at an increased salary of 30 shillings a week. Outwardly he could be said to have had very few assets at this juncture, other than his association with Sir Humphry Davy as lab boy and general factotum. But he already had a deep love of science, dating from before he knew Davy, and he had a strength of character and a faith, founded on his spiritual convictions, which proved a far more powerful asset than superior education or worldly advantages could have done. From then onwards he devoted himself to his experiments and to the pursuit of scientific truth.

He was soon working with Davy on the invention of the miner's safety lamp. A year later he gave his first lecture and his first small research paper, written jointly with Davy, was published. We cannot go into all his scientific achievements in this account, but they are dazzling in their variety and importance, although it was not until the age of twenty-five that he ever expected to

An Example of Greatness

do anything in research and he was twenty-nine before his first important discovery was published.

To begin with, he produced some very simple papers in collaboration with, or annotated by, Davy, but gradually he became more independent and in 1823, eight years after he had got back to London, he was proposed as a candidate for Fellowship of the Royal Society by one of the other members, called Wollaston. Davy, who by this time was President, far from supporting the proposal, vigorously opposed it. One can call this small-mindedness or jealousy or just a typical example of a prophet not being recognized in his own country. Presumably, Davy still regarded Faraday merely as a particularly bright lab boy whom he had benevolently patronized, although Faraday had already by this time made many important independent contributions to science. Davy even asked Faraday himself to withdraw his name, but Faraday said that, as he had not proposed himself, he could not have it withdrawn. Davy then said that, as President, he would remove the name from the list himself. Faraday did not react to Davy's hidden jealousy and vanity; he simply replied that he was sure Davy would do what was best for the Royal Society.

Parenthetically, it may be said that one could hardly ask for a clearer example of someone practising the teachings of Yoga on not being concerned with the fruits of action, as expressed in the *Bhagavad Gita* (II.48):

> Do thy work, abandoning attachment, with an even mind in success and failure, for evenness of mind is called Yoga.

In spite of Davy's opposition, Faraday was elected a Fellow in the following year. There was only one vote against him at the election. It was apparent that no one else but Davy had any doubts about his worthiness for the honour! In the following year (1825) Faraday's position at the Royal Institution was much improved when he was appointed Director of the laboratory under the Professor of Chemistry, Brande. Faraday started evening meetings, at which members could see experiments and discuss researches which were being carried out at the Institution and elsewhere. He also started a Christmas series of children's lectures. Contemporaries spoke of the grace, earnestness and refinement of his whole demeanour when lecturing, his lucidity being at its best when lecturing to children.

The Royal Institution had been founded in March 1799 following a proposal by Count Rumford

> ...for forming in London by private subscription an establishment for feeding the poor, and giving them useful employment, and also for furnishing food at a cheap rate to others who may stand in need of such assistance, connected with an institution for introducing and bringing forward into general use new inventions and improvements, particularly such as relate to the management of heat and the saving of fuel, and to various other mechanical contrivances by which domestic comfort and economy may be promoted.

Rumford particularly wanted to make it fashionable to care for the poor and indigent. In the end the Society for Bettering the Condition of the Poor was separated from the Research Institution and the latter was set up in a house in Albemarle Street, where it still is. By the time that Faraday was appointed to the staff, some sixteen years later, the Institution was still in considerable financial difficulties and this state of things continued for some time, so that when at the age of thirty-four he was appointed Director, as well as lecturing and carrying on his scientific researches, he had to devote a great deal of time to trying to keep it financially afloat. Two years later, in 1827, he was offered the relatively well-paid Chair of Chemistry in the newly founded London University, but he refused it because (as he said)

> I think it is a matter of duty and gratitude on my part to do what I can for the good of the Royal Institution in the present attempt to establish it firmly. The Institution has been a source of knowledge and pleasure to me for the last full fourteen years; and though it does not pay me in salary what I now strive to do for it, yet I possess the kind feelings and goodwill of its authorities and members, and all the privileges it can grant or I require; and, moreover, I remember the protection it has afforded me during the past years of my scientific life.

Things did not get better, however, and he had to tell the Board of Management that 'we are living at the parings of our skin' (or, as we might now say, by the skin of our teeth!). The Committee considered that they could not make any reduction in Mr Faraday's salary which was at that time £100 per annum plus a house, and a supply of coals and candles for heat and light. Thus Faraday as Director of the Institution was getting less than twice as much as when he was first employed by Davy as a lab boy. The Committee expressed their regret that the circumstances of the Institution did not justify them increasing his salary to what he undoubtedly merited. Faraday was then forty-one, having made his most famous discovery the year before and having received by that time the highest honours bestowed by international learning. He never complained about his salary.

Faraday throughout this period remained true to his religious conviction. John Tyndall, his successor, said that he came nearer than anybody else that he knew to the fulfilment of the Christian precept: 'Take no thought for the morrow'. He had absolute confidence that, in case of need, the Lord would provide. With such feeling and such faith he was naturally heedless of laying anything by for the future. He used to have his dinner each day at two o'clock and would begin his meal by lifting both hands over the dish before him, and in the tones of a son addressing a father, of whose love he was sure, asked the blessing on the food. In his earlier years at the Royal Institution, he used to make a little extra money by what he called 'commercial work', advising people on scientific and chemical problems. Between 1823 and 1837 he made between £240 and £310 per annum from this source, but he then gave this up altogether in favour of concentrating on his scientific research on electromagnetism. He wanted to concentrate all his time and effort on what he considered to be worth-while in the search for truth. It was the period of his greatest discoveries in science.

Faraday can truly be said to have demonstrated his faith in the spiritual principle enunciated by the Lord in the *Gita*: 'O Arjuna, in the case of my devotees I provide what they need and protect what they have'. We can find essentially the same teaching in the Christian Gospels in the passage on the lilies of the field.[3]

At the age of thirty, in 1821, Faraday married a twenty-one year old girl called Sarah Barnhard, who was also a member of the Sandemanian Church. He had the formal ceremony in which he seriously committed himself to enter the life of the community a month later. Although he had been brought up in the group and had long been an attender, this was a definite step undertaken by serious members to commit their future life to following the way of Christ in accordance with its tenets. At the same time he was, in his scientific work, determinedly tackling the problem of electromagnetism; and on Christmas Day, 1821, he took his young wife into the laboratory to show her the rotation of a magnetic needle round an electric current passing through a wire, the first demonstration of this particular effect, which was to be the origin of the electric motor.

He was also researching very actively in chemistry, working on the vaporisation of mercury and preparing liquid chlorine for the first time. He went on to liquefy a number of other gases and demonstrated clearly the principle that all gases were simply substances in a gaseous state which could be liquefied by lowering the temperature or increasing the pressure. He experimented with alloys of steel and made the first stainless steel. In 1825 he discovered the new compound of carbon and hydrogen ('bicarburet of hydrogen'), which later came to be called benzene and led in time to the development of aniline dyes. He also turned his attention to the production of different kinds of glass with varying optical properties, presenting the results in three lectures in 1829.

But his main theme—and his most important contribution to future knowledge—lay in his studies of electricity and magnetism and the induction of one by the other. He steadily worked on these problems for over ten years, trying (but without success) to see if magnetism could be converted into electricity in the same way that magnets could be deflected by currents flowing in wires in their vicinity. He also tried to see if a current flowing in one wire could induce a current in a second nearby wire connected to a sensitive galvanometer. No matter how large the steady currents he used he was unable to do this. It was not until 1831 that he discovered that it was only at the moment when a steady current was turned on or off that a current could be induced in a nearby 'secondary' coil of wire and that this effect could be increased by the introduction of an iron core (e.g., in the form of an iron ring round which the two coils were wound). The iron became magnetized with the steady current, and produced a surrounding magnetic field, which was built up or collapsed at the moment when the current was turned on or off, inducing the current in the secondary wire. Similarly, when a magnet was *moved* in the neighbourhood of a coil of wire, a current was induced in the wire at the time of the movement. This was when (what Faraday called) the 'lines of force' of the magnetic field surrounding the magnet were moving relative to the nearby wire. It was therefore the relative movement or change of the electromagnetic fields surrounding a current or magnet which caused the interaction and induced the effects. Electromagnetic forces interacted when there was a *change of strength, direction or movement,* either of the current or the magnet, correlating with the movement of the lines of force making up the surrounding electro-magnetic field.

This discovery, made by Faraday in 1831, showed how electricity could be generated from mechanical movement and led to the dynamo. It was the most important of all his many discoveries, the result of long and intense enquiry and experiment, which had gradually revealed the fundamental nature of electricity and magnetism as forces characteristic of a single all-pervading field underlying the physical world.

In 1833 at the age of forty-two he read a paper to the Royal Society on the fundamental identity of the electricity which manifested itself in many different phenomena. His work on electrochemistry had suggested that electricity was in some way made up of definite 'packets' as if it were composed of particles, atoms or corpuscles, an observation which foreshadowed the discovery of the electron. He had worked out the quantity of electricity needed to bring about chemical changes such as the release of iodine from potassium iodide through electrolysis. He studied the production of gases during electrolysis and showed that it depended solely on the amount of electric current passed irrespective of the size of the battery or the composition of the plates, and that the same law applied to the decomposition of all chemical substances by electrolysis, when one also took into account their chemical equivalents (i.e. the proportions in which they were combined in different substances). He thus showed that 'the decompositions of the voltaic battery are as definite in their character as those chemical combinations which gave birth to the atomic theory'. He commented in a paper in 1834:

> Although we know nothing of what an atom is, yet we cannot resist forming some idea of a small particle which represents it to the mind; and though we are in equal, if not greater, ignorance of electricity, so as to be unable to say whether it is a particular[4] matter or matters, or mere motion of ordinary matter, or some other kind of power or agent, yet there is an immensity of facts which justify us in believing that the atoms of matter are in some way endowed or associated with electrical powers, to which they owe their most striking qualities, and amongst them their mutual chemical affinity. As soon as we perceive, through the teaching of Dalton, that chemical powers are, however varied the circumstances in which they are exerted, definite for each body, we learn to estimate the relative degree of force which resides in such bodies; and when upon that knowledge comes the fact that the electricity we appear to be capable of loosening from its habitation for a while and conveying from place to place, whilst it retains its

chemical force, can be measured out, and being so measured is found to be as definite in its action as any of those portions which, remaining associated with the particles of matter, give them their chemical relations, we seem to have found the link which connects the proportion of that we have evolved to the proportion of that belonging to the particles in their natural state.[5]

Faraday continued his investigations of electricity throughout the 1830's, turning to the problem of the nature of static as distinct from current electricity. He studied the charges induced in two concentric spheres separated either by air or by other substances and demonstrated the properties of what we would now call capacitative charge and the dielectric of capacitors.

In 1841 at the age of fifty his health broke down under the strain of overwork and he did no science for three years. During this time he went to Switzerland with his wife and brother-in-law and, since he was still physically robust, went on long excursions. On 12th August 1841 he visited the falls at Giessbach and noted in his journal:

> The sun shone brightly, and the rainbows seen from various points were very beautiful. One, at the bottom of a fine but furious fall, was very pleasant—there it remained motionless while the gusts of cloud and spray swept furiously across its place, and were dashed against the rock. It looked like a spirit strong in faith and steadfast in the midst of a storm of passions sweeping across it; and, though it might fade and revive, still it held on to the rock, as in hope, and giving hope.

As soon as his health permitted he returned and resumed his work and soon became equally productive. He demonstrated that the plane of polarized light passing through glass could be rotated by a magnetic field. And he then proceeded to the discovery of what is called diamagnetism. He studied the effects of a magnetic field on a flame and on the flow of gases, establishing that oxygen was strongly magnetic but that nitrogen was neutral 'like space'. This led on to an investigation of the effect of the atmosphere on the earth's magnetism. He applied the findings to the effect of magnetic storms and to the annual and diurnal variations in the earth's magnetism and also to the effect of temperature on the earth's magnetic field. In 1850 he sent papers to the Royal Society on these topics.

It has been said that 'a strong vein of metaphysics runs through the speculations of Faraday, but his experiments are always handled with regal power'. In fact Faraday saw beyond the atomic theory of his contemporaries, realizing that the atom was not the hard solid object which they imagined, but a centre of force. He held that in the conception of molecules or atoms separated by inter-molecular space 'space must be taken as the only continuous part of a body so constituted'. If space is a conductor (he argues) it cannot exist in insulating bodies, and if it is an insulator it cannot exist in conducting bodies. So it cannot be either. He recognized chemical combinations as being due to electric forces of attraction and repulsion between atoms, quantified in definite and characteristic amounts, anticipating in this (as Helmholtz was later to point out) the existence of the electron as the unit of charge in ion exchanges during electrolysis. He also conceived of particles as concentrations in fields of force and amounting to that alone. In 1846 he suggested the electromagnetic theory of light and expressed doubt about the existence of the ether, asking 'whether it was not possible that the vibrations which...are assumed to account for radiation and radiant phenomena may not occur in the lines of force which connect particles and consequently masses of matter together; a notion which, as far as it is admitted, will dispense with the ether which, in another view, is supposed to be the medium in which these vibrations take place'. He points out that the velocity of light and electricity are known to be approximately the same. In these prophetic words he presages the findings of the experiment of Michelson and Morley in 1877 and the Theory of Relativity. The existence of electromagnetic waves was not experimentally established and generally accepted until Hertz discovered radio waves, also in 1877.

Perhaps these few short indications can give an idea of how it could be said that 'Faraday was the greatest physicist of the nineteenth century and the greatest of all experimental investigators of physical nature'.

His friend and successor John Tyndall says that Faraday was a man of strong emotions, generous, charitable, sympathizing with human suffering.

> His five pound note was ever ready for the meritorious man who had been overtaken by calamity. The tenderness of his nature rendered it difficult for him to refuse the appeal of distress. Still,

he knew the evil of indiscriminate alms-giving, and had many times detected imposture; so that he usually distributed his gifts through some charity organisation which insured him that they would be well bestowed. He used to give a large part of his meagre income to charity.

His faith never wavered, but remained to the end as fresh as in 1821 when he made his profession of faith on formally joining his Church; and in later life, when questioned about his religious belief by Lady Lovelace, he described himself as belonging to 'a very small and despised sort of Christians, known—if known at all—as Sandemanians; and our hope is founded on the faith as it is in Christ'. He made a strict distinction between his religion and his science, believing that man could not know God by means of his reason, but that the soul could have direct communion with God.

He could not bear indecision and said that even a bad decision was better than no decision. Later in his life he was given a pension of £300 by Sir Robert Peel and was also, through the initiative of Prince Albert, given a grace and favour house at Hampton Court. He resigned from the Royal Institution at the age of seventy in 1861 and died aged 75 in 1867.

John Tyndall, who was appointed Professor of Natural Philosophy at the Royal Institution under Faraday in May 1853 and had a long and harmonious collaboration with him, wrote of Faraday's character:

> Faraday's intellectual power cannot be traced to definite antecedents; and it is still more difficult to

account by inheritance for the extraordinary delicacy of his character. On a memorable occasion, a friend who knew him well, described him thus: 'Nature, not education, made Faraday strong and refined. A favourite experiment of his own was representative of himself. He loved to show that water, in crystallising, excluded all foreign ingredients however intimately they might be mixed with it. Out of acids, alkalis, or saline solutions, the crystals came sweet and pure. By some such natural process in the formation of this man, beauty and nobleness coalesced, to the exclusion of everything vulgar and low.

The experiment could stand as representative of that transformation of the human personality of which the yogis speak, in which the pure Self of man emerges, as if crystallized from the personality with all its impurities, by the process of meditation and spiritual enquiry (*vichara*), culminating in self-realization.

12

Seeing is Believing*

Among the doctors who graduated in the year 1766 from the University of Vienna was a young man who had been born thirty-three years before in a small Swiss village on Lake Constance, which lies on the borders of what is now Germany, Austria and Switzerland. It was a time when the scientific ideas propounded in the previous century were spreading widely, but often mixed with older superstitions. The young graduate wrote his thesis on the influence of the planets on the human body. Later, he became interested in the ideas of a Jesuit professor of astronomy called Hehl who was studying magnetism and had been trying to see if he could use it to cure certain diseases. The young man's name was Franz Anton Mesmer. Mesmer confirmed for himself that the use of a magnet could have beneficial effects on some patients, but he soon found that you did not need the magnet and that the same results could be more easily achieved by means of the laying on of hands. Nonetheless, he developed a theory to explain the effects he had observed which held that all animals and bodies were permeated by what he called 'animal magnetism'.

Mesmer had an enormous success with his method in both Vienna and Paris, also incurring the animosity of most of the local doctors in the process. However, both the Austrian Empress, Maria Theresa, and the French

* A lecture given on 17th March 1989.

Queen, Marie Antoinette, were interested in his powers and sent their protégés to be treated by him. Such was his fame that Mozart (who knew him well) was making fun of him in his opera *Cosi Fan Tutte*, first staged in Vienna in 1790, 24 years after Mesmer graduated.

Because of its association with unorthodox medicine and the fact that it was exploited both then and more recently by charlatans and knaves to make a fortune for themselves, Mesmerism got a bad name. During his time in Paris, King Louis appointed a Royal Commission to report on Mesmer's claims. It concluded that he had brought about many cures, but denied that there was any such thing as 'animal magnetism', an eminently sensible conclusion. After his death in 1815 Mesmer's work was carried on by one of his disciples, the Count de Puységur. He noted that the patients who responded well to this treatment 'heard only what the magnetiser said to them and were oblivious to all else; but they accepted the magnetiser's suggestions without questioning them; and that they could recall nothing of what had happened after their return to an ordinary state of consciousness.'[1]

In this way the modern history of hypnotism was born. The word hypnotism itself was coined later by a Scottish surgeon named James Braid, practising in Manchester in the nineteenth century, who was originally deeply suspicious of Mesmerism, considering it fraudulent, but became convinced after he conducted his own experiments. He found that sleep or trance could be self-induced by staring fixedly at a bright light. A British Army surgeon in India, James Esdaile, used hypnotically induced anaesthesia to carry out 73 operations successfully, without the patients feeling pain. He published his results in 1846 in a monograph entitled *Mesmerism in India*, which greatly influenced John Elliotson, a London surgeon working at University College Hospital. Elliotson started to introduce the method in London, but encountered such opposition from his colleagues that he was forced to resign his appointment. The further acceptance of hypnotic anaesthesia was brought to a halt for the time being by the arrival at this period of the first anaesthetic drugs: ether, nitrous oxide and chloroform. But today hypnotism is recognized as a respectable and familiar (if rather unusual) way of inducing anaesthesia. One of the most prestigious British medical organisations, the Royal Society of Medicine, which in 1780 passed a decree depriving any qualified doctor of his diploma if he should advocate or practise Mesmer's treatment by 'animal magnetism', today has an established section of its members devoted to the study and practice of medical hypnosis.

Now that hypnosis can be looked at scientifically and objectively, divorced from the nonsense which became associated with it while it was being practised by charlatans and professional entertainers, we can see that it represents a dramatic example of the power of suggestion over the mind. As such, we can learn much about the mind itself by looking at this phenomenon and its implications.

Hypnotism was taken up by the famous neurologist Charcot working at the Salpetrière Hospital in Paris in the second half of the nineteenth century. He regarded hysteria or hysterical symptoms as closely akin to the phenomena produced by hypnotic suggestion. Charcot became a noted teacher, and in 1885 a young medical graduate from Vienna arrived to spend some time studying with him in Paris. His name was Sigmund Freud and he was so impressed with what he learnt while there that he decided to devote himself entirely to the treatment of nervous diseases. He and another (later famous) physician called Breuer tried treating patients with hysterical symptoms by hypnosis and found that when they probed into the mind of the patient under hypnosis and brought back some painful experiences from early life, the symptoms disappeared. As a result of this, Freud came to the conclusion that there were powerful forces working in the mind, of which the individual was unconscious, and that some of the contents of the unconscious represent painful or unwelcome experiences which have been repressed by a kind of censorship exerted by the conscious mind on its memories. In this way the phenomenon of hypnosis led directly to many of the ideas which are now generally accepted about the way the mind operates and its manifestation in certain psychosomatic disorders and mental illnesses.

This is the briefest of thumb-nail sketches of the history of ideas about hypnotism and mental suggestion as they developed in the West. Their interest from the point of view of the practice of Yoga is that they confirm many of the things that the yogis had been saying about the mind long before 1766: for instance, that—in addition to the body and the mind familar to us all in our own experience—there is an unconscious store of memories, impressions and urges, called in the Yoga classics the *anandamaya kosha* or causal sheath; and that the conscious operations of the mind, both in perception and in thought, are influenced by these latent impressions in an important way. In fact, the idea that the phenomena of suggestion, seen in such dramatic form in hypnosis, are unusual or exceptional phenomena could not be further from the case. Sensitivity to suggestion is a constant characteristic of the mind and its operation, and we cannot fully understand the mind unless we recognize this.

Even the kind of phenomena that Mesmer encountered were not really new or unfamiliar to earlier generations. Since the time of Edward the Confessor and before, thousands of people had come to be cured of the King's Evil by the Royal Touch, not only in England, but elsewhere. Louis XIV is said to have 'touched' 2,500 persons, and in the Stuart period, when the custom reached its zenith, poor King Charles II actually touched, on an average, 4,000 persons per year. From his restoration in 1660 to his death in 1685 he clocked up the amazing total of 92,107 treated. This may have been in part due to the fact that, as part of the ceremony, each patient received a gold coin or 'touchpiece' as it was called. As one ancient writer put it, rather sweetly: 'Some were cured of the king's evil, who never had any other evil than that of poverty, which brought more patients and more fame to those royal practitioners than they deserved'. But Richard Wiseman, a naval surgeon who became Surgeon to Charles II and has been called the

Father of English Surgery, wrote: 'I have myself been an eye witness of hundreds of cures performed by His Majestie's Touch alone, without any assistance of Chirurgery'. King William, when he came to the throne, was not so enthusiastic as Charles about his own powers of healing and is said to have 'touched but few', saying as he did so: 'God grant you better health and more sense', but after him Queen Anne restored the custom and is recorded as having actually touched the sickly two-year-old who was later to become Dr Samuel Johnson. However, she was the last English monarch to carry on the practice.

Still further back in history, we cannot help being reminded of those incidents described in the New Testament in which people came to Christ to be healed. There are accounts in all except the fourth Gospel of a woman who came to Jesus to be cured of an issue of blood which she had had for 10-12 years, believing that if she could but touch the hem of his garment, she would be cured. She did and she was cured. But Jesus' remark to her was not an acknowledgement that *he* had cured her, but rather that her own belief had done so: 'Thy faith has made thee whole'.[2] And he said exactly the same to the blind beggar who successfully asked to have his sight restored[3], and to the ten lepers who were 'cleansed'[4]. St Mark describes a man in the crowd following Jesus and bringing his son, who was said (in the contemporary phrase) to be 'possessed of a dumb spirit' which made him fall on the ground and foam at the mouth and gnash his teeth. In other words he was having (or appears to have been having) what we should now call severe epileptic fits. Jesus' response to the father who asks for his help in 'casting out the spirit' was to tell him: 'If thou canst believe, all things are possible to him that believeth'. To which the father rather pathetically answered, with tears in his eyes: 'Lord, I believe; help thou mine unbelief!'.[5]

Orthodox medical opinion nowadays would have no difficulty in accepting that many cures are produced by suggestion, but it would regard these as mainly occurring in the domain of what is called psychosomatic illness, and particularly (but by no means exclusively) in the realm of those hysterical phenomena which so interested Charcot, Freud and Breuer. But there are limits to what the methods of Mesmer or the modern hypnotist can achieve. As we all know in our everyday life, many of our cherished beliefs come up against the apparently granite resistance of hard ineluctable facts. It is said that Anatole France, when he was shown the hundreds of crutches left behind at Lourdes by those who had been miraculously cured before they left, looked round at them all and remarked to his companion: 'Even *one* wooden leg would have been more to the point!' He was making the perfectly valid point that you may be able to cure many things by suggestion, but only a miracle can restore a lost limb.

What then can we learn from the phenomena of suggestion and hypnosis? And how does it relate to what we call belief? What is the real significance of faith or belief in mental life? In ordinary parlance we loosely use the words 'faith' or 'belief' to refer to our religious or political convictions, but the yogis use the word 'faith' in a different sense as meaning 'that basic tendency in the nature of each individual which gives rise to, and colours, his thought and action. Our mental, emotional and physical activities are actuated by this deep mystic tendency which is called Faith. It is the aggregate of the subtle impressions left by our past lives on our causal body. Man can create, control and change this tendency; it is not an unalterable fate.'[6]

But there is also a much wider sense in which belief enters into our mental life. In his book on *Human Knowledge: Its Scope and Limits*, Bertrand Russell shows that virtually all our thoughts can be described as beliefs. Even sensation, memories or expectations have the characteristics of beliefs.

In perception the interpretation of the sense impressions involves the production of a belief about what is perceived, and this is influenced by past experience at a conscious, unconscious or semi-conscious level. Expectations, which may be entirely unverbalized (as they are in animals) similarly depend on the beliefs induced by sensations combined with past experience (e.g., the smell of smoke leads one to expect a fire in the vicinity).

It may be objected that in sensation there is a direct awareness of what is there in front of one, and that this is not a matter of belief at all, but of direct perception. But, in fact, seeing *is* believing. This can be very easily demonstrated.

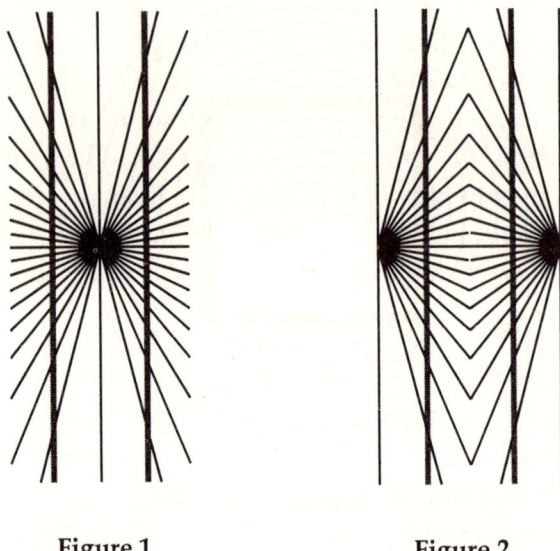

Figure 1   **Figure 2**

The two straight lines shown in Figures 1 and 2 appear bent, because they are distorted by the lines in the background (which are interpreted wrongly at quite a simple level by sensory mechanisms used to getting clues from any 'straight' contours in the background when seeing objects in perspective in space).

In this way it is relatively easy to distort the apparent shape of things that we see by adding background lines, as in Figures 3 and 4. They work by suggestion, because such contours are normally used by us as clues to recognizing the real shape of objects in space which we see from different perspectives as we move from one

Seeing is Believing

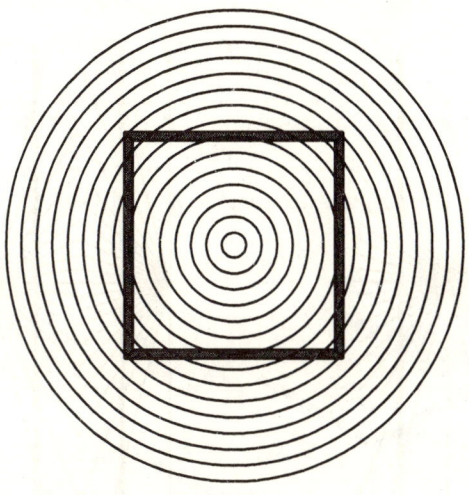

Figure 3

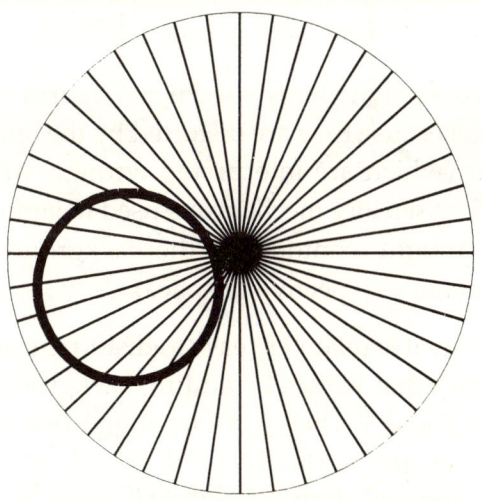

Figure 4

place to another, and we have certain expectations (operating at an almost unconscious or semi-conscious level) as to how they will appear. The background 'suggests' something to us, which is different from what our senses expect to see from a straight edge in space, so we interpret the circle and square as not being what they actually are.

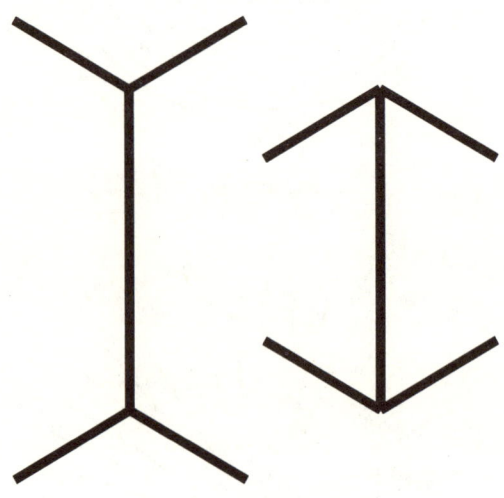

Figure 5

The two vertical lines in Figure 5 don't appear to be of the same length, because of what the 'arrows' suggest to us. In fact, you can see the same effect with the 'arrows' alone (Figure 6).

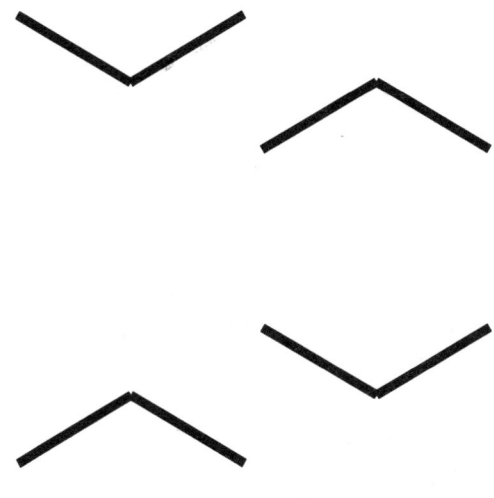

Figure 6

What is further away from us usually looks relatively smaller than it is, while nearer things look larger. This is what we expect from long experience. It is (as we say) habitual. So we compensate when seeing something which other clues suggest is further away (e.g., in the corner of the room), and judge it to be really larger than it seems to be, whereas the opposite is true of nearer objects—they appear relatively larger than they are (like the near corner of a building) and we judge it to be relatively smaller than it seems (Figure 7). Of course we are misinterpreting the clues here, but we can't help doing it. What we actually see is changed.

This well-known effect is known to psychologists as

'size constancy'. We actually see far objects as being larger than they strictly appear from the image on our retina and near objects as smaller than their image. This 'correction' operates at the perceptual level in the brain, but at a fairly early and simple stage in the process, since it requires only the kind of contours shown in Figures 1 to 6 to produce it. We jump to conclusions about what we are seeing on what is obviously inadequate evidence, although the clues we employ usually lead us to the right interpretation more often than not.

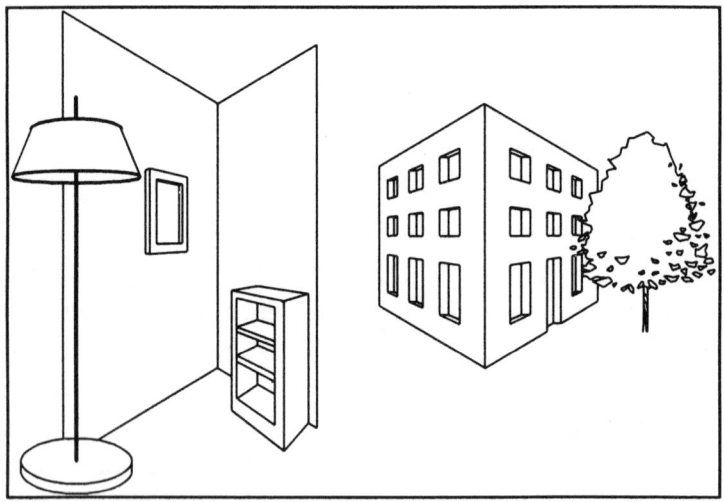

Figure 7

The same applies to two objects on the road or railway track in front of us (Figure 8). If the surrounding clues in the background suggest that one object may be

Figure 8

further away than another, we compensate by actually seeing it as larger than a near object, although its objective size is identical. Again this perceptual distortion must act at a very early and fundamental level, because even the simplest contours associated with a receding

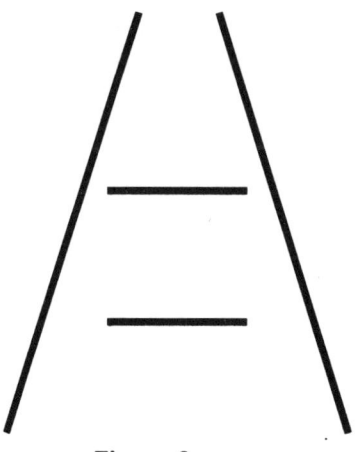

Figure 9

road or railtrack will bring it about (Figure 9). It is not a question of reasoning it out. We just see it that way! We believe it to be different in size, even though it isn't.

In these so-called optical illusions, or tricks played on us by the senses, we cannot help accepting the suggestion and seeing things incorrectly, even when we know it is wrong and may indeed reject the suggestion at the intellectual level.

But if we actually *see* the lines as bent or of unequal length, what right have we to reject this evidence as an illusion? This brings us to another important point that Russell makes in his account of human knowledge. It is that (as we all know) *beliefs can be true or false*; and we then have to ask what it is that makes them so.

Russell's reply is that it is *facts* which make beliefs true or false. Any sensation or idea refers to something outside itself; it is a sensation *of* something or an idea *about* something, either in the outside world or in the mind. What makes a belief true is if it corresponds to the fact to which it refers—in other words, if what we believe really is the case. If we believe that the lines are really bent, our belief is false. If we believe that the circle really is distorted, we believe a lie. As Wittgenstein said: 'The world is everything that is the case'.

The reason that all our sensation and knowledge has this unsatisfactory character of not giving us certainty is that we can only find out what the world is really like by what the senses tell us, aided by our past experience in the form of memory and expectation. Often the evidence of the senses is too inadequate to allow us to decide definitely what is what, and our past experience or habits of thought lead us astray.

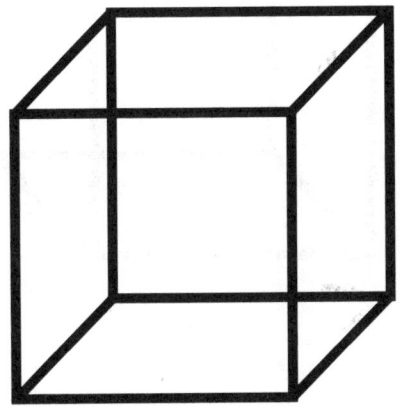

Figure 10

In Figure 10, for instance, there is no definitive clue as to whether the cube has its front surface above or below the back one. But we don't remain neutral; we jump to conclusions on totally inadequate evidence. We can't help seeing it one way or the other. But, because we can equally well see it in two different ways, the way that we see it is unstable, and it can switch between one possibility and the other. However, you can influence how you see it by where you focus your attention, as you can verify by looking steadily, first, at the point **X**, and then at the point **Y** in Figure 11.

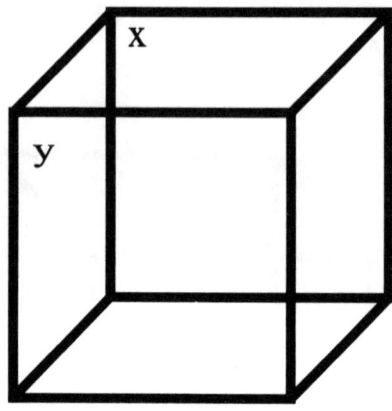

Figure 11

This is a simple example, but there are many other occasions in everyday experience where we are equally puzzled and uncertain about the facts which face us. Yet it is very difficult for us not to jump to conclusions and make up our minds about things, even when we don't really have any good reason to do so. People are, all too often, more inclined to make up their minds about things for which there is really no good evidence, than about things which can definitely be decided fairly easily!

There are many other ways in which we are subject to the suggestions of the senses, interpreted in the light of past experience, and are misled by them. Some of these arise from the fact that the senses only give us *relative* knowledge of things as larger or smaller, hotter or colder,

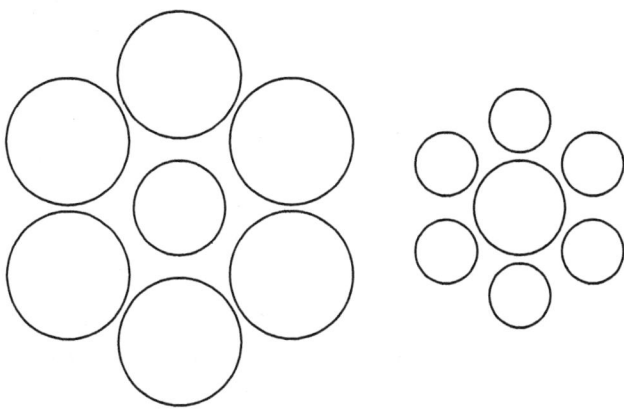

Figure 12

softer or harder than other things. There is a story of Emperor Akbar drawing a line on the ground and challenging his courtiers to shorten it without cutting it, and of how Birbal solved the problem by drawing a longer line beside it.

It is equally easy to change the size of a circle by suggestion. The two central circles of Figure 12 are of exactly the same size, but the one on the left looks smaller. This reduction in apparent size is produced by the surrounding circles, which make it look so. But, of course, we are not really making the line or circle any smaller. The true size of each of them remains unchanged. It is our belief about them which has altered and also (it may be added) the way we actually see them.

This visual illusion is analogous to the well-known fact that a bowl of tepid water will feel cold to one hand which has just been immersed in hot water and yet hot to the other hand which has just been immersed in cold water. The same water at the same time produces the opposite impression on the two hands.

This ability to distort the perception of things by subtle suggestion is not limited to geometrical figures; you can equally well alter the apparent size of real people—even when you know that what you are seeing is nonsense.

Figure 13[7] shows the same two people—father and son—on opposite sides of the same room on two different occasions. Deprived of all binocular stereoscopic clues to depth, the single eye or camera is misled by an apparently normal room into compelling misjudgements about the relative size of the objects seen in it. The clues provided by the room mislead the brain into misjudging the size of objects.

The idea for this form of perceptual distortion was first suggested by Helmholtz, but it was an American psychologist, Adelbert Ames, who actually constructed a room of this kind and confirmed the illusion.

How is it done? By making use of the fact that we rely much more than we realize on our normal expectations about the shape of rooms and on the size and uniformity of walls and windows in interpreting what we see in rooms. We expect windows to be regular

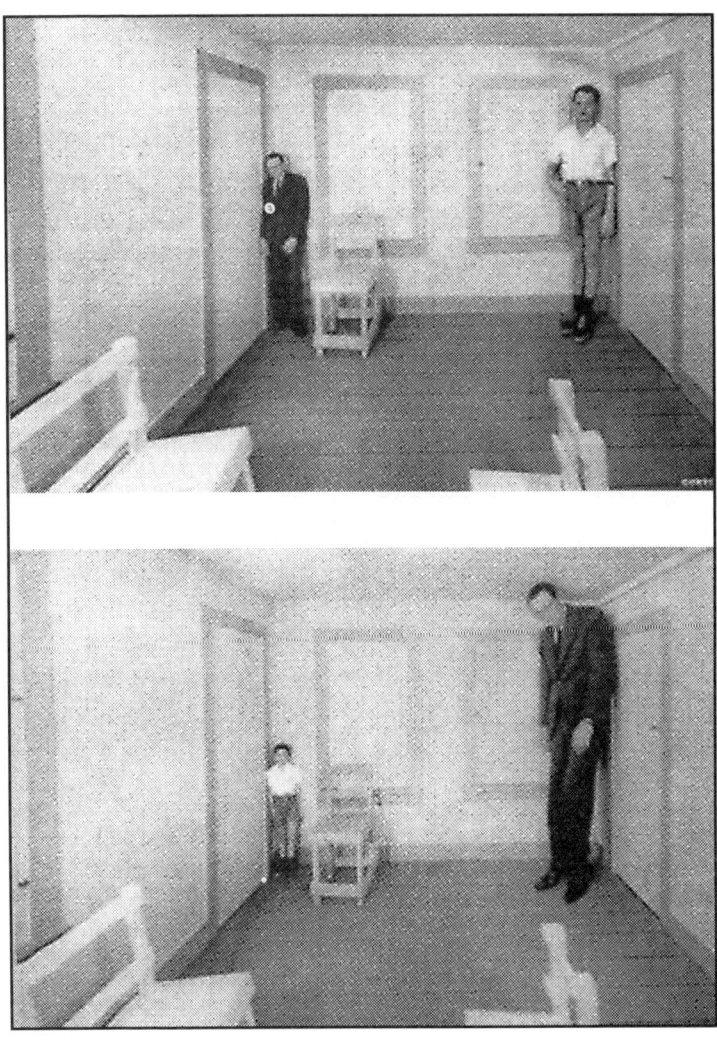

Figure 13 Father and son photographed in an Ames Room

in shape and walls to be regular in outline. This is what we are used to. Where these clues are manipulated to mislead us, our judgements may be totally wrong and yet compelling. The perceptual mechanisms of the brain continually and unconsciously gamble on the most likely interpretation of what we are seeing, but fail to limit their confidence with caution in extrapolating far beyond the evidence provided by what they actually see. As Figure 10 demonstrates, a definite decision about what we are seeing is favoured as against a suspension of judgement. In fact, as in Figure 13, we can jump to conclusions which we accept at the perceptual level even when we know that they are crazy! Figure 14 shows how the camera/eye view is actually produced.

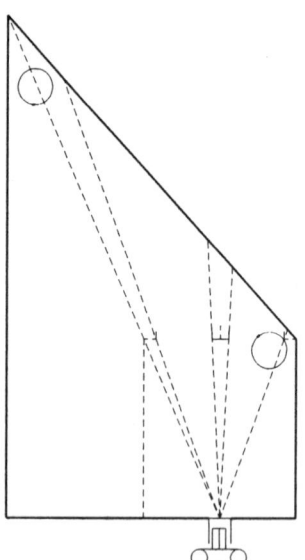

Figure 14

These examples are not given simply to amuse or divert you, but to demonstrate a very important principle about the way that the mind works, and the ability of the suggestions made by the sense-impressions to induce beliefs about the nature of reality. These beliefs can give either a true or a false view of reality, according to whether those suggestions which we accept correspond to the facts or not.

In the fourth chapter of *Panchadashi*[8], a Yoga classic written in the fourteenth century, you can find a detailed discussion of the way in which the mind of the individual imposes on the outer objects its own distorted view of what they are like. The terms *Jiva shrishti* and *Ishvara shrishti* are used by the author, Swami Vidyaranya, to describe the two viewpoints: (1) things as we see them and (2) things as they really are, empirically speaking, in the universe at large. And it is the mental suggestions in the form of beliefs that subtly change the object in the outer world into the picture which the mind makes of it.

According to the yogis we are unwise if we accept uncritically the suggestions of the senses, because they are not even self-consistent and are clearly, in some important respects, misleading. Maya is said to make the impossible possible; and not a bad analogy of ordinary life in the world is given in the impossible figure shown in Figure 15. One goes on endlessly climbing up the stairs, but never seeming to reach the top, and finding in the end that one has got nowhere and is back where one started!

Wherever one looks in the picture shown in Figure 15 the steps seem to be continuous but never-ending, and—although we know after careful examination and reflection that what we are presented with is impossible—the impossibility of the situation is too abstract to overcome what is actually seen at each particular point on which we focus our attention. Reason is defeated by what we see at each glance.

It is a fundamental feature of our mind that it has a shifting focus of attention which is directed, at any one moment, to a particular local feature in the field on which the eye or the ear or one of the other senses is concentrating, and, although it can very rapidly scan a whole array of features in different parts of the field of the incoming sense data, everywhere it looks in Figure 15 presents it with the appearance of the same apparently unidirectional steps. It is only when reason and judgement attempt to interpret the scene as a whole that something is realized to be wrong.

One of the main reasons why the brain is so easily misled under these circumstances arises from the way it is organized to analyse experience. The brain consists of many areas—what Pavlov originally called 'the cortical analysers', although they are probably not exclusively limited to the cerebral cortex. These operate in parallel. Each specializes in the detection of a particular feature.

The sensory messages for sight, hearing, smell, taste and touch are dealt with in different areas of the brain, quite widely separated from each other; but even within an area dealing with one modality of sensation, different

Seeing is Believing

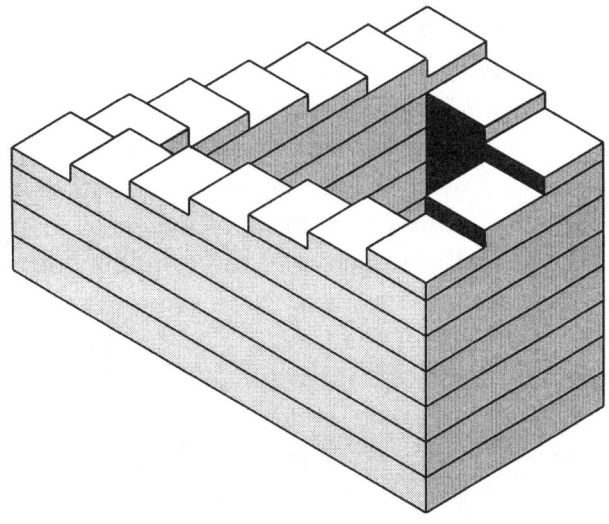

Figure 15

parts of the cortex are specialized to analyse the input for different features and different sensory qualities.

For instance, in the visual cortex, there are separate areas devoted to the analysis of incoming visual data for shape and form, colour, movement, three-dimensional stereoscopic depth and so forth. The incoming nervous messages from the eye are distributed to each and every one of these areas which independently examine them for the particular feature of the input with which the area deals.

The brain is thus equipped with many independent detectors operating in parallel to analyse experience in terms of many different features at one and the same time. Conscious attention is free to focus on one or other of the analysers, to the exclusion of the rest and to reach a quick consensus. In modern parlance the brain is a device which uses 'parallel distributed processing' rather than acting like a single channel analyser. This has the advantage of allowing a very rapid assessment of new and unexpected stimuli in terms of a consensus arrived at from the overall assessment of the combined inputs, speedily providing the most likely interpretation in the minimum time, rather than aiming at a slower, more precise and reliable recognition taking full account of the whole of what is to be seen. This fast method of assessment—allowing a quick sizing up of the situation— is no doubt a matter of considerable biological importance for survival, but it has the disadvantage that strong local clues or features may acquire an undue weight, forcing one to jump to conclusions which may override reason or common sense. Wiser counsels do not always necessarily prevail, nor will second thoughts—which are proverbially best—always be able to override the strength of the first impressions.

The 'impossible figures' such as the endless staircase of Figure 15 depend on the operation of such local clues. Wherever you look on the stairs, they are going in the same direction. The eye cannot find a break anywhere. Hence the whole staircase is impossible even though clearly seen.

Figure 16 shows a similar type of illusion. The apparently spiral pattern is not a spiral at all, although it is difficult to convince oneself of this. The local clues

Figure 16

suggest a spiral and disguise the fact that the figure is, in fact, made up fundamentally of a pattern of what are concentric circles—a truth which you can verify for yourself by tracing any one of them round with your finger or the tip of a pencil! Even when you know it to be so, you cannot cease to see it as a spiral pattern, because of the overwhelming influence of the 'local' suggestions of spirality, incorporated in the detail of the interruption of the essentially circular pattern, made up of what the

British psychologist, James Frazer, called 'twisted threads'. This particular illusion was described by him in 1908.[9]

Frazer described another version of what he called 'an illusion of direction', an example of which is shown in Figure 17. Here again, the effect of the 'local clues' as to non-verticality overwhelm the recognition of the fact that the whole letters making up the word LIFE are themselves quite vertical in orientation, as is clear from

Figure 17

an examination of how they lie along the vertical lines of the diamonds on which they are superimposed. The organization of the visuo-sensory areas of the brain, with its network of feature analyzers working as parallel distributed processors, makes it easy to understand how this can happen.

All these examples emphasize how intimately

suggestions of the simplest and most unreliable kind can enter into perception and how much what is actually perceived depends upon the almost instinctive interpretative habits of our sense-organs and nervous system. Perception is a very different thing from sensation, if the latter is taken to be the reception and acceptance of the raw, unaltered sense-data as it comes in through the eyes, ears and other senses. An understanding of how profound a rôle suggestion plays in the interpretation of the sense data which produces our sense experience is perhaps one important element in the beginning of wisdom, and it points to the powerful effect which suggestion has on our whole mental life.

* * * *

We have now to consider what is the relation of the beliefs which we hold in the mind to *knowledge*. As has been said, a belief can be true or false. Russell puts it very clearly, and what he says can be briefly summarized:

1. Beliefs can be expressed in statements or propositions.
2. Facts are what make statements true or false.
3. Everything that there is in the world is fact.
4. A fact is something which is there, whether anybody thinks so or not.
5. Beliefs are true when they correspond to the facts.

Russell speaks of *knowledge* as being a sub-class of true belief, making the point that it is not sufficient simply for a belief to be true for it to constitute knowledge. It may *happen* to be true, even though we have no very good grounds for believing it. But to constitute knowledge, we must also have 'sound evidence' for believing it. Russell points out that, in ordinary life, knowledge is a matter of degree, since we have a varying degree of certainty and confidence in different beliefs and (even more important) a varying degree of reliable evidence to support them. He holds that there is no definite and unambiguous answer to the question 'what do we mean by knowledge?', any more than there is to the question 'what do we mean by baldness'.[10]

Vedanta speaks of knowledge (meaning true knowledge) and also of (i) the absence or lack of knowledge, (ii) doubt and (iii) false knowledge, but adds an important rider to what Russell says—that while all that he says may apply to empirical knowledge of the world of time, space and causation, which is the region of uncertainty and doubt, there is one fact about which absolute knowledge and certainty is possible, and that is knowledge of the nature of the knowing entity itself.

In what does 'sound evidence' consist and how does one recognize it? There are three possible criteria which Russell considers for distinguishing true knowledge from mere true belief. The latter may be purely fortuitous, like the correct time indicated by a clock which has stopped, but which one happens to see at one of the two instants during the day when it is showing the correct time! Russell's three possible criteria for distinguishing genuine knowledge are: *self-evidence*, the *coherence* of a whole body of beliefs, and the pragmatic view which abandons the idea of knowledge in favour of *beliefs which promote success*.[11]

Self-evidence is often thought to apply particularly to sensation. It is held that through perceptual experience we come to know matters of fact, but (as has been made clear) it can be easily demonstrated that the senses readily mislead us. According to the yogis *the one really self-evident principle is the principle of knowing itself*. The real Self, *Atman*, is said to be *svayam prakasha*, self-shining, a light requiring no other thing to reveal it. This is also, of course, the point being made by Descartes, but he mistakenly applies it to thought, which is a function of the mind, rather than to consciousness *per se*, the knower of knowing.

Russell says of self-evidence as a criterion of truth:

> If, however, self-evidence is to be accepted as a guarantee of truth, the concept must be carefully distinguished from others that have a subjective resemblance to it. I think we must bear it in mind as relevant to the definition of 'knowledge', but as not in itself sufficient.[12]

The coherence criterion of truth is seen at work when we come to believe the testimony of a group of people because (as we say) 'it hangs together'. Science relies on the criterion heavily, since we expect the new laws to be consistent with, and fit into, the body of knowledge which is already established. But there are apparent inconsistencies even in accepted scientific knowledge. Some of these probably indicate things which have yet to be understood, and they can be an important spur to further progress. But there are also more puzzling inconsistencies which look as if they won't go away so easily, like the strange behaviour of electrons, which sometime seem to behave as if they were waves and at other times as particles.[13]

The third pragmatic criterion, of 'beliefs which promote success', is criticized and rejected by Russell as half-hearted and useless in practice for the purpose for which its proponents attempt to justify it, because you cannot know in practice which the successful beliefs are.

The ideas in the mind, then, are of the nature of beliefs, and these beliefs (or many of them) are produced by the suggestions made by the sensations which impinge on the mind from its perception of the outer world. Others arise from the influence of memory, either influencing the way we perceive things—that is to say, our interpretation of sense impressions—or, on their own, by their direct influence on our thoughts. Others again arise from the influence of what we are told by other people (verbal testimony is a powerful source of suggestions which influence our thought and action). Still other beliefs or ideas concern our expectations as to what is going to happen in the future, and these beliefs or suggestions powerfully affect our present conduct. For instance, they may give rise to apprehension or hope or pleasurable anticipation and many other states of mind.

Russell makes the point that these beliefs of many kinds may arise even without any language. We can see this clearly in the case of babies or animals, in which language has not yet developed, but it is equally true in ourselves. When a baby catches sight of a dog and says 'doggy!', it is expressing a belief about what it is seeing, but it may also say 'doggy!', when it goes to the zoo and sees a lion or a wolf; so these primitive and simple forms of belief can also be seen to be correct or erroneous, true or false. Russell makes the point that even without any language, we can see such beliefs operating in animals, as when a cat sits watching intensely in front of a mousehole with her tail swishing in savage expectation.[14] The cat has an idea or belief that there is a mouse. Even at this level one can see at least three clear characteristics of beliefs: firstly, beliefs refer to something outside the believer themselves (i.e. they have something external to which they refer, they are an idea or a belief about something else); secondly, they are often preparations for future action and influence how we behave, particularly as they may lead to certain expectations; thirdly, it is worth noting that they may concern things not present to our senses, as in the case of the cat which has not yet actually seen the mouse. The cat has an idea of the mouse, and this belief is 'true' if there is a mouse down the hole and 'false' if not.[15]

All these characteristics of belief at the pre-linguistic level are also characteristic of human ideas or thoughts. Moreover, human thought also exists without language in the human adult. We may have an idea or belief long before we put it into words. Russell gives the example of believing that we are going to miss the train when we are at the station. If we are on our own this belief may never be formulated in words even in our own minds, but it is a powerful spur to action, and we hurry to make sure that we do not miss it. This means that belief exists long before the development of language, although language enables us to express much more subtle and complicated ideas than we could manage to do without it. Moreover, without language, we can only detect those beliefs in other people which actually lead to action. As Russell says:

> In an animal or a young child, believing is shown by an action or a series of actions. The beliefs of the hound about the fox are shown by his following the scent. But in human beings, as a result of language and of the practice of suspended reactions, believing often becomes a more or less static condition, consisting perhaps in pronouncing or imagining appropriate words, together with one of the feelings that constitute different kinds of belief. As to these, we may enumerate: first, the kind of belief that consists in filling out sensations by animal inferences; second, memory; third, expectation; fourth, the kind of belief generated unreflectingly by testimony; and fifth, the kind of belief resulting from conscious inference… 'Belief', therefore, is a wide generic term, and a state of believing is not sharply separated from cognate states which would not naturally be described as believings.[16]

Russell further says:

> Every belief which is not merely an impulse to action is in the nature of a picture, combined with a yes-feeling or a no-feeling; in the case of a yes-feeling it is 'true' if there is a fact having to the picture the kind of similarity that a prototype has to

> an image; in the case of a no-feeling it is 'true' if there is no such fact. A belief which is not true is called 'false'.[17]
>
> What would commonly be called a man's 'mental' life is entirely made up of ideas and attitudes towards them. Imagination, memory, desire, thought and belief all involve ideas, and ideas are connected with suspended reactions. Ideas, in fact, are parts of causes of actions, which become complete causes when a suitable stimulus is applied. They are like explosives waiting to be exploded. In fact, the similarity may be very close. Trained soldiers, hearing the word 'fire!' (which already existed in them as an idea) proceed to cause explosions. The similarity of language to explosives lies in the fact that a very small additional stimulus can produce a tremendous effect. Consider the effects which flowed from Hitler's pronouncing the word 'war!'[18].

In this passage Russell emphasizes the important rôle that the ideas and beliefs implanted in the mind play in determining our future action. This again is a confirmation of what the yogis have always maintained.

One of the great modern yogis, Swami Rama Tirtha, who died in 1906—forty-two years before Russell's great work was published—has written a very short essay on 'Hypnotism and Vedanta', which is published along with his lectures *In Woods of God-Realization*. He begins it by quoting the saying of Emerson: 'Call someone a thief and he will steal'. In other words, make any kind of suggestion and you will see the corresponding result in action.

But he goes on to qualify this as being true only in

some cases and not invariably, because suggestions can either be accepted or resisted by the mind. If they are resisted, then the result may be the exact contrary of what was intended. He draws an analogy with an electric current which, if it flows freely into another conductor, will produce a spread of the same current, flowing in the same direction, but if it encounters an impermeable resistance interposed between the two conductors, will induce an equal and opposite current in the second conductor. He says that in the same way there is *hypnotism by conduction*, where the suggestion is freely accepted, and *hypnotism by induction* where it is resisted. These two could be said to correspond, of course, with the yes-feeling and the no-feeling associated with the belief, of which Russell speaks.

Swami Rama goes on to speak of the causal body as the subconscious storehouse for all the impressions and latent energies of man, all the actions, movements and behaviour of man being simply the working out of the hidden material in the causal body. When any act is done by the physical body, it generates mental energy or thought, and this in turn passes into the causal body or unconscious mind; from there it emerges much later in the form of mental energy, influencing our conscious mind through our dreams or our inner emotions, as the inner inclinations, tendencies and propensities.

Swami Rama Tirtha cites the phenomenon of post-hypnotic suggestion as a demonstration of this power of the implanted suggestions to influence future action. When a person is hypnotized, it is well-known that he can be given what is called a post-hypnotic suggestion, requiring him to do a particular thing at a particular time after he wakes up from his hypnotic trance. Such a suggestion 'will unfailingly bear fruit at the proper time in the shape of a strong inclination to do the deed'. In ordinary life, of course, when the phenomenon of hypnosis is not obviously at work, the suggestions which are active (he says) 'are due to the hypnotism of the senses, to the hypnotism of the inner impressions (in the form of memory) or from any form of hypnotism of which the whole world is made, according to Vedanta.'[19]

It is interesting that we also find Russell recognizing something of this fact, when he writes:

> There has been a great deal of study by psychologists of the operation of the unconscious upon the conscious, but much less of the operation of the conscious upon the unconscious. Yet the latter is of vast importance in the subject of mental hygiene, and must be understood if rational convictions are ever to operate in the realm of the unconscious... My own belief is that a conscious thought can be planted into the unconscious if a sufficient amount of vigour and intensity is put into it. Most of the unconscious consists of what were once highly emotional conscious thoughts, which have now become buried. It is possible to do this process of burying deliberately, and in this way the unconscious can be led to do a lot of useful work. I have found, for example, that if I have to write upon some rather difficult topic the best plan is to think about it with very great intensity—the greatest intensity of which I am capable—for a few hours or

days, and at the end of that time give orders, so to speak, that the work is to proceed underground. After some months I return consciously to the topic and find that the work has been done. Before I had discovered this technique, I used to spend the intervening months worrying because I was making no progress; I arrived at the solution none the sooner for this worry, and the intervening months were wasted, whereas now I can devote them to other pursuits.[20]

It is easy to understand the importance attached by the yogis to the practice of meditation when one realizes this principle. Swami Rama says that we can greatly improve the quality of our life by consciously burying thoughts.

> Let the causal body be instilled with the suggestion of health, and the physical body is bound to be healthy. Let the causal body be saturated with the suggestion of Godhead, and the man is bound to be a prophet. Let the causal body be imbued with the suggestion of slavery and weakness, and the physical body must be weak and slavish. A man is the architect of his own product, in as much as it is his own causal body that is responsible for all his environment.[21]

More fundamentally and radically, Swami Rama Tirtha tells us that:

> all the people in the world are thrown into a queer hypnotism of the world and they will take a long, long time to be de-hypnotised till there comes a free

man of God-consciousness and he de-hypnotises them to their real Godhead and they wake up. That which is substantial and which underlies all the phenomena must be the Reality, and all that which is imposed upon it must be the hypnotic phenomena. Now the substratum of the causal body, remaining the same under all states—the state of hypnotism, the state of wakefulness, the state of dreaming and deep sleep, etc.—is the real Self or one Reality. Everything else is imposed upon it and is a hypnotic phenomenon. Self-realisation means to get rid of the helplessness, the hypnotism, and merge the phenomena into this final Reality.

Through the suggestion of the mother and father, born out by the suggestion of the senses, was the hypnotic sleep of the world brought on, and through the counter-suggestion in the right way it is shaken off.[22]

Our teacher, Dr Shastri, wrote in a paper on mental health:

Suggestion and autosuggestion have a great effect on the mind... suggestion can also be inaudible... By suggestion and autosuggestion (of the right kind, in particular visualizing success in your efforts to live the spiritual life) your will-power is increased... Use autosuggestion in the form of meditation to overcome the cosmic illusion, *sansara*.[23]

But it is also important to remember that he distinguishes clearly between meditation and knowledge:

It is written: 'Without *knowledge* there is no salvation', not 'Without *meditation* there is no salvation'. Meditation *per se* is valueless. It is merely the method whereby the knowledge of God is attained, and therein lies its real value. Meditation itself is a technique for purifying the psychological instruments of knowledge, and for awakening their faculty of spiritual intuition.[24]

13

Tolstoi's Questions*

When we look at the events which have been occurring in Eastern Europe over the last few weeks, it could truly be said that we are living through one of the most momentous periods of history.[1] The seeds of those events have been germinating for a long time, but now they have suddenly sprung into an unexpected and vigorous life, like a smouldering fire bursting out into a great conflagration. Both the active participants and the onlookers have been equally amazed and taken aback by the speed of developments. And these are not limited to Eastern Europe. The two giant states, Russia and China, have both been experiencing manifestations of the same process, as the human spirit tries to shake itself free from the shackles of totalitarianism and struggles to release itself from the strait-jacket of Marxist ideology. The words of Abraham Lincoln have proved their truth:

> You can fool all the people some of the time, and some of the people all of the time, but you can't fool all the people all of the time.

It has become increasingly clear and self-evident that the people have not been fooled, in spite of any appearances to the contrary, and that, once they were able to express themselves freely, they have left no one in doubt about their views of life in the so-called 'Workers' Paradise'.

As the Upanishad proclaims, truth triumphs in the

---

* A lecture given on 8th December 1989.

end and not falsehood. But the half-truth or the falsehood has had a long and uncomfortable run in Communist Russia and its satellites. Even to have established itself and lasted so long suggests that there was at least a half-truth in the Communist doctrine, which was able originally to appeal to the aspirations and self-interest of those who felt themselves to be among the deprived and exploited. Just as Hitler's doctrine of Nazism found a ready audience among those in Germany, who were suffering under the severe economic depression and unemployment which followed on the unenlightened treaty of Versailles concluded by the victors at the end of the First World War; so the Russian masses' experience of past serfdom and economic deprivation provided a fertile field for sowing the doctrine of the Communist Manifesto.

One is reminded of the verse of Coventry Patmore:

> When all its work is done the lie shall rot.
> The truth is great and shall prevail
> When none care whether it prevail or not.

We must hope that the work of the lie is indeed now done and that a wiser, less oppressive and freer epoch of truly democratic government will now begin for the inhabitants of Russia and the Eastern bloc.

In yogic terms 'the lie', or half-truth, is the result and manifestation of *rajasic* vision, of the delusive power of desire-imagination in the mind, which clouds the judgement and conceals wisdom, making us see one small part of the picture as if it were the whole truth. It is what Maulana Rumi in the *Mathnavi* likens to 'the toggle in the nose of the camel', the force which leads the individual blindly on even against his better judgement.

> As the light of a fire is hidden by smoke..., so is wisdom enveloped and obscured by this insatiable fire of desire, which is the constant foe of the wise

says the third chapter of the *Bhagavad Gita*[2], and later it brings home the point by instancing the example of the promised pleasures which are sought through the contact of the senses with their objects, which are transient and fleeting and which become ultimately the source of suffering, saying that 'No wise man delights in them'.[3] Perhaps an even more graphic example is provided by the so-called 'highs' which people seek through the use of drugs—fixes which lead all too rapidly to the ruin of life and the destruction of the personality.

Just as the French Revolution arose in the last decade of the eighteenth century as a result of the glaring inequalities in French society between the rich and pampered aristocracy and the struggling masses of the poor, so the Russian Revolution took its impetus from similar glaring inequalities in Russian society. In France, there were a number of writers and thinkers who had appeared within the previous fifty years, like Voltaire and Rousseau, who are recognized as forerunners of the French Revolution in 1793, because their thoughts acted as seeds germinating in the national consciousness. Rousseau's book *The Social Contract*, published in 1762, thirty-one years before the French Revolution broke out, advocated democracy and denied the divine right of kings, and, as a result of its publication, he was forced to leave France and take refuge under Frederick the Great in Prussia.

It could be said that a comparable forerunner to the Russian Revolution was the novelist Leo Tolstoi. Although he was not in any sense a Marxist, he was one of the most influential figures in Russia to launch into a major criticism of the State and of the organization of society as it existed at his time and, in the course of it, to raise the whole question of the morality of property-owning. But his particular interest to us is that this critique arose out of what was fundamentally a personal spiritual quest, the course of which he has expressed with great eloquence in his writings.

Tolstoi describes in his book *My Confession* how he was brought up as a Christian but lost his faith as he grew up. By the time that he left the University, after his second year there, at the age of eighteen, he had lost all his former beliefs. He did not deny the existence of God, nor the validity of Christ's teachings, but (as he says) 'all the faith I had, the only belief which, apart from mere animal instinct, swayed my life, was the belief in the possibility of perfection, though what it was in itself, or what would be its results, I could not have said'.[4]

From the age of fifteen onwards he had begun to read philosophical works and tried to reach intellectual and moral perfection, by giving himself principles or rules to follow to strengthen his will and subjecting himself to many voluntary hardships and trials. In a revealing passage he goes on to say:

Tolstoi's Questions

I think that many and many have had the same experiences that I did. I desired with all my soul to be good; but I was young, I had passions, and I was alone, wholly alone, in my search after goodness. Every time I tried to express the longings of my heart to be morally good, I was met with contempt and ridicule, but as soon as I gave way to low passions, I was praised and encouraged.

Ambition, love of power, love of gain, lechery, pride, anger, vengeance, were held in high esteem.

As I gave way to these passions, I became like my elders, and I felt that they were satisfied with me. A kind-hearted aunt of mine, a really good woman with whom I lived, used to say to me that there was one thing above all others that she wished for me — an intrigue with a married woman: '*Rien ne forme un jeune homme, comme une liaison avec une femme comme il faut*'. Another of her wishes for my happiness was that I should become an adjutant, and, if possible, to the Emperor; the greatest piece of good fortune of all, she thought, would be that I should find a very wealthy bride, who would bring me as her dowry as many slaves as could be.

I cannot now recall those years without a painful feeling of horror and loathing.

I put men to death in war, I fought duels to slay others, I lost at cards, wasted my substance wrung from the sweat of peasants, punished the latter cruelly, rioted with loose women, and deceived men. Lying, robbery, adultery of all kinds, drunkenness, violence, murder... There was not one crime which I did not commit, and yet I was not the less considered by my equals a comparatively moral man. Such was my life during ten years.[5]

Tolstoi's *My Confession* reminds one of St Augustine's *Confessions*. Augustine, too, never lost his faith in the search for perfection, but succumbed early in his career to a way of life in which he gave himself up to sensuality and the empirical pursuit of pleasure in much the same way.

Tolstoi described how he began to write primarily from ambition, following

> as a writer the same path which I had chosen as a man. In order to obtain the fame and the money for which I wrote, I was obliged to hide what was good and to say what was evil. Thus I did. How often while writing have I cudgelled my brains to conceal under the mask of indifference or pleasantry those yearnings for something better which formed the real thought of my life. I succeeded in this also, and was praised.[6]

At the age of twenty-six, at the end of the Crimean War which was waged during that year at Sebastopol between Russia and the French and English armies, Tolstoi went to St Petersburg and mixed with the writers and poets there who considered themselves the leaders of thought. Tolstoi was welcomed by this coterie and received much flattery. Of this time he writes:

> Before I had time to look around, the prejudices and views of life common to the writers of the class with which I associated became my own, and completely

put an end to all my former struggles after a better life.[7]

The view of life, or theory, which was developed by this group to justify its dissipated and self-indulgent life-style, was that life was a development, in which the principal part was played by the thinkers, writers and poets, whose vocation was to teach mankind:

> In order to avoid answering the very natural question 'What do I know, and what can I teach?' the theory in question is made to contain the formula that it is not necessary to know this, but that the artist and the poet teach unconsciously.
>
> I was myself considered a marvellous artist and poet, and I therefore very naturally adopted this theory. I, an artist and poet, wrote and taught I knew not what. For doing this I received money; I kept a splendid table, had excellent lodgings, women, society; I had fame. Naturally what I taught was very good.
>
> When I now think over that time, and remember my own state of mind and that of these men (a state of mind common enough among thousands still), it seems to me pitiful, terrible and ridiculous; it excites the feelings which overcome us as we pass through a madhouse...
>
> Quite unconscious that we ourselves knew nothing, that to the simplest of all problems in life—what is right and what is wrong—we had no answer, we all went on talking together without one to listen, at times abetting and praising one another on condition that we were abetted and praised in turn,

and again turning upon one another in wrath—in short, we reproduced the scenes in a madhouse.

Thousands of labourers worked day and night, to the limit of their strength, setting up the type and printing millions of words to be spread by the post all over Russia... The real motive that inspired all our reasoning was the desire for money and praise, to obtain which we knew of no other means than writing books and newspapers, and so we did. But in order to hold fast to the conviction that while thus uselessly employed we were very important men, it was necessary to justify our occupation to ourselves by another theory, and the following one was adopted:

Whatever is, is right; everything that is, is due to development; development comes from civilization; the measure of civilization is the diffusion of books and newspapers; we are paid and honoured for the books and newspapers which we write, and we are therefore the most useful and best of men![8]

Tolstoi concludes:

It is now clear to me that between ourselves and the inhabitants of a madhouse there was no difference: at the time I only vaguely suspected this, and, like all madmen, thought all were mad except myself... I lived in this senseless manner another six years up to the time of my marriage.[9]

Tolstoi then went abroad and travelled in Europe. He found the dominant belief among the eminent and learned at that time was in what was called 'progress'. He accepted this for the time being because (he says):

> I did not as yet understand that, tormented like every other man by the question 'How was I to live better?', when I answered that I must live for progress, I was only repeating the answer of a man carried away in a boat by the waves and the wind, who to the one important question for him, 'Where are we to steer?' should answer, 'We are being carried somewhere'.[10]

He had a rude shock to his belief in progress, which outraged his feelings rather than his reason, when he saw a public execution in Paris.

> I understood not with my reason, but with my whole being, that no theory of the wisdom of all established things, nor of progress, could justify such an act; ...and that therefore I must judge what was right and necessary, not by what men said and did, not by progress, but by what I felt to be true in my heart.[11]

He returned to Russia and settled in the country and occupied himself in the organization of schools for the peasants. He also got married. Things seemed to be going very well for him, but he felt that his mind was not in a normal state and that a change was near. But for the time being his new circumstances led him away from the search after the meaning of life as a whole.

> The effort to effect my own individual perfection, already replaced by the striving after general progress, was again changed into an effort to secure the particular happiness of my family.
>
> In this way fifteen years passed. In my writings I taught what for me was the only truth—that the

object of life should be our highest happiness and that of our family.

Thus I lived: but, five years ago, a strange state of mind began to grow upon me: I had moments of perplexity, of a stoppage, as it were, of life, as if I did not know how I was to live, what I was to do, and I began to wander, and was a victim to low spirits. But this passed, and I continued to live as before. Later, these periods of perplexity began to return more and more frequently, and invariably took the same form. These stoppages of life always presented themselves to me with the same questions: 'Why?' and 'What after?'

At first it seemed to me that these were aimless, unmeaning questions; it seemed to me that all they asked about was well known, and that if at any time when I wished to find answers to them I could do so without much trouble—that just at that time I could not be bothered with this, but whenever I should stop to think them over I should find an answer. But these questions presented themselves to my mind with ever-increasing frequency, demanding an answer with still greater and greater persistence, and like dots grouped themselves into one black spot.[12]

Tolstoi tried to answer the questions, but without success; they seemed so foolish, so simple, so childish; but when he attempted to grapple with them he became convinced that they concerned the deepest problems of life. These questions kept intruding in what he was doing.

When considering by what means the well-being of

> the people might best be promoted, I suddenly exclaimed, 'But what concern have I with it?' When I thought of the fame which my works were gaining me, I said to myself: 'Well, what if I should be more famous than Gogol, Pushkin, Shakespeare, Molière—than all the writers of the world—well, and what then?'... I could find no reply... I felt that the ground on which I stood was crumbling, that there was nothing for me to stand on, that what I had been living for was nothing, that I had no reason for living...[13]

He felt that life was meaningless, that he, a healthy and a happy man, had been taken hold of by some irresistible force which was dragging him onward to escape from life. He adds here that he does not mean that he wanted to kill himself.

> The force that drew me away from life was stronger, fuller and more universal than any wish; it was a force like that of my previous attachment to life, only in a contrary direction... I knew not what I wanted; I was afraid of life; I struggled to get away from it, and yet there *was* something I hoped for from it.

> Such was the condition I had come to, at a time when all the circumstances of my life were pre-eminently happy ones, and when I had not reached my fiftieth year. I had a good, loving and beloved wife, good children and a large estate, which, without much trouble on my part, was growing and increasing; I was more than ever respected by my friends and acquaintances; I was praised by strangers, and could lay claim to having made my

> name famous without much self-deception. Moreover, I was not mad or in an unhealthy mental state; on the contrary, I enjoyed a mental and physical strength which I have seldom found in men of my class and pursuits; I could keep up with a peasant in mowing, and could continue mental labour for eight or ten hours at a stretch, without any evil consequences. And in this state of things it came to this—that I could not live, and that as I feared death I was obliged to employ ruses against myself so as not to put an end to my life.[14]

At this stage life seemed to Tolstoi like a foolish and wicked joke played on him by someone, notwithstanding the fact that he did not recognize the existence of a someone who might have created him! Like Faust, he sought an explanation of the questions which tormented him in every branch of human knowledge, but only convinced himself that all those who had searched like himself, had, like him, found nothing, either in the clear horizon opened out by mathematics and experimental sciences or in the murky darkness of philosophy. Whether clear or murky, they did not answer his question.

At this point he abandoned reliance on the knowledge to be found through the intellect or reason and his whole enquiry took a different turn. In his own words:

> When I had come to this conclusion, I understood that it was useless to seek an answer to my question from knowledge founded on reason, and that the answer given by this form of knowledge is only an

indication that no answer can be obtained till the question is put differently—till the question be made to include the relation between the finite and the infinite. I also understood that, however unreasonable and monstrous the answers given by faith, they have the advantage of bringing into every question the relation of the finite to the infinite, without which there can be no answer.[15]

He studied Buddhism, Islam and Christianity and sought out the believers in the Russian Church. He remained unconvinced by those whom he talked to from his own stratum of society—members of the educated classes—because he felt that only that faith would convince him which enabled men to prove through their action that they had destroyed the fear of poverty, illness and death, which he felt so strongly in himself. He found such fearlessness more characteristic of the life of the open unbelievers of his own class than among the so-called believers.

> I understood, then, that the faith of these men was not the faith which I sought; that it was no faith at all, but only one of the Epicurean consolations of life...
>
> I began to draw nearer to the believers, among the poor, the simple and the ignorant, the pilgrims, the monks, the *raskolniks* (Old Believers) and the peasants. The doctrines of these men of the people, like those of the pretended believers of my own class, were Christian. Here also much that was superstitious was mingled with the truths of Christianity, but with this difference, that the superstition of the believers of our class was entirely

unnecessary to them, and never influenced their lives beyond serving as a kind of Epicurean distraction; while the superstition of the believing labouring class was so interwoven with their lives that it was impossible to conceive them without it—it was a necessary condition of their living at all. The whole life of the believers of our class was in flat contradiction with their faith, and the whole life of the believers of the people was a confirmation of the meaning of life which their faith gave them.[16]

Tolstoi began to see a major difference between what were appropriately then called the leisured classes and the toiling masses in his own country and he became more and more convinced that, in the Russia of his time at least, the life of the ordinary poor people had a spiritual dimension which was not to be found among the idle rich. He himself puts it in this way:

Thus I began to study the lives and the doctrines of the people, and the more I studied the more I became convinced that a true faith was among them, that their faith was for them a necessary thing, and alone gave them a meaning in life and a possibility of living. In direct opposition to what I saw in our circle—where life without faith was possible, and where not one in a thousand professed himself a believer—amongst the people there was not a single unbeliever in a thousand. In direct opposition to what I saw in our circle—where a whole life is spent in idleness, amusement, and dissatisfaction with life —I saw among the people whole lives passed in heavy labour and unrepining contentment. In direct opposition to what I saw in our circle—men resisting and indignant with the privations and sufferings of their lot—the people unhesitatingly and unresistingly accepting illness and sorrow, in the quiet and firm conviction that all these must be and could not be otherwise, and that all was for the best. In contradiction to the theory that the less learned we are the less we understand the meaning of life, and see in our sufferings and death but an evil joke, these men of the people live, suffer and draw near to death, in quiet confidence and oftenest with joy. In contradiction to the fact that an easy death, without terror or despair, is a rare exception in our class, a death which is uneasy, rebellious and sorrowful is among the people the rarest exception of all.

These people, deprived of all that for us and for Solomon makes the only good in life, and experiencing at the same time the highest happiness, form the great majority of mankind. I looked more widely around me, I studied the lives of the past and contemporary masses of humanity, and I saw that, not two or three, or ten, but hundreds, thousands, millions had so understood the meaning of life that they were able both to live and to die. All these men, infinitely divided by manners, powers of mind, education and position, all alike in opposition to my ignorance, were well acquainted with the meaning of life and death, quietly laboured, endured privation and suffering, lived and died, and saw in all this, not a vain, but a good thing.[17]

Tolstoi described how he began to grow attached to these people, the more he learned of their lives, and over the next two years a great change came about in his attitude. He tried to live in accordance with what he now felt and, as a result, the life of his own circle of rich and learned friends lost all meaning for him. All the science and art and reasoning which they indulged in seemed to be mere child's play, in which it was useless to seek a meaning. On the other hand he felt that the life of the working classes, of the mass of mankind, was truly signnificant and gave a meaning to life. He then understood (he said) how he himself had erred in his earlier thinking.

> I had erred, not so much through having thought incorrectly, as through having lived ill. I understood that the truth had been hidden from me, not so much because I had erred in my reasoning, as because I had led the exceptional life of an epicure bent on satisfying the lusts of the flesh. I understood that my question, 'What is my life?', and the answer, 'An evil', were in accordance with the truth of things. The mistake lay in my having applied to life in general an answer which only concerned myself. I had asked what my own life was, and the answer was 'An evil and absurdity'. Exactly so, my life—a life of indulgence, of sensuality—was an absurdity and an evil; and the answer, 'Life is meaningless and evil', therefore, referred only to my own life and not to human life in general.
>
> I understood the truth which I afterwards found in the Gospel: 'That men loved darkness rather than light because their deeds were evil. For every man that doeth evil hateth the light, neither cometh to the light, lest his deeds should be reproved.'[18]

Tolstoi goes on to say that he realized finally that he had lived only when he believed in a God and not otherwise. In his own words:

> What was this discouragement and revival? I do not live when I lose faith in the existence of a God; I should long ago have killed myself, if I had not had a dim hope of finding Him. I really live only when I am conscious of Him and seek Him. 'What more then, do I seek?' A voice seemed to cry within me, 'This is He, He without whom there is no life. To know God and to live are one. God is life'.
>
> Live to seek God, and life will not be without God. And stronger than ever rose up life within and around me, and the light that then shone never left me again.[19]

Tolstoi's powerful testament of his own spiritual struggles also had a wider social dimension, because it led him to a criticism of the state of the society in which he lived. His criticism of his own class—rich, educated and largely idle—suggested to him that there was a fault at the heart of society. He regarded wealth or property as a wall between the rich and the poor and thought that the organisation of the state had been largely created to protect private property. In this he shows that he lived before the age of the great modern Communist States, who have outlawed capitalism and property-owning, but have turned out to be far more oppressive in the treatment of their subjects than the so-called capitalist societies.

But where Tolstoi is certainly right is in pointing out that States and Nations behave far worse than any individual would dare to, and also far worse than any individual would get away with without being stopped and punished for it by the law or public opinion. Unfortunately, International Law is too weak and has no teeth, and public opinion can be fooled much of the time, because it is ill-informed and subject to manipulation by false propaganda. On the positive side, however, the modern media and means of communication are beginning to change this.

Tolstoi himself has affinities with the great stream of thought in Russia which was anarchist rather than Bolshevik. This was the movement led and inspired by such figures as Bakunin and his disciple, Kropotkin.

Mikhail Bakunin, the originator of modern anarchism, was fourteen years older than Tolstoi. Like Tolstoi he came from an aristocratic family. He joined the Russian Army at the age of fifteen and was horrified by the brutal crushing of the Polish insurrection of 1830 a year later. This led him to give up his military career four years later in order to study philosophy, first at Moscow and then in Berlin. He became a revolutionary and moved to Dresden, but had to leave there, going first to Switzerland and then Paris. In Paris, between the years 1843 and 1847, Bakunin made the acquaintance of Marx, and was later to write of him:

> It was just at this time that he elaborated the first foundations of his present system. We saw each other fairly often... and I sought eagerly his conversation, which was always instructive and clever, when it was not inspired by paltry hate, which alas! happened only too often. But there was never any frank intimacy between us. Our

temperaments would not suffer it. He called me a sentimental idealist, and he was right; I called him a vain man, perfidious and crafty, and I was also right.[20]

As a result of a speech which he made praising the Polish rising of 1830, Bakunin was expelled from France at the request of the Russian Embassy. He went to Brussels, where he renewed his association with Marx. In a letter at the time he writes:

> The Germans, artisans, Bornstedt, Marx and Engels —and above all, Marx—are here, doing their ordinary mischief. Vanity, spite, gossip, theoretical overbearingness and practical pusillanimity— reflections on life, action and simplicity, and complete absence of life, action and simplicity— literary and argumentative artisans and repulsive coquetry with them: 'Feuerbach is a bourgeois', and the word 'bourgeois' grown into an epithet repeated *ad nauseam*, but all of them themselves from head to foot, through and through, provincial bourgeois. With one word, lying and stupidity, stupidity and lying. In this society there is no possibility of drawing a free, full breath. I hold myself aloof from them, and have declared quite decidedly that I will not join their communistic union of artisans, and will have nothing to do with it.[21]

After the Revolution in 1848, Bakunin found himself again in Dresden, this time in company with Richard Wagner. He was arrested when the two of them and a companion were trying to escape the authorities (Wagner got away) and Bakunin spent from 1850 to 1864 in prison and exile in Siberia, eventually escaping to Japan. He died in 1876.

Tolstoi was *not* an active revolutionary; he believed in a moral and spiritual revolution within the individual. But, like Bakunin, he felt that the State itself could become an even worse tyrant than the rich capitalist over the mass of its population. He held that the State was largely invented to protect property and that it was the arch criminal, shielding all the injustices of present-day society. And one of its worst features, in his view, was its invention of universal military service. Both he and Bakunin, like Rousseau before them, wanted to limit the power of the State and ideally to abolish it. But in this they seemed to have got hold of another half-truth. They overlooked the fact that a return to Nature, if it means the law of the jungle, is anything but a state of freedom and peace for many of the inhabitants of the forest. Anyone who has a dog with a bone will know that it is not so easy to abolish the sense of private property, and it is certainly not simply a matter of abolishing the government!

In his reaction against the defects of the educated classes of his time in Russia, Tolstoi idealized the masses. In this it is interesting to compare him with his contemporary Nietzsche, who (on the contrary) idealized the superior man who rose above the values of the common herd. But these two apparently opposing streams of thought go back much further than that. The two great formative thinkers of Ancient China in the sixth century BC were Lao Tzu and Confucius, who could be said to perfectly epitomize the two opposing views— that the government bungles things and actually gets in the way of man expressing the best in him, which was the view propounded by Lao Tzu, and the Confucian ideal which holds up the example of the superior man who lives in society, following the ideal of the good in his conduct and refining his mind through scholarship and art and wise government. The great difference in traditional Chinese society, however, was that the higher ranks of the civil service (or as we would say officialdom) were democratically open to all through competitive examination, so that genuine ability was the criterion for social advancement.

A third major feature of Tolstoi's thought is his insistence on the idea of passive resistance, which he based on the teaching of Christ—that we should not resist evil by force, but turn the other cheek. Tolstoi's eloquent preaching of this particular doctrine was a decisive influence on Mahatma Gandhi in his political struggles for Indian independence. It is one of the curiosities of history that Gandhi got his inspiration, not from India where the Buddha had taught the doctrine of harmlessness or *ahimsa* more than two thousand years before, but from the writings of Tolstoi, his near contemporary in the West. Gandhi was at this time a practising lawyer in South Africa, where he had gone after training in England. Gandhi was not the only Indian to be influenced by Tolstoi's ideas. So too was the Indian poet, Rabindranath Tagore, who founded his ideal community, *Shanti Niketan*, largely on the Tolstoyan ideal.

We have seen an impressive adoption of this principle of passive resistance—in the emergence of what is now called 'people power'—in the current overthrow of the totalitarian Communist regimes in Eastern Europe.

This first started in Hungary in 1956, and in Czechoslovakia in the Prague spring of 1968, and has now spread to Poland, East Germany, and Russia itself. It was also evident in the great popular uprising in China earlier this year, which was so brutally put down by the army of the totalitarian government. All these are manifestations of the inextinguishable desire of the human spirit for freedom.

Tolstoi's criticism of the State as the great criminal finds an echo in the events which are sweeping the countries of Eastern Europe at the present time, but it is ironically the governments supposed to be representing the interests, not of the property-owners (as in Tolstoi's day), but of the proletariat, which have now taken on this rôle; and it is the proletariat which is rising in protest against them! This shows us clearly that it is not a particular class which is the real enemy of freedom, progress and enlightenment, as Marx supposed, but the narrow self-interest of the unenlightened power-loving individuals who seize power in the name of this or that ideology, whether Fascist or Communist, and then try and impose their will by the crude exercise of military force and the secret police. This is political gangsterdom and there is little essential difference in principle between the methods of such governments, whether of the Right or the Left, and the drug-barons or the Mafia.

Equally one can see that the forces which have been effective in keeping alive and fostering the spirit of truth and freedom in these situations are the enlightened individuals who have heroically remained true to their own conscience. Men like Solzhenitsyn, Father Poppiewsku, Jan Palach, Václav Havel, Sakharov and many others have done more to keep the torch of freedom alight in the totalitarian world than any of the diplomatic or political initiatives. And the spiritually-minded, whether members of the Church or not, have been in the forefront of the struggle to free the mind from the shackles of false propaganda and Marxist brainwashing. Indeed one of the major factors leading to the present events in Eastern Europe must be accounted the election of a Polish Pope a few years ago.

All this re-confirms the view of the yogis that the sources of inner strength and independence reside in the inner light to be sought by the individual within his own personality.

The real solution to the ills of society is neither anarchism nor Communism, nor any regime imposed by a totalitarian state. It is to return to the spiritual ideal, which taught liberty, equality and fraternity long before the French Revolution, and the end of oppression and exploitation long before Marx arrived on the scene. In this respect Tolstoi was at least looking for the solution to these problems in the right way—through a spiritual quest for perfection carried out largely within his own personality. We can do real good to society if our efforts are based on universal benevolence.

As Shri Dada says:

> The only service to society you can render is to live the ideal laid down in the *Gita* and invite other people's attention to the necessity and importance of holy living.[22]

The ideal of universal social justice and equality follows naturally from the words of the Lord in the *Gita*: 'O Arjuna, I abide deep in the hearts of all beings', echoed by the words of Christ in the Gospels: 'Inasmuch as ye (serve and) do good to the least of these my children, ye do it unto Me'.

Unlike the political agitators, who put their trust in altering the government or the outer circumstances, the spiritual teachers tell us to alter our own lives, to turn within and change the world by ushering in the inner light of wisdom within our personality. The life of a Shri Dada or a Mother Theresa does far more for humanity than the life of a Marx because it is based on a truly universal love and sympathy and not on class hatred or the struggle for power.

Tolstoi held the same view about the need for the individual to seek light within and to return to live by the word of the Christian Gospel, but he did not enjoy the benefit of a traditional spiritual path, such as Yoga. His own tradition, the Russian Church, totally rejected him. The first book in which he set forth his principles, *My Confession*, was banned by the censors; the second, called *My Faith*, was banned by the Holy Synod of the Church. Later the Church excommunicated Tolstoi himself for heresy.

The speaker remembers hearing of a lecture by the great Spanish exile and thinker, Salvador de Madariaga, in which he traced the two most important influences on Western civilization back to two individuals, Christ and Socrates, who had given it the spiritual ideals and the ideals of truth, justice and virtue. Señor de Madariaga ended his lecture by asking his audience: 'Has it ever occurred to you that both of them were put to death by the State?'

It is worth remembering the wise words of Shri Dadaji to his English disciple, Brother Allnutt, when they visited the spot where the Indian Mutiny broke out in Meerut:

> All that is accomplished by means of arms is comparable to a building of straw erected on the sea-shore. The real foundation of a social or inter-social structure is a spiritual understanding, a deeper vision of the fundamental unity of all. The service of the part must be based on the service of the whole.[21]

14

Living in Truth*

The *Book of Common Prayer* adjures us to lead an honest, sober and upright life and there is a verse in the *Book of Ecclesiastes* which says: 'God has made man upright; but they have sought out many inventions'. The speaker was forcibly reminded of the truth of this verse on a recent visit to Gothenburg in Sweden. He was there at the University teaching a group of students who had come from other parts of Scandinavia to attend a course. As a relaxation after the day's study, they were entertained by their Swedish hosts to a dinner and a stroll through the large amusement park which is a feature of the town and which is apparently well-known and visited by Swedish people from all over the country. Such places are really temples of illusion, which exert an attraction to children of all ages, but there can have been few better illustrations of the deceiving power of the world of Maya than the particular attraction which we were taken to sample.

On approach it appeared to be a very large wooden house with windows and doors of a quite traditional kind, except that they and the whole front of the house were set at a crazy angle pointing up in the air to the right, so that the right hand end was perhaps twenty feet higher than the left and, as a consequence, the whole giddily-tilted house appeared to be balanced precariously on its left hand end. But this was only the outer sheath!

---

* A lecture given on June 15th 1990.

Climbing up the steps to the front door, we entered a dim corridor which led one through a horizontal rotating tunnel the whole inner surface of which was covered with a highly-coloured pattern of brightly-coloured blobs on a neutral background rotating anti-clockwise to one's left. Almost at once one lost all sense of what was vertical and what was horizontal and, with it, all clear idea of what was and was not upright. As a consequence, one found oneself leaning dizzily to the right. Thankfully emerging from this tube by passing through a narrow door, one was soon walking along on what was apparently a flat path, but feeling it curiously hard work as if you were going uphill. The cunning of the disorienting manipulations to which one was being subjected was revealed when in the next room there were a series of casks joined by intervening gutters along one wall, in which the water was quite clearly and obviously flowing steeply uphill. In a further room one was amazed to see all one's companions standing not vertically but at the same oblique angle to the floor. It looked so bizarre that everyone was reduced to laughter at the sight of this group of improbable figures, all emulating the Leaning Tower of Pisa. After many more such illusions the tour of the house ended in what appeared to be an enormously long descent in a lift. Through two windows in the wall, one could see the side of the shaft hurtling upwards during the bumpy descent, which ended with a resounding crash, after which the doors opened to allow us to emerge, only to find ourselves on the same level at which we had started!

The makers of the crazy house had used great

ingenuity, not only in destroying one's confident and familiar sense of the vertical, but also in using false but powerful clues to suggest to one what the vertical was in the other parts of the house. But they were only able to do so because they knew that each of us is all the time using things like the angles of doors and windows and walls to infer this information and to jump to what is usually the right conclusion. Since this process is largely unconscious and is second nature to us in ordinary life, we are totally unaware of how much we depend on these clues to orient ourselves. It is only nowadays, when we have become used to seeing astronauts floating head downwards in their capsules, that we can realize that the whole concept of vertical depends on the operation of gravity in the little local region of the universe in which we live. It has none of the unquestioned universal validity which we normally attribute to it quite unconsciously. It is therefore disturbing when we come across circumstances which bring this home to us and deprive us of some of the unquestioned assumptions of our everyday empirical world.

These challenges as to how we see things in everyday life are valuable, because they remind us that we live in a world of appearances. Those appearances are often deceptive and they are not always worthy of the confidence which we put in them. The mind is an unreliable guide. If it is to arrive at truth, we have to subject what it tells us to a critical enquiry and not simply accept first appearances at their face value.

There is a verse in the short yogic classic called *Atma*

Bodha, Knowledge of Self, which says: 'The knowledge that arises from the realization of one's own true nature, directly destroys the illusion of I and mine, which resembles the sort of confusion about the directions which is experienced by a man who is disoriented'. He does not know which is north and south, or even whether he is standing upright, like the visitor to the crazy house.

To know where one is it is necessary to get one's bearings. In order to know whether one is standing on one's head or on one's feet it is necessary to have a sense of the vertical and of *terra firma*, which the astronaut lacks. When there is a discrepancy or conflict between the evidence of one's senses, when one seems to *see* one thing and to *feel* another, then one becomes confused and disoriented. It is a powerful reminder of the fact that knowing where we are and where we stand is not quite so straightforward or easy as we commonly suppose. The yogis say that to answer the question 'What am I?' is a similar challenge, because we are far from unconfused about what we really are. It is not for nothing that one of the greatest scientists of the modern era, Erwin Schrödinger, has said that to carry out the command of the Delphic oracle 'Know thyself!' was not only the main task of science, but the main task of all man's undertakings.

It is like asking the question: 'Where is the centre of the universe?' In a certain real sense each man feels that it is himself. Although we may not all be so immodest as to admit it, for each of us the centre of our own universe is this 'I' which we feel within us. But what is this 'I'?

There are many different views on the matter. Some regard man as a miserable worm wriggling in the mud. Beckett, who has expressed the views of the existentialists in his plays, pictures life as lived on the edge of despair and nihilism. Then there are the views of the thorough-going materialists, who can offer nothing to man but the advice to eat, drink and be merry, for tomorrow we die. Then there are those who hold to the Cartesian philosophy: that the real man is the disembodied mind, which thinks and inhabits a particular body, but is really unconnected to it. What is the yogic view? It is expressed by Shri Shankara in his commentary on the *Bhagavad Gita*. The Self (he says) is what at the outset appears as the suffering, active individual in the body, and turns out in the end (after enquiry and experiment to discover its real nature) to be one with the spiritual reality behind appearances. How are we to decide between these different views of the Self?

In the late fifteenth and early sixteenth centuries practically everyone believed that the earth was the centre of all things, and that all the heavenly bodies moved in cycles and epicycles around it. But at this time there was a renewed interest in what the ancient Greeks taught and it was discovered that there were other views in the ancient world. While Ptolemy and Hipparchus believed that the earth was the centre of the universe, and Aristotle, who was a great authority, followed them in this, the Neo-Platonist philosophers and the Pythagoreans had another idea—that the earth itself moved round a central fire. A Polish German mathematician called Nicolaus Koppernigk went to Italy to study as a pupil of Novarra in Bologna for six years and he found mention in Plutarch and Cicero of the thinker Aristarchus who held that the earth moved round the sun. Nicolaus Koppernigk's Latin name was Copernicus and he was attracted to the idea of Aristarchus, because it made the movement of the heavenly bodies easier to understand. He set about devising a mathematical model to account for the movements of the planets in circular orbits about the sun, in line with this idea. Unfortunately it was marred, not only by his lack of reliable data, but also by the fact that the orbits were actually elliptical, as Kepler was to show more than fifty years after Copernicus' death in 1543. He published a short account of this view in 1530 and a complete book in 1543 and (needless to say) it evoked a good deal of criticism from his contemporaries. If the earth really revolved once a day, they said, reviving an old argument used by Ptolemy, there would be a terrific wind always blowing from West to East and a bird which left its nest would never be able to get back to it again! Copernicus replied that the air rotated with the earth. Ptolemy had also objected that, if the earth really rotated so rapidly, it would fall apart and disintegrate. In reply Copernicus asked how it was then that the other heavenly bodies did not do the same, since they were held to be rotating just as rapidly by his opponents!

The whole argument centred round how you interpreted what you saw moving around you in the heavens. It was rather like someone on a merry-go-round or a big dipper trying to decide whether it was they or the world around them which was moving!

The authorities did not worry too much about Copernicus' ideas, until, in the seventeenth century, Galileo, using his newly invented telescope, observed the satellites of Jupiter, which were a clear example of a solar system in miniature. By 1616 the Catholic authorities had become alarmed and the theory was condemned as 'false and altogether opposed to holy scripture'. Galileo had already ruffled the feathers of the authorities by his experiments on gravity. The traditional view, based on Aristotle's physics, was that a body weighing ten pounds would fall through a given distance in one tenth of the time that would be taken by a body weighing one pound. Galileo went to the top of the leaning tower of Pisa with a ten pound and one pound shot. He demonstrated that the two weights arrived at the ground almost simultaneously. The learned professors, however, would not believe that Aristotle could be wrong. In the end Galileo was hauled before the Inquisition and made to recant his views and to undergo a period of penance in prison for his impiety.

In spite of this, the Copernican revolution triumphed because it was based on a re-discovery of an ancient truth. It, once and for all, humbled man's overweening pride in regarding the earth on which his body happened to live as the centre of the universe. But it still did not answer the question of what he was, or of why what Shakespeare calls such a poor forked animal as man should have these innate feelings of his own value. What the yogis stress is that he does not really know who he is and that, like Galileo, he needs to undertake the necessary enquiry and to examine the evidence so that he can discover and realize the truth about himself and thus decide which of the many theories and hypotheses current in the world is the true one.

The yogis call the world the realm of *avidya* or ignorance of the Truth and there are many influences leading us to get the wrong ideas about things. In many ways, for instance, the situation of going into the crazy house can be compared with what it has been like to live under the totalitarian regimes in Eastern Europe for the last few decades. As in the experience of disorientation in the crazy house, people may have a very strong feeling of confusion and conflict within themselves. They may know that things are not right and that the view of man which their environment is trying to impose on them is somehow totally wrong, but only those with a strong inner sense of independence and a strong desire to live in accordance with truth can remain properly oriented under the circumstances. Only those who were able to maintain (by listening to the voice of their conscience) a sense of the absolute standards, the true uprightness, could fully appreciate and resist what was happening to them, not in the sense that they did not suffer from the appearances, but in the sense that they knew that they were false and based on lies.

One individual who managed to do this, in spite of intense pressure by the secret police and persecution culminating in long periods in prison, was the Czech playwright Václav Havel, now President of Czechoslovakia. He has written a testimony to the principles which enabled him to resist this treatment in a book which is appropriately called *Living in Truth*.[1] It was this principle that enabled him to found the Charter 77 movement in Czechoslovakia and to play a major part in bringing about the popular awakening which led to the overthrow of the Communist regime in his country. In 1979, after being for many years the object of harassment, detentions and close surveillance by the secret police, he was sentenced to four and a half years of hard labour together with the other members of the Committee which had been set up to defend the unjustly prosecuted. In prison he was allowed to write only one four-page letter home each week. It had to be legible, with nothing corrected or crossed out; there were strict rules banning the use of quotation marks or underlining or foreign expressions. Prisoners were allowed only to write about family matters and humour was banned.

Havel's letters to his wife, Olga, were published in *samizdat* form after his release, and it is interesting to discover in their pages frequent references to the practice of Yoga. One is reminded of the verse in the *Bhagavad Gita* which says: 'Even a little practice of this Yoga saves one from great fear'. His first letter contains the following:

> Dear Olga,
>
> It appears the astrologers were right when they predicted prison for me again this year and when they said the summer would be a hot one. As a matter of fact, it's stifling hot here, like being in a perpetual sauna. I feel sorry about the many complications my new stint in jail will probably cause you. I think you should stay in Hrádeček and

look after the place—tend the meadow, make improvements to the house, take the dogs for walks to the pond, etc. There are always family or friends who might want to spend their holidays there with you. There's no reason to stay in Prague—you can't be of any help to me here and what would you do all day? And anyway, we've sublet the flat. Of course, you should learn to drive so you can do the shopping and so on without having to rely on someone else all the time. In short, you should lead a completely normal life, as though I were off on a trip somewhere. This is how you can help me the most, if I know you're well and taken care of. I don't know, of course, how long this trip will last; I am not harbouring any illusions, and in fact I hardly think about it at all. I don't think much about our 'case' either—since there's nothing to think about. The matter is clear and it is also clear to me (after all we've been through) what I have to do and how... I am trying to do a little yoga, but quarters are cramped and every movement must be worked out to within a millimetre...'[2]

In the course of the seventh letter two months later he writes:

What can I say about my life here? In recent days I've been bothered by lumbago or rheumatism or whatever it is; it's hard for me to stand up, sit down, etc, and impossible to do yoga. I hope I'll be over it soon; my colleague is giving me massages. I'm now even more introverted than before, if that's possible, since I have a new colleague with whom I can't converse the way I could with the previous one...[3]

But by the next letter he is writing:

> My lumbago is on the mend—thanks to the massages. It was probably caused by inactivity, so I'm trying to be more active and tomorrow I'll start doing yoga again...

A few days later he is saying that he has a new colleague, so that the massages have come to an end, adding:

> But it doesn't matter; my lumbago is improving and it was obviously nothing serious... Write me... about how the roses are blooming and how all those special plants we set out are doing. BE CHEERFUL, LEVELHEADED, HEALTHY AND SOCIABLE, DO YOUR TASKS CONSCIENTIOUSLY, KEEP TRACK OF WHAT GOES ON, DON'T LET TRIVIAL MATTERS UPSET YOU, THINK ABOUT ME AND KEEP YOUR FINGERS CROSSED FOR ME, TRY TO GET ALONG WELL WITH EVERYONE.
>
> > Greetings, and I kiss you,
> >
> > Vašek.[4]

Three months later he is writing:

> I had a good day today: a good bath, a marvellous session of yoga.[5]

Again he is full of positive advice:

> BE CALM, SERENE, CHEERFUL, INDUSTRIOUS, SOCIABLE, KIND TO EVERYONE, OPTIMISTIC, TAKE CARE OF YOURSELF, DRESS NICELY. SAY ONLY CLEVER THINGS. DON'T PUT OFF

UNPLEASANT DUTIES, STUDY MY LETTERS CAREFULLY AND TRY AND CARRY OUT THE TASKS I SET YOU. BE BRAVE, YET PRUDENT. THINK WELL OF ME, FEEL SORRY FOR ME, BUT NOT ENOUGH TO MAKE YOURSELF SAD. DON'T LOSE HOPE AND LOVE ME![6]

What is remarkable about these letters is the indomitability of his spirit and the positive attitude which he went on advocating, no doubt as much for himself as for his wife, in contrast to the appalling circumstances in which he found himself. Of course, as a sensitive person, he was not altogether unaffected by his circumstances. One finds him writing, for instance, in December 1979:

> When hopelessness comes over me, I do yoga and it helps. It's the trivial details that depress me, never the general situation. I read a very interesting book by Byrd, the explorer, *Alone*, about how he lived for half a year by himself at the South Pole. Many of his observations about isolation are consistent with my own experience![7]

On New Year's Eve, 1979, he writes:

> In his last letter Puzuk [a childhood nickname for his brother, Ivan Havel] asked me to write more about the play I'm working on. I've abandoned the original Faustian conception and left only the basic theme, which I have shifted to a different milieu—prison. Yet it is not going to be a play about prison but—in a manner of speaking—about life in general; the prison milieu should serve only as a metaphor of the general human condition (the state of 'thrownness'

into the world; the existential significance of the past, of recollection, and of the future, the spinning of hopes; the theme of isolation and pseudohope, the discovery of 'naked values,' etc). It will be a Beckettian comedy about life; all that remains of Faust is the theme of temptation (the swapping of one's own identity for the 'world of entities').[8]

Later in the same letter he remarks:

I've just had a good session of yoga (I'm delighted by the sun, thanks to which I now have light)...[9]

It is now ten years since he wrote that letter and Václav Havel is President of the new Czechoslovakia, but one has the sense of someone who will not be disoriented or made dizzy by the whirligig of time. Shakespeare somewhere has a character saying: 'O world, but that thy strange mutations make us hate thee, youth would not yield to age'[10]. But someone like Havel showed an inner strength which was not affected by the vagaries of time and change, because he had at least some sense of the truth of Yoga—that man has an inner source of light, power and independence which he can tap even in the most adverse outer circumstances.

So long as man thinks of himself only as a physical body, he is limited and subject to the physical circumstances in which the body finds itself. But if he can contact the inner spirit, then his whole perspective changes and he has a new, reliable spiritual dimension against which to judge the deceptive appearances of outer events. Shri Shankara makes this point again and again in his great classic *Direct Experience of Reality*:

> For the person who is travelling in a boat, everything appears to be in motion; so does one perceive the Self as the body by virtue of ignorance. (76)
>
> Just as, when the eyes are dizzy, everything appears as wandering, so does one perceive the Self as the body by virtue of ignorance. (78)
>
> Just as the directions seem to be changed for one who has been in a swoon and has lost his sense of direction, so does one perceive the Self as the body by virtue of ignorance. (85)
>
> Thus is the Self mistaken for the body owing to ignorance. But when the true Self is realized, this mistake disappears in the spiritual reality, Brahman. (87)

What these verses make clear is that we are grievously wrong so long as we regard the centre of our universe and its interests as the physical body, and as long as we do so we shall be spiritually disoriented, lacking the right perspective by which to understand the world and our life in it aright.

What we need is a new revolution, not the outer Copernican one, which identified the sun as the centre of the universe instead of the earth, but the inner one to identify the true centre of our being, not as the limited individuality identified with the body and the mind, which we mistake for it, but as the real Self, *Atman*, the spirit within. It is a mistake to imagine the body to be immortal; but our real 'I', the spirit, is. We are doomed to ultimate disappointment if we seek complete freedom for the ego, because it can never escape the limitations of its empirical nature and circumstances, but our real 'I' is free by its very nature. In the same way it is no good seeking lasting happiness as if it resided in outer objects, when the real source of happiness lies hidden within our own hearts in the infinite *Atman*.

Yoga involves the inner enquiry into truth, relying on the old spiritual promise: 'Seek and ye shall find; knock and it shall be opened unto you'. In some of the later letters Václav Havel describes how he arrived at a deeper understanding of himself through his sufferings in prison and his deep cogitation on what he regarded as his own moral failings in having compromised with the totalitarian regime. In a letter of July 25th 1982, he writes to his wife about the starting point of his own spiritual enquiry.

> Five years ago something happened to me that in many regards had a key significance in my subsequent life. It began rather inconspicuously: I was in detention for the first time and one evening, after interrogation, I wrote out a request to the Public Prosecutor for my release. Prisoners in detention are always writing such requests, and I too treated it as something routine and unimportant, more in the nature of mental hygiene: I knew, of course, that my eventual release or non-release would be decided by factors having nothing to do with whether I wrote the appropriate request or not. Still, the interrogations weren't going anywhere and it seemed proper to use the opportunity and let myself be heard. I wrote my request in a way that at the time seemed extremely tactical and cunning: while

saying nothing I did not believe or that wasn't true, I simply 'overlooked' the fact that truth lies not only in what is said, but also in who says it, and to whom, why, how and under what circumstances it is expressed. Thanks to this minor 'oversight' (more precisely, this minor self-deception) what I said came dangerously close—by chance, as it were—to what the authorities wanted to hear. What was particularly absurd was the fact that my motive—at least my conscious and admitted motive—was not the hope that it would produce results, but merely a kind of professionally intellectualistic and somewhat perverse delight in my own—or so I thought—'honourable cleverness'. (I should add, to complete the picture, that when I read it some years later, the honour in that cleverness made my hair stand on end.) I sent the request off the following day and because no one responded to it and my detention was prolonged again, I assumed it had ended up where such requests usually end up, and I more or less forgot about it. And then one day lightning struck: I was given to know that I would probably be released, and that in the process, 'political use' would be made of my request. Of course I knew right away what that meant: (1) that with appropriate 'recasting', 'additions' and widespread publicity, the impression would be created that I had not held out, that I had given in to pressure and backed down from my positions, opinions and all my previous work; in short, that I had betrayed my cause, all for a trivial reason—to get myself out of jail; (2) no denial or correction on my part could alter that impression because I had undeniably written something that 'met them halfway' and anything I could add would, quite rightly, seem like an attempt to worm my way out of it; (3) that the approaching catastrophe was unavoidable; (4) that the blot it would leave on me and everything I had taken part in would haunt me for years to come, that it would cause me measureless inner suffering, and that I would probably try to erase it with several years in prison (which in fact happened), but that not even that would rid me entirely of the stigma; (5) that I had no one but myself to blame: I was neither forced to do it, nor offered a bribe; I was not, in fact, in a dilemma and it was only because I'd unforgivably let down my moral guard that I'd given the other side— voluntarily and quite pointlessly—a weapon that amounted to a heaven-sent gift.[11]

Havel said that this incomprehensible lapse thrust him 'into a drastic but, for that very reason, crucial confrontation with myself; it shook, as it were, my entire "I", "shook out of it" a deeper insight into itself, a more serious acceptance and understanding of my situation, of my thrownnesses and my horizons, and led me, ultimately, to a new and more coherent consideration of the problem of human responsibility…'

> The central question I came back to again and again was this: how could it have happened? How could I have done something so transparently dubious? …Was it a major error in thinking, an expression of subconscious physiological fear, or was it simply a wrong assessment, a kind anyone could have made (usually without such far-reaching consequences)? In this and other ways, then, I interrogated myself,

but regardless of how I responded, I still felt I had left the essence untouched, that I was getting no closer to an explanation and that this way would never bring me even relative peace of mind. I've known for some time now why this was, but only now have I learned, perhaps, how to articulate it: the mistake lay not in answering the questions wrongly,... but rather in the very way I posed the questions, which originated in an unconscious effort to localize the essential cause of my failure somewhere 'outside', beyond the borders of my real 'I' (the 'I' of my 'I'), in 'circumstances', 'conditions', external factors or influences, into some alienating 'psychological process'—that typically modern way of excluding the self from the 'category of blame'. Yes, my questioning was essentially only a desperate attempt to hide from myself the hard fact that the failure was mine—exclusively, essentially and fully mine.....Today, the hidden motives behind this attempt are clear to me: accepting full responsibility for one's own failure is extraordinarily difficult, from the point of view of the 'interests of our existence-in-the-world', and frequently it is virtually unbearable and impossible, and if one wants to live even slightly 'normally'—i.e., exist in the world (guided by the so-called instinct for self-preservation)—one is irresistibly driven to ease the situation by dividing the self, turning the matter into an unfortunate 'misunderstanding': those entirely warranted reproaches cannot possibly be addressed to me, but to the other, who has been mistakenly identified with me. Obviously if one stuck complacently to this approach, it would lead to the disintegration of one's own identity.[12]

This insight led Havel to realize that his questioning was only a desperate attempt to hide from himself the fact that the failure was his.

> It is not hard to stand behind one's successes. But to accept responsibility for one's failures… is devilishly hard! But only thence does the road lead—as my experience, I hope, has persuaded me—to a renewal of sovereignty over my own affairs, to a radically new insight into the mysterious gravity of my existence as an uncertain enterprise, and to its transcendental meaning. And only this kind of inner understanding can ultimately lead to what might be called true 'peace of mind', to that highest delight, to genuine meaningfulness, to that endless 'joy of Being'. If one manages to achieve that, then all one's worldly privations cease to be privations, and become what Christians call grace.[13]

He goes on to speak of the inner voice which caused him to agonize over his moral failure, speaking of it as

> the mysterious 'voice of Being' that reaches my 'I' 'from outside' more clearly (so clearly that it is usually described as coming 'from above') than anything else, but which, at the same time—paradoxically—penetrates to a deeper level than anything else, because it comes through the 'I' itself: not only because I hear it in myself, but above all because it is the voice of my own being, torn away from the integrity of Being and thus intrinsically bound to it…[14]

He speaks of the fact that good has emerged from what seemed bad:

I have my failure to thank for the fact that for the first time in my life I stood—if I may be allowed such a comparison—directly in the study of the Lord God himself: never before had I looked into his face or heard his reproachful voice from such proximity, never had I stood before him in such profound embarrassment, so humiliated and confused, never before had I been so deeply ashamed and felt so powerfully how unseemly anything I could say in my own defence would be. And the most interesting thing about that confrontation... was this: if my request had ended up in the chief prosecutor's waste basket and I had come out of prison a hero, I might never have experienced it at all! In other words: it was shame... that, to my astonishment, put me in the sharpest confrontation I have ever experienced with the 'absolute horizon' of my relating, i.e. with the Being of the world and my own being, with that 'personal face' which Being, in moments like this, turns towards me. Thus it is not so at all that there are two separate and remote worlds, the earthly world of erring people who are of small account, and the heavenly world of God, the only one who counts. Quite the contrary: Being is one, it is everywhere and behind everything; it is the Being of everything and the only way to it is the one that leads through this world of mine and through this 'I' of mine. The 'voice of Being' does not come 'from elsewhere' (i.e., from some transcendental heaven) ... it is the 'unuttered in the language of the world' that Heidegger writes about...[15]

Havel goes on to say that the shock of this experience meant that 'Everything I was, for myself and for others, suddenly found itself open to question... I had to ask... who I really was'. To this question he arrived at an existential answer:

> I understood that my identity is what I seek, do, choose and define, today and every day; that it is not a path I once chose and now merely proceed along, but one which I must redefine at every step, wherein each misstep or wrong turn, though caused only by neglecting one's bearings in the terrain, remains an irradicable part of it, one that requires vast and complex effort to set right. The maturing of the 'I' into itself is not, therefore, merely an accumulation of bits of knowledge and action that cover one's original state of nakedness and vulnerability with layers of clothing and armour, but a constant confrontation with one's own source,... demanding each instant to return in full seriousness to the 'core of things', to pose the primordial questions again and again, and from the beginning, constantly, to examine the direction one is going in.[16]

Havel speaks of the self as related both to the concrete horizon of the finite world in which it lives and also to what he calls the absolute horizon.

> My family, friends, acquaintances, fellow prisoners, the unknown weatherwoman, my fellow passengers in the streetcar, the transport commission, those who go to see my plays, the public, my homeland and the state power-structure; countless relationships, tensions, loves, dependencies, confrontations, atmospheres, milieus, experiences, acts, predilections, aims and things with which I am loosely or

closely connected—all that forms the 'concrete horizon' of my relating, because all of it is my world, the world as my home, the world in which I am rooted in a complex way... It is the world of my existing, such as it presents and opens itself to me, as I make myself at home in it, as it constitutes itself for me through my experiences and as I—in one way or another—make it meaningful. Thus my 'I' creates this world and this world creates my 'I'.

And yet: my existence in this world and the way I relate to my 'concrete horizon' cannot be explained, as it may seem at first, by some one-sided and unqualified clinging to them as such, by surrendering to their actually existing, isolated, relative, self-exhausting, phenomenal and superficial manifestations. It depends, rather, on something else: on the extent to which I direct my existence-in-the-world toward... its own Being, to the very Being of this world. This can only mean that through my life, through the experiences and trials I undergo, I gradually penetrate beyond the different horizons of my 'concrete horizon', I attempt to widen them, to step past them, to see beyond them, to get to what is on the other side of them—until ultimately I aspire towards a place beyond its ultimate, conceivable limit, the 'horizon of all my horizons', to what I call 'the absolute horizon' of my relating.[17]

First of all, then: my only true certain and indisputable experience is the experience of Being in the simplest sense of the word, that is, the experience that something is. At the very least, there is I, the one having the experience, there is the experience as such, and there is, and must be, intrinsically, something that I experience;... If I try, in all honesty, to examine this trivial experience of Being more closely and describe it, if possible, in words, then it seems more appropriate to divide it ...essentially into two basic layers. The first layer—apparently more definite, more tangible, but in fact rather problematic because it is relative—includes all my direct experience of the world and myself as they manifest themselves to me on various levels of perception. The second layer—far less direct and vivid, yet incomparably more profound and essential—is the experience of 'Being' in the sense that I am using it here. The first of those layers is related, obviously, to my state of separation, my thrownness into the world. The second, on the contrary, grows out of my thrownness into the source in Being, my recollections of it and my longing for it. But what does the second experience—evidently the more primordial and firmer, however deeply concealed it may be and drowned out by the incessant clamour of everyday life—what in fact does it mean or say? Essentially, it is... a conviction... that everything I experience on the first level is not, somehow, exhausted by itself, is not 'just that' with 'nothing more to it', but rather is a situational, partial, superficial assembly (limited by my perspective and locked into it) of fleeting, confusing, isolated—or once again, merely superficially and accidentally linked—expressions of something infinitely more consistent, absolute and absolutely self-defining. There is here an undeniable intimation not only that 'there is something behind it all', but also that somewhere in the fathomless depths (i.e., fathomless to me) of everything that exists there is something beyond which there are no more 'beyonds' and beyond which there is, therefore, nothing to be, because it is the 'last of everything', of every entity... it is the essence of the existence of everything that exists; it is what joins everything that exists together,...[18]

He goes on to say that this is not just a philosophical thesis but a matter of experience, manifest as

an intrinsic longing to arouse, through the conduct of one's existence in the world, one's own hidden, slumbering, forgotten and betrayed being and through this being—which is anchored in the integrity of 'absolute Being' and separated from the 'I' that is constituted from it and to which that 'I' is intrinsically oriented—to touch once again that fullness and integrity of Being,... In other words: the experience of Being is not merely an idea or an opinion: it is a state of the spirit and of the heart, the key to life and one's orientation in life, to one's way of existence; it is not merely one experience among many: it is the experience of all experiences, their veiled starting point and their veiled end. It is a genuinely human journey, arduous and beautiful for what it entails—all the way from the injunction to pay attention to the incorruptible voice that is everywhere calling us to responsibility (which exists even where we are out of sight of the world of our existence) to that highest delight, as we experience it fully and completely in those fleeting moments when the meaning of Being is brought home to us, when we find ourselves on the very 'edge of finitude'—face to face with the miracle of the world and the miracle of our own 'I'.[19]

The revolution that Václav Havel has led in Czechoslovakia has certainly inaugurated a new freedom for the peoples of that country, but the revolution he speaks of here is a much more profound one, akin to that Copernican revolution of the spirit which we so badly need to usher in a real age of enlightenment. It is the recognition that man's life should not revolve round the body and its individual interests, but those of the spirit, and that the real freedom and immortality which he desires for himself is to be found, not in the finite ego or the fallible mind, but in seeking and finding the inner light of the spirit, *Atman*, of which the yogis speak.

> Just as when the eyes are dizzy, everything appears as wandering, so does one perceive the Self as the body by virtue of ignorance...
>
> Thus is the body mistaken for the Self owing to ignorance. But when the Self is realized, this mistake disappears in the absolute Being, Brahman.[20]

15

Learning from Experience*

A cynic remarked that experience is what you usually acquire in life two or three seconds immediately after the time when it would have been really useful to you! Certainly we can all think of occasions on which we would not have acted as we did if we had only known beforehand what we knew afterwards. On such occasions, when we have learnt quickly and painfully from our own mistakes, all we can do afterwards is to shrug our shoulders philosophically and reflect that we have learnt something from it.

But can we learn from the experience of others? Samuel Taylor Coleridge wrote rather pessimistically:

> If men could learn from history, what lessons it might teach us! But passion and party blind our eyes, and the light which experience gives is a lantern on the stern, which shines only on the way behind us!

His view was that, although we could in principle benefit by studying the past experience of others, in practice our own prejudices get in the way and make it difficult for us to do so. Hegel took an equally gloomy view of the ability of mankind in general to learn from the past experience of others when he said: 'What experience and history teach is this: that people and governments never have learnt anything from history, or acted on principles deduced from it.'

---

* A lecture given on 21st June 1991.

But these provocative, and apparently negative, sentiments are perhaps more properly regarded, not as statements of what the author actually believed, but as veiled protests against the slowness and unwillingness of people to take advantage of what they could learn from history. The fact is that the whole of our life depends on what mankind has learnt from the past, particularly from the contributions made by the great pioneers of human thought. We acknowledge this truth in one of the frequently heard catch-phrases of today, when we protest against the idea that we have to start from scratch by saying: 'We don't want to try and re-invent the wheel!' It is an implicit recognition of the fact that our whole life depends on a thousand-and-one things which we take for granted, but which have been achieved for us by those who lived before us.

It is worth asking how these conflicting views compare with the conclusions reached by one of the greatest of modern historians who deliberately set out to see if he could discover the meaning of history; that is to say, whether there were any great principles underlying the pattern of historical events which we could learn by studying this record of past human experience.

The historian in question was Arnold Toynbee who published his ten-volume *Study of History* between 1934 and 1954. When the last four volumes of the original ten appeared in 1954, one reviewer wrote: 'We are here in the presence of one of the 'Great Books' of our century, or of any century'[1]. Toynbee has a particular interest for the members of Shanti Sadan, as our teacher, Dr Shastri, read his *Study* with keen appreciation as it appeared from 1934 onwards. He later met Toynbee and corresponded with him and always spoke with particular admiration of Toynbee's achievement.

Toynbee believed that 'the job of making sense of history is one of the crying needs of our day'[2], and he wrote:

> I do not think that history, in the objective sense of the word, is a succession of facts, nor history-writing a narration of these facts. Historians, like all human observers, have to make reality comprehensible, and this involves them in continuous judgements about what is true and what is significant.[3]

Toynbee goes on to point out that those who attempt to learn from history are in danger of erecting deterministic explanations (as, for instance, Marx did in his analysis of history as the fixed and inevitable transition from feudalism through industrialism to the dictatorship of the proletariat). This suggests that history is governed by inexorable laws over which man has no control, in which case there can be no question of learning from past mistakes and avoiding them in the future. Toynbee says that this does not need to be so. He writes:

> I believe that human beings are free to make choices within the limitations of their human capacity. I also believe that history shows us how men may learn to make choices that are not only free but effective, by learning to achieve harmony with a supra-human reality that makes itself felt although it is impalpable.

But what about the personal history of Arnold Toynbee himself? What can we learn from this?[4]

Arnold Toynbee was born 102 years ago, on 14th April 1889, in his great uncle's house near Paddington Station. The family had originally come from Lincolnshire, where Toynbee's great grandfather, George, was a prosperous farmer. Farmer George's third son, Joseph, became a fashionable London doctor in the first half of the nineteenth century (1815-1866). He was a specialist in ear and throat problems and successfully treated Queen Victoria for deafness. But he was not just a successful specialist. He was keenly interested in medical research and published many papers in that area. He met his death at the age of fifty-one by exposing himself experimentally to an overdose of chloroform. He numbered among his friends people like Michael Faraday, John Stuart Mill, Ruskin and Jowett, as well as Giuseppe Mazzini, the 'father' of modern Italy.

Joseph's second son was called Arnold (1852-1883), but he was not the Arnold Toynbee whom we know as the historian; he was his uncle. The first Arnold Toynbee, like his father, died tragically young, in his case, at the age of thirty, from 'brain fever' (encephalitis). He was, by all accounts, a remarkable person and made a great impression on all his contemporaries and teachers, when he went up to Oxford as an undergraduate in 1873. After getting his degree he returned to his College, Balliol, as a special tutor. Jowett, who was Master of the College, said of him: 'The really interesting and striking thing in his life was not what he actually produced, but himself, that is to say... his unlikeness to everyone else'. And he wrote in a letter to Arnold's sister: 'I am sure he was one of the best persons I have ever known'.

He became the animating spirit of a group of young men from Balliol who aspired to reform Church and society in such a way as to bridge the gap between themselves and the working class. This involved living among the poor in London during university vacations, and discussing 'the laws of nature and of God' with working men. This led to a group of his admirers establishing Toynbee Hall in the East End of London. It was the first settlement house there and was intended to replicate within its walls something of the life of an Oxford college, thus propagating at least some of the benefits of university education among people hitherto excluded from it.

The other thing that the first Arnold Toynbee did was to try and reform the science of economics and, by doing so, to bridge the gap between rich and poor, both in theory and in practice. He wrote in his lectures on the industrial revolution in England: 'Morality must be united with economics as a practical science'. He was not a socialist, and it is difficult to know now what exactly his ideas were, because his early death prevented him from leaving much in the way of writing, but he clearly had a major influence for good on those with whom he came into contact.

Arnold Toynbee the historian, who was born in Paddington in 1889, was the nephew of his earlier namesake, the son of a younger brother. He was also lucky in the choice of his mother who was an early student of what was later to become Newnham College, Cambridge, where she got a First in history. This must have been an important factor in determining Arnold Toynbee's own choice of history as his life-long field of study when he went to University. In a paper read to an undergraduate club at Oxford at the age of twenty-one, he wrote that 'art and history resemble each other in being both activities of the imagination working upon experience'. And he also maintained that 'the historian must have second sight, which is called intuition', two views which remained with him for the rest of his life.[5] After a brilliant academic career at Oxford from 1907 onwards, where he came under the influence of Gilbert Murray, the Professor of Greek, Toynbee became a don and spent two years travelling in Italy and Greece (1911-1912) before coming back to Oxford and marrying Murray's daughter, Rosalind, in 1913.

His early preoccupation with understanding history developed into a master passion which persisted for the rest of his long life and which made him one of the most erudite and creative historians of modern times. Even before he had completed his undergraduate career, Toynbee had conceived 'the ambition of writing a great book that would comprise ancient and modern times, as well as the East and Europe, in a single conspectus. He called it a philosophy of history but (at that time) remained entirely unclear about the guiding principles he would need to make so much detail intelligible.'[6] But it was to be many years before he could get down to it in earnest.

Toynbee's life was anything but a life of retirement or inactivity; he devoted himself indefatigably to the study of history, both ancient and contemporary. He was very actively involved in the negotiations over the Peace Treaty after the First World War and was bitterly disappointed at the outcome, which he later regarded as leading to the conditions which fostered the rise of Fascism and ultimately the Second World War. Afterwards, as Director of the Royal Institute for International Affairs, it was his job single-handed to write an account of contemporary world affairs in the form of an annual volume surveying international events, which he wrote personally for each year from 1924 until 1938, a truly monumental achievement. At the same time he was working on the material for his *Study of History*.

Arnold Toynbee was the first historian to take the whole tapestry of human history as his subject matter. He identified within it the rise and fall of about thirty civilisations and he then looked to see if there were any common features in their history. He chose to consider civilizations, because to study nations, as is often done, seemed to him to be unnecessarily fragmentary and parochial. Nations, on the whole, he regarded as fragments of something larger, and that something was a civilization. Even as early as 1920, Toynbee, who was already familiar with Greek, Roman and Persian history, began to wonder whether all civilizations known to us follow the same pattern of growth, breakdown and dissolution.[7] In tracing the development of each civilization, he found that their birth appeared to originate in some challenge posed by circumstances, which required a creative response. In a sense, his idea is like the Darwinian one that the evolution of higher forms of life is driven by the need to adapt to changes in the environment or perish.

In one respect, however, the progress of civilization is different to that of evolution in Nature, because it involves human choice. As Toynbee wrote:

> I believe human development is a process in which human individuals are moulded less and less by their environment... and adapt their environment more and more to their own will. And one can discern, I think, a point at which, rather suddenly, the human will takes the place of the mechanical laws of the environment as the governing factor in the relationship.

That point (comments his biographer) constituted for Toynbee the beginning of civilization and of history too, for 'the impress made by human beings on their environment creates a record which enables later generations of human beings to reconstruct in their minds their predecessors' activities'. Civilization and human freedom are therefore closely akin. Both are opposed to 'mechanical laws' of the environment—and Toynbee explicitly pointed out that what he called 'environment' included mechanical laws of human society that allowed one class or group of human beings to oppress others.'[8] Toynbee was promulgating these ideas in his lectures as early as 1919 to 1920[9].

By 1921 Toynbee had come to the conclusion that 'the great civilizations that have been created by the spirit of man may all reveal the same plot, if we analyse them rightly'. By studying the civilizations which he knew in the ancient world of Greece and Rome and in Europe, he had come to the conclusion that there were seven stages in their rise and fall. This was in 1921, but for the next ten years he devoted all his spare time to mastering the histories of China, Japan, India and other parts of the earth. In doing so he acquired an entirely new (and at that time unique) view of world history, encompassing a breadth of vision which had never before been attempted. And when he came to write the *Study* he was able to quote detailed examples from this whole comprehensive body of knowledge to illustrate the parallels between the many civilizations which he had identified.

Toynbee's widening views meant that he became less and less inclined to subscribe to traditional orthodox creeds. When still an undergraduate, he had already abandoned the doctrines of the Christian Church in which he had been brought up, particularly under the influence of Gilbert Murray who was a life-long agnostic. He wrote to his mother-in-law in 1930:

> For myself, I steadily become more undogmatic. I simply can't conceive of myself belonging to any religious institution.[10]

But Toynbee also speaks of mystical experiences which he had when meditating on his historical studies. On three occasions, for instance, he describes remarkable mystic encounters with the past: 'On 10th January 1912, when contemplating the site of the ancient battle of Cynocephalae he "saw" in his mind's eye how the

Romans had defeated the Macedonians there in 197 BC, and the re-enactment was so vivid that Toynbee asked himself more than forty years afterwards: "Can the dreamer really have sunk, for that instant, those twenty-one centuries deep below the current of Time's waters, on which he now finds himself riding, once again, in his normal waking life?" Three months later he had a similar experience in Crete when he caught sight of an abandoned Venetian Villa—a mute testament to the Turkish victory of 1669; and for the third time visiting the Moreote citadel of Momenvasia, he "fell again into the deep trough of Time" on seeing abandoned bronze cannon littering the site.'[11]

These were not the first such experiences, carrying him beyond the ordinary states of consciousness. He remembered in 1911, when preparing for his examinations at Oxford, a few words from Livy describing the death of one of the leaders of the so-called social war against Rome produced an infinitesimally brief yet intensely poignant experience which brought him 'into a momentary communion with the actors in a particular historic event. He himself said that other similar experiences happened to him on six separate occasions. He clearly felt that this visionary communion with the past was in some sense real.'[12]

One of his most vivid mystical experiences occurred in 1919. He describes it as follows:

> In London, in the southern section of the Buckingham Palace Road, walking southward along the pavement skirting the west wall of Victoria

I personally believe that the principal cause of war in our world today is the idolatrous worship which is paid by human beings to nations and communities or States. This tribe-worship is the oldest religion of mankind, and it has only been overcome in so far as human beings have been genuinely converted to Christianity or one of the other higher religions... The spirit of man abhors a spiritual vacuum; and if it loses sight of God as He is revealed in Christianity it will inevitably relapse into the worship of Juggernaut and Moloch...[17]

By 1940 Toynbee's whole interpretation of history had undergone this major change. Whereas, lecturing in Oxford in 1920, he had suggested 'that all civilizations followed the tragic pattern he had read into Graeco-Roman history', lecturing again there in 1940 'he set forth the theme that was to dominate the last volumes of his great work, by suggesting instead that spiritual progress, achieved largely through suffering, gave meaning to human history on earth'. His biographer Professor McNeill writes that as his life went on after the Second World War 'his respect for Buddhism and other non-Western religions became more apparent' and 'By the time he got back to writing his great book, Toynbee's faith had become more ecumenical, embracing all the world's higher religions...'[18] 'He continued to believe that humanity's evolving relation to God constituted the central drama of history, (and in)... a spiritual reality that became less and less like the God of Christian theology and a good deal more Indian... as he grew older'.[19]

To a Catholic friend he wrote in 1947:

> Christians don't effectively become humble by transferring their pride to the Church... All the higher religions make the same claim to unconditional allegiance of all mankind and declare they have absolute authority. I think they are all revelations of different aspects of the same truth, and all of them are clogged with silt and flotsam and jetsam that they have picked up on their way through the world.

Writing to his father-in-law, Gilbert Murray, he was more explicit:

> What all the religions need is a great winnowing out of permanent truth in them from the accidental accretions... This kind of truth can only be expressed in myth, and myth has to take its colours from the everyday life of the particular time and place, so that the eternal truths are always needing new suits of mythical clothes. Unfortunately this doctrine is detestable to ecclesiastical administrators.

> I should, I am sure, be burnt by all the representatives of all the traditional forms of religion if they had a free hand again for that—and, of course, by the Communists, who are superstitious as well as dogmatic and practical.[20]

He himself was consistently modest and willing to listen to criticism. As his biographer says, even when late in life people began to try and make him into a prophet, his 'private conduct showed no sign of megalomania.

Instead, he remained courteous, even hesitant, when meeting strangers, listened to what others had to say, and expressed his own opinions moderately. His religious faith had much to do with his demeanour. "To break out of self-centredness seems to me, more and more, [he wrote to a friend in 1960] to be the whole of the Law and the Prophets".... "To get rid of self-centredness implies, I think, finding a true and better positive centre: Nirvana or God (two names for the same reality, I believe). One cannot replace something so positive as the self except by something still more positive. 'Trying to get rid' is the road, the reality behind the phenomena is the goal...'"

He said he was trying 'to encourage people to take more interest in looking at history as a whole, as part of a unified study of human affairs. The more people who enter this field, the sooner my own work will be superseded, and this is what I should regard as a sign of success'.[21] Toynbee listened carefully to all that his critics said about his *Study* when it was completed with the publication of volumes VII to X in 1954, and he attempted to correct any genuine errors that had been pointed out and to answer what he described to a friend as a 'trunkful of criticisms' which he took with him on a visit to America where he planned to go through them. This he did in a further volume which he called *Reconsiderations*, published in 1961. One of his most persistent critics, Pieter Geyl, wrote of this volume with patronising condescension: 'Toynbee appears to be more accessible to reason than I had expected... He is doing his best to be a historian, but first and foremost he is still a prophet'.[22]

In the *Study*, Toynbee wrote:

> Human emotions, consciousness, and will are not collective; they are faculties of an individual human being; and the inner spiritual life of a person—of each and every person who is a participant in social relations—is the field in which the spiritual battle for self-mastery is to be fought. This is Man's most urgent, and also his most difficult, task. It is difficult because Man is a living being, and every living being is self-centred by nature. Self-centredness is, indeed, another name for life itself, and the overcoming of self-centredness is therefore a *tour de force*... In human life, self-centredness can be prevented from causing social disasters only in so far as it is mastered in the inner spiritual life... salvation can be won only by self-mastery. This is the reason why [the founders of the higher religions] taught that self-mastery is the indispensable prerequisite for the establishment of the right relationship between a human person and the ultimate spiritual reality.[23]

Toynbee died, after suffering a stroke the previous year, on 22nd October, 1975. Among the last words in his *Study of History* are these:[24]

> Death is the universal, inescapable, and conclusive retort to the audacious declaration of independence that is made by every living being. The creature sets itself up as the centre of a counter-universe. Death demolishes this pretension. Thus the awe induced by the pursuit of historical curiosity is an indication that the inquisitive explorer has caught a glimpse of the reality behind the phenomena. His awe is his reaction to what he has seen. It is Arjuna's reaction

to Krishna's terrifying disclosure of his naked self at Arjuna's importunate request. But awe is not the only emotion that is aroused in the explorer by his quest. The spectacle of the enigmatic phenomena also evokes two other emotions—compassion and exultation—and these, like awe, are responses to glimpses of the reality that the phenomena veil...

How is it possible for the ultimate reality behind the phenomena to reveal itself in such different guises? What is there in common between an annihilation through death, an exit into nirvana through self-extinction, and an entry into a communion of saints? On first thoughts, these three visions of ultimate reality look as if they were irreconcilable with each other, but on second thoughts we can see that they each present a picture of an identical goal. They each testify that the cause of sin and suffering and sorrow is the separation of sentient beings, in their brief passage through the phenomenal world, from the timeless reality behind the phenomena, and that a reunion with this reality is the sole but sovereign cure for our ailing world's ills. Communion, extinguishedness, and annihilation are alternative images of reintegration. They are symbols of a consummation that is ineffable because it is the antithesis of Man's experience in his ephemeral life on Earth. They are variations on a single theme: the return from discord to harmony, or, in Sinic terms, from Yang to Yin. 'To Him return ye, one and all'. Or in Goethe's words in Faust: 'Das Unbeschreibliche, Hier ist's getan'.[25]

16

The Mind in Society*

Biologically speaking, life starts with the single-celled organism needing to do everything for itself. But this way of life can only support a simple and rudimentary form of existence—and a very vulnerable and uncertain one. Evolution gets under way when cells combine together in a common symbiotic bond—*'living together'* —each contributing something to the good of the whole and receiving help and aid from the whole organism. It implies each part (organ) taking on particular duties and becoming specialized for them, while it depends on the rest of the cells to do the other jobs for it. It means that everything can be done more efficiently, but at the price of interdependence. The skin protects us from the elements, the alimentary system nourishes us, the brain thinks for us, and the circulation keeps us supplied with what we need by transporting food and oxygen to each cell and taking away the waste products of metabolic combustion and giving them to the kidneys and gut to eliminate. If our lungs do not function, providing the oxygen we need and eliminating the carbon dioxide we produce, we shall die within a few minutes.

Man began his evolution as a lone hunter, self-reliant and depending on no one else, but he soon learnt the advantage of joining forces with his fellow men and forming societies in which the members of the group help

* A lecture given on 27th October 1991.

each other. It at once led to an enormous improvement in the quality and safety of his life, but at the cost of becoming dependent on others. The essential feature of society, and of the civilizations to which it has given rise, is mutual aid, and in society (as in the multi-celled organism) there has to be a contribution made by the individual to the good of the whole, from which he derives so many benefits. In successful societies there is a harmonious interaction between the apparently conflicting interests and activities of the parts, based on a spirit of unity and common purpose. This principle, which should govern the life of the individual in society, is called *dharma* in the Yoga classics. It can be very roughly translated as duty and implies doing what one ought to do for one's fellow men. Neglect of this great principle, if severe, is said to lead to the breakdown of society. The 'law of *dharma*' also implies that each individual has a rôle to carry out as his contribution to the general well-being. For instance, we find the third chapter of the *Bhagavad Gita* saying: 'Better is one's own *dharma* (duty to society), even though imperfectly carried out, than the *dharma* of another carried out perfectly.'[1]

The whole idea of struggle between individuals as the natural basis of society is wrong. If we want to compete, we can compete by trying to do better than our neighbour in carrying out our job, to make a more worthwhile contribution to the good of our fellow men, to excel in being a better member of the society in which we live. This is real success. The fact is that each and everyone can make their own contribution to the common weal, even if it is at the level of ordinary everyday life. We have the wrong conception of Darwin's Struggle for Existence and Survival of the Fittest as it applies to human society. Swami Rama Tirtha says in his notebooks: '[The] struggle [for existence] does not mean [a fight] with teeth, claws, fists, brute strength, trickery or war. Through all the ages love has been stronger than force, and those creatures who could help each other have been stronger than those who could only fight'.[2] The secret of success in society is for the different, apparently conflicting, elements to work together harmoniously for the good of the whole.

The same principle applies to man's mind too. It is a mass of conflicting desires and emotions, driven this way and that by the impressions of the outer sense world which impinge on it. Lurking in it there is a good deal which is primitive, anarchic and anti-social; and the mind needs to be civilized and directed to a common worthwhile purpose if it is to realize its potential for peace and be transformed into an ally in life! Shri Dadaji, our teacher's teacher, who lived a simple life among the poor of Northern India about 100 years ago, said that

> Most of the misfits in society, who are called criminals and sinners, are people who have not received right guidance in their early life. Man ought to create first and foremost, harmony, peace and order within himself. His instruments of creation are his thoughts and feelings; he must refine them and keep them in good order. Religion, if taught without sectarianism and narrowness, teaches man self-control, eradication of hatred and

inordinate affection, and, above all, devotion of the heart to the one universal and eternal fountain of beauty and bliss, the all-pervading spiritual entity.[3]

Modern life all too often gives us a feeling of powerlessness. It makes us feel that we are in the grip of events which we can't really influence. But it *is* in our power to change things. Man is the master of his fate, the captain of his soul. And there are very good examples to prove it.

When I was younger, London was famous for its pea-souper fogs and people actually had to wear masks which they bought to protect themselves from what was called 'the smog'. Now we quite often see skies which are as blue as those in the Mediterranean and the air is relatively clear and pleasant to breathe. We have discovered to our immense surprise, that it was we ourselves who were largely producing the smog, by the wasteful burning of coal in open fires in a thousand homes and in our factories and powerhouses. By applying a little practical scientific knowledge combined with common sense we have found a much more efficient and economical way of using the fuel to produce the energy we need, and at the same time improving our health and our environment.

This is not an isolated example. Are we not now all waking up to the realization that it is we ourselves in the West, driven largely by the selfish desires for money and success, irrespective of the consequences to others, who have created the monster which emerged in the form of

Saddam Hussein and his Iraq, a monster who was well on the way to success in developing nuclear bombs, chemical and biological weapons with which to try and conquer his neighbours and, no doubt, ultimately (in his own mind at least) the rest of the world. We were effectively helping to build up the future source of war and destruction and letting ourselves in for a frightful regime of tyranny and terror. Even as it was, we had to endure a major war to prevent things developing that way before it was too late.

These are only examples to underline the fact that, if we are to build a better society for the future, we have to tackle the more anarchic aspects of our own mind and ensure a more enlightened social conscience in society at large. But we tend to forget these important principles in practice, and the result is unrest in society and an absence of inner peace and contentment.

The yogis tell us that what we need to do is to start improving things where we have the real power to do so, within our own personality. The Greek scientist Archimedes is reported to have said: 'If I can find a fulcrum—(by which he meant a firm point of leverage against which I can exert my influence)—I can move the world'. That firm point, say the yogis, is to be found in the human mind as the real Self of man. It is the point which enabled Socrates to withstand the power of the Athenian politicians in the cause of truth; that enabled Solzhenitsyn to withstand the might of Stalin against the lies of Communism, that made it possible for Václav Havel to emerge and be recognized as the true voice of Czechoslovakia even during his long period as the lone prisoner. Social problems have their true origin in the human mind and its antisocial urges, the most dominant of which is rampant individualism. As such, they are symptoms of a spiritual problem, not merely of a sociological or ethical one, and this has to be solved in the human mind where it originates.

Bertrand Russell writes that:

> One of the sources of unhappiness, fatigue and nervous strain is inability to be interested in anything which is not of practical importance in one's own life. The result of this is that the conscious mind gets no rest from a certain small number of matters, each of which probably involves some anxiety and some element of worry. Except in sleep the conscious mind is never allowed to lie fallow while subconscious thought matures its gradual wisdom. The result is excitability, lack of sagacity, irritability and a loss of sense of proportion. All these are both causes and effects of fatigue...[4]

Selfishness can manifest itself within the group as well as in the individual. Party or group interests can be just as ruthlessly pursued at the expense of society as a whole as individual advantage. And in the larger world nationalism can become a kind of cancer in the body politic, as it did in the case of Hitler and is threatening to do now in Eastern Europe. Toynbee wrote in 1935 that worship of the tribe or nation is the principal cause of war in the world today, and that it has only been successfully overcome in so far as mankind has been converted by spiritual traditions to a more universal outlook.

It is easy to think that these broad statements of

general principle are too vague and abstract to apply to our own lives. But just consider the experience one meets when driving a car these days. Isn't there a real change in the way people drive in recent years? A few years ago, one used to expect drivers to stop for pedestrians crossing the road, particularly children or the elderly, and it was not unheard of to see a driver stop his car, get out and help a blind man who was waiting to cross the road before driving on. Now no one has time for such niceties and they are mainly concerned with hooting at the driver in front if he is holding them up by keeping within the legal speed limit!

Consideration for other road users has given way to trying to overtake the person in front on either side, irrespective of safety and, all too often, even of common sense or sanity! The steep rise in car insurance premiums is eloquent evidence of the real change which has taken place in this aspect of social life. Living together in harmony implies consideration for others. Empirically it is a recognition, at its lowest, of the principle 'Do as you would be done by'; and the recognition that a misfortune affecting someone else is in some real sense a shared misfortune. To disidentify oneself totally from it is to fail to recognize that 'There but for the grace of God go I!' That society in which the weakest are allowed to go to the wall on the principle that 'I'm alright, Jack!' is denying the very basis of social health and well-being.

Einstein wrote to an old friend of his in April 1946:

> I believe the horrifying deterioration in the ethical conduct of people today stems from the

mechanization and dehumanization of our lives—a disastrous by-product of the development of the scientific and technical mentality... Man grows cold faster than the planet he inhabits.[5]

In one of his books Russell has an interesting discussion on the difference between knowledge and wisdom[6], posing the question as to what it is which distinguishes them, and starting out from the recognition that (in his own words): 'Most people would agree that, although our age far surpasses all previous ages in knowledge, there has been no correlative increase in wisdom'. He says that one thing that is implied by wisdom is a wide perspective, which gives a sense of proportion, which is often lacking in the outlook of the learned but narrow specialist. But he goes on to say that comprehensiveness of knowledge is not, in itself, enough to confer wisdom, and that there must also be 'a certain awareness of the ends of human life'. He illustrates this by pointing out that if one's outlook is viewed by even the greatest of experts through 'the distorting medium of their own passions', it will lack wisdom. And he illustrates this by the example of Hegel, who had an encyclopaedic knowledge of history, but thought that its chief lesson was that his own nation, Germany, was the most important one and the standard-bearer of progress in the world. Russell makes the perceptive observation that the wideness or comprehensiveness must include not only knowledge but also feeling. 'It is by no means uncommon (he says) to find men whose knowledge is wide but whose feelings are narrow. Such men lack what I am calling wisdom'. In this Russell talks like a yogi, for it is the teaching of Yoga that our sympathies and understanding should be universalized.

Russell here directly addresses the problem raised by Einstein about the 'horrifying deterioration in the ethical conduct of people today' stemming from the 'dehumanizing' influence of 'the scientific and technical mentality'. And Russell makes essentially the same point when he says:

> Even the best technicians should also be good citizens; and when I say 'citizens', I mean citizens of the world and not of this or that sect or nation. With every increase of knowledge and skill, wisdom becomes more necessary, for every such increase augments our capacity for realizing our purposes, and therefore augments our capacity for evil, if our purposes are unwise. The world needs wisdom as it has never needed it before; and if knowledge continues to increase, the world will need wisdom in the future even more than it does now.[7]

The universal outlook that Russell advocates here is precisely that which is recommended by the Yoga, but in Yoga it is based on a more fundamental spiritual principle, namely, on the vision of the inner unity of all in the spirit. As the Lord says in the *Bhagavad Gita*: 'O Arjuna, I am seated deep within the hearts of all beings'. It is the same message that we find in the Christian Gospel. Christ indicated that when our lives came to be judged it would be, to the surprise of many, on whether we had done or not done something to help our fellow men. His recognition of the spiritual unity of all is summarized in the principle: 'Inasmuch as ye have done it to the least of these, my children, ye have done it unto Me', and he went on to illustrate what he meant by the parable of the Good Samaritan as the example of good neighbourliness.

Arnold Toynbee wrote to a friend in 1960:

> To break out of self-centredness seems to me more and more the whole of the Law and the Prophets. To get rid of self-centredness implies, I think, finding a true and better positive centre: Nirvana or God (two names for the same Reality, I believe). One cannot replace something so positive as the self, except by something still more positive. 'Trying to get rid' is the road, the reality behind the phenomena is the goal....[8]

We can only tackle these all too real and pressing problems effectively if we find some way of altering the way people think. We have to change the mental outlook. Can one actually learn to become wiser by effort? The yogis say that we can. And it is impressive to find Russell (who knew nothing of Yoga and was not interested in such things) asking the same question about his conception of wisdom and coming to much the same conclusion:

> Can wisdom in this sense be taught? And, if it can, should the teaching of it be one of the aims of education? I should answer both these questions in the affirmative.[9]

And he goes on:

We are told on Sundays that we should love our neighbour as ourselves. On the other six days of the week, we are exhorted to hate him. You may say this is nonsense, since it is not our neighbour whom we are exhorted to hate. But you will remember that the precept was exemplified by saying that the Samaritan was our neighbour. We no longer have any wish to hate Samaritans and so we are apt to miss the point of the parable.

(No doubt today we should be thinking in terms of Protestants and Catholics, Croatians and Serbians, Arabs and Jews, or Azerbaijanis and Armenians, to name only a few.) Russell goes on to say that, 'It might be objected that it is right to hate those who do harm'. But to this he replies:

> I do not think so. If you hate them, it is only too likely that you will become equally harmful; and it is very unlikely that you will induce them to abandon their evil ways. Hatred of evil is a kind of bondage. The way out is through understanding, not through hate.

Our mind gets soiled, and our vision dimmed and contracted, by hatred or animosity against anyone, and we lose the capacity for wise judgement. It is for this reason that we need to practise the control and purification of the mind. Swami Rama Tirtha speaks of the great value of 'washing and refreshing the mind' by stilling it and immersing it in meditation after it has become soiled by being plunged throughout the day in the outer world. It is also a good preparation for the day.

But Yoga can be practised also in active daily life, not only in meditation. Swami Rama makes the point that, in our dealing with others, we all too often approach people in the wrong way, and he says that here it is often not so much our ideas, as our feelings, that are wrong. He says we misread what is written on the door of the human heart as 'Push' and imagine that this is the way to open it, when what it actually says is 'Pull'. If we can adopt a positive, cheerful and encouraging spirit, we can more easily create the atmosphere in which differences can be resolved and disagreements can be friendly. It may sound simple, but it is something which can help to improve the quality of life for everyone.

Let us consider two other simple principles which are given by the *Bhagavad Gita* as among the most important ways of changing our thinking for the better. The first is the principle of *yajna*, or what may be very roughly translated as 'sacrifice', or perhaps more nearly 'self-sacrifice', although that sounds a bit too much like a grand romantic gesture—the sort we associate with Sidney Carton in Charles Dickens' *Tale of Two Cities*, where he goes to the guillotine to die for another man saying: 'It is a far, far better thing that I do, than I have ever done!' That may make a good curtain line in a Victorian melodrama, but it is not what is meant by *yajna*. But *yajna* does have the connotation of something which (unlike so much in our life) is done not simply to satisfy some personal desire or ambition, but for the good of others as well as ourselves. At its lowest it is a recognition of what we owe to society and an attempt to make some return for it.

The third chapter of the *Gita* speaks of the need for such sacrifice, for doing something unselfishly for the greater good:

> Whoso enjoys (the fruits of the sacrifice made by others) without offering something in return is a thief![10]

> He who does not follow this active principle (of the circulation and exchange of sacrifice, *yajna*) is of sinful life.[11]

And it makes clear that it is through such mutual aid that human society prospers.

> Nourishing one another (by self-sacrifice, *yajna*) ye shall obtain the supreme good.[12]

As we have already made clear, this is a universal principle which has deep roots in biological evolution itself and in the development of human society and civilization.

The second principle recommended in the *Gita* is that of trying to act disinterestedly, in the way which we feel to be right, without concerning ourselves with our success or failure. The Chinese have a saying:

> He who plays for counters, plays with all his skill; he who plays for gold stumbles in his play and makes mistakes; while he who plays for his life, loses his wits.

It expresses the psychological truth that if we are too deeply invested in our success or failure, it interferes with our action and clouds our judgement, whereas if we can act with interest only in what we are doing for its own sake, without worrying whether we are going to be successful or not, but nonetheless doing our best, we will make a better job of it.

If you have ever had to walk on a beam while doing gym at school, you will know what is meant. When the beam is at floor level, there is really nothing to it. You just walk along the top of it. But when it is two feet above the ground, it becomes curiously much more difficult and a bit of a balancing act. As a consequence one is much more liable to lose one's balance and fall off, particularly if others are watching and *amour propre* is involved! And when the beam is raised to six feet or more in the air, it is a real challenge, and, for those with no head for heights, even an ordeal. Yet the task is essentially the same in all three cases. It is what is at stake that changes, and the mind's vivid imagination and fear of the possibility of failure!

The mind enters into even the simplest of our social activities and to understand it and control it is the beginning of wisdom. And if we can get it to provide its greatest benefit, the realization of the inner spiritual unity of all, of which the yogis speak, it can be transformed into a real source of wisdom and inner peace. It is this spirit of unity and common purpose which society needs if it is to prosper. To achieve it is what Yoga is about. As our teacher, Dr Shastri writes in his book *Teachings from the Bhagavad Gita*:

> The word Yoga means union, and any teaching which leads to the realization of that Truth which is perfect unity, is Yoga.[13]

17

A Critical Ailment*

At this time of year we have to expect the increased occurrence of epidemics of one sort or another, and the media have recently been warning us of the potentially serious epidemic of Beijing 'flu sweeping through the general population. This lecture is concerned with an outbreak of a different kind which appears to be affecting society at the present time, no less serious and more difficult to counter effectively, since those experts competent in its treatment appear to be few and far between and most of the sufferers have no access to them. Like 'flu, the epidemic manifests itself in a number of different ways, sometimes as excessive criticism, sometimes as contempt for others, sometimes as envy, and in a variety of other forms.

The epidemic, which we tend to overlook until it is too late for effective treatment, arises from the fact that we pay too little attention to the fact that our minds are as susceptible to infection as our bodies. Indeed our minds are in many ways much more vulnerable and much more sensitive to undesirable and ultimately unpleasant infections than our bodies. This week there was a talk on television by an Oxford psychologist on the topic of 'viruses of the mind', pointing out quite rightly that there were ideas which spread like wildfire through society in a similar way to that in which viruses spread through the population, or computer viruses reproduce

---

* A lecture given on 3rd December 1993.

themselves in computers. In the case of computer viruses we know that these fragments of programs (which are made up of a few instructions) get into the system and, by tricking the host computer into aiding their reproduction, rapidly multiply themselves, taking over and destroying the rightful contents of the computer's memory, so that the machine is corrupted and becomes useless. Physical viruses invade the body in a similar way, entering the cells and taking over their controlling mechanism, so that they gradually overwhelm the normal life of the cell. Of course, the body has developed defence mechanisms for many of the less virulent infections, and can often limit their spread or even eradicate them altogether by mobilizing its protective forces. But there are particularly virulent infections, such as those causing AIDS, which lead to chronic progressive illness with the patient steadily wasting away and eventually dying.

Dr Dawkins, the TV speaker on viruses and the mind, was pointing out that ideas can enter the mind and begin to take it over in somewhat the same way. A very trivial example of this sensitivity of the mind to outer influences (which must be familiar to virtually all of us) is the way in which one may hear a catchy tune or song, and find that one can't get it out of one's mind. Another example is the way that—and one remembers this particularly from one's schooldays—there would suddenly be a craze for some particular game or toy which would sweep through the whole of the group and then die away, almost as suddenly as it had appeared. Computer games seem to have taken over today the rôle played by toy cars or yo-yos fifty years ago and by hula-hoops somewhat more recently. These examples, harmless enough in themselves, illustrate well the phenomenon of a 'craze' spreading (like a transient mental infection) through the group, and they portray a more general and more important principle: the sensitivity and vulnerability of the mind to outer influences. They should serve to remind us of how susceptible the mind is to the quality and character of what we feed into it.

Nowadays, the standard of physical hygiene and sanitation enjoyed by the bulk of the population is much higher than was the case even as recently as the 1930's, but the standard of *mental* hygiene, particularly in the moral and spiritual spheres, is in many ways far worse than it used to be, to a great extent because of the decline in religious belief and the absence of spiritual and moral education, both in the schools, but even more importantly in the family and the home. Whereas in the thirties the traditional Christian values of Western society still pervaded the education and upbringing of children in our society, the minds of the vast majority of the young are today far more influenced by the new phenomenon of pop culture, by the morals of the permissive society, and (sadly) by the pervasive influence of the drug culture. Instead of the sane and healthy influence of the wisdom of the great spiritual traditions, they are exposed almost daily to ideas of violence, degrading sado-masochistic fantasies and crude sexuality, purveyed on freely available videos, and to some extent even on the national and satellite TV channels. The social accompaniments of all this, rising crime, gratuitous violence even against the weak and the defenceless, drug abuse and resurgence of racism, are all too clear to see.

But the psychological malaise enters into the life of all of us in subtler ways as well. There are many less obvious wrong and unhealthy ideas which are widely accepted without question. The Archbishop of York has recently been talking about the climate of contempt which pervades society at the present time, saying that Christians must reject this insidious cultivation of contempt.[1] He instances the contemptuous way in which Lady Thatcher talks about her cabinet colleagues in her recently published memoirs and the self-satisfaction with which newspaper editors are willing to publish dishonestly acquired photographs denigrating people in the public eye. As he says: 'Contemptuousness breeds contemptibility, and if contempt flows from those in power, in the end it reflects back on themselves'. He very rightly says that 'the media must accept their share of blame for this'. And he points out that 'learning to value people for what they are, to listen to them, to speak to them with respect and to safeguard their dignity, could begin to break this vicious circle of contempt...' (which) '...entails a refusal to listen and to learn, because the contemptuous assume they know better than they whom they despise'. We can see the truth in all this, but it does not seem to get to the heart of the problem.

In yesterday's *Times*, on the other hand, we find Janet Daley drawing attention to the way in which the Church leaders have totally failed to give a lead in emphasizing the importance of teaching the concept of right and wrong to the individual.[2] Instead they have gone along with the fashionable habit of blaming all crime and anti-social behaviour on the policies pursued by the government, blaming poverty or deprivation rather than moral turpitude. Yet it is obvious (as she points out) that poverty, which was far worse in the thirties, did not produce the present level of crime when the moral guidance of Christianity and the churches was still influential in educating and influencing social behaviour of individuals.

Amid all this criticism and counter-criticism we seem to have very nearly arrived at the state of mind described by Samuel Butler in his mythical state of Erewhon, where those who committed crimes were regarded as invalids and sent to hospital (to be cured, in current terms, of the illnesses supposedly induced by deprivation, unemployment and poverty) rather than being seen as free individuals morally responsible for their actions; while those inhabitants of Erewhon who were so perverse and wrong-headed as to become ill were tried, sentenced and sent to prison to reform them of such bad and anti-social habits. It is surely a reflection on the moral blindness of our society that the purveying of sado-masochistic violence or crude sexuality on videos or the media is given the full protection of the permissive society, and defended on the specious grounds of the individual's right to freedom of choice and civil liberties, while everyone knows that behind the scenes vast illicit fortunes are being made by the criminal elements supplying these things. No wonder that such a society can offer so little effective resistance to the spread of drugs. If the rate at which crime is increasing each year becomes less steep than it was in the previous year, we congratulate ourselves nowadays on the success of the efforts to counter crime, when all that is actually happening is that the increase is slightly less fast than it was the year before!

If we consider, even cursorily, what we are constantly seeing and hearing in the media and having drummed into us by public commentators, we find that contempt, envy and jealousy are rife, although they are often hidden (somewhat hypocritically) under the cloak of criticism. Far from rejoicing in the good fortune of others, we all too often pillory them. The climate of contempt, which the Archbishop of York was speaking about, is certainly something we can all recognize every time we turn to the media or listen to the commentators speaking about (or even to!) our leaders, or about virtually anyone who challenges our entrenched self-interests in one way or another.

The media are so influential nowadays that this general climate of contempt has gradually percolated through society to become almost unconsciously accepted as the norm, and it has led to a pervasive flavour of destructive criticism which dominates, not only serious comment, and what passes for objective investigative journalism, but even the content of light entertainment, comedy and quiz shows. So it is more than high time to remind ourselves of what the wiser members of society, and (even more important) the spiritual teachers of mankind, have done to try and protect us against this critical ailment, which has serious side-effects on our own mental outlook and enlightenment.

The first essential point emphasized by the yogis is that the education of the individual in moral and spiritual hygiene is neglected at our peril, and that it is high time we started cleaning up the mental environment with as much energy and motivation as we are currently directing towards cleaning up the physical environment. But the process has to begin with spiritual education, and, like charity, spiritual education begins at home —with ourselves!

This is one of the most striking points made about the moral and spiritual ailments which affect the mind, but we shall find that it is proclaimed unanimously by all the spiritual teachers: it is no good trying to eliminate the apparent source of the infection in society at large, before one has cured oneself to some extent or at least got over the worst of the current attack from which one is suffering! And the reason for this (we are told) is that we are literally not fit to treat others effectively until we have acquired enough insight to recognize the manifestations of this polymorphic disease in ourselves, and enough wisdom to know how to deal with it effectively in our own mind and then in others.

One of the great modern yogis, Swami Rama Tirtha, has said:

> To escape the plague, the only way is to live up to the laws of hygiene. To be saved from 'foreign politics' [the alienating feeling of 'us' and 'them'

A Critical Ailment

which underlies all criticism], the only remedy is to live the law of spiritual health—the law of love for your neighbour.[3]

He is here quoting, not simply the Indian tradition, but the central message of our own Christian tradition. Christ's summing up of his message was:

You should love the Lord your God with all your heart, and with all your soul and with all your might, and your neighbour as yourself.[4]

The fact is that it is easy for us to diagnose the malaise of others and of society at large, but much more difficult to diagnose one's own malady or to see how one's own judgement is being distorted by it. At first sight this may be difficult for us to accept, but we should take seriously the warning given by Mencius, which is striking in its simplicity and directness.

What trouble is he not laying up for himself who discourses on other people's faults![5]

Mencius is talking from the point of view of a Confucianist gentleman living in the society of ancient China. But we can find the same message in Jesus' Sermon on the Mount:

Judge not, and ye shall not be judged: condemn not and ye shall not be condemned: forgive, and ye shall be forgiven:

Give, and it shall be given unto you; good measure, pressed down, and shaken together, and running over, shall men give into your bosom. For with the same measure that ye mete withal it shall be

> measured to you again… Can the blind lead the blind? Shall they not both fall into the ditch?… And why beholdest thou the mote that is in thy brother's eye, but perceivest not the beam that is in thine own eye?
>
> And how canst thou say to thy brother, Brother, let me pull out the mote that is in thine eye, when thou thyself beholdest not the beam that is in thine own eye? Thou hypocrite, cast out first the beam out of thine own eye, and then shalt thou see clearly to pull out the mote that is in thy brother's eye.
>
> For a good tree bringeth not forth corrupt fruit; neither does a corrupt tree bring forth good fruit.
>
> For every tree is known by his own fruit. For men do not gather figs from thorns, nor grapes from a bramble bush.
>
> A good man out of the good treasure of his heart bringeth forth that which is good; and an evil man out of the evil treasure of his heart bringeth forth that which is evil: for of the abundance of the heart his mouth speaketh.[6]

This teaching from the Christian Gospel could not be more explicit. And Jesus emphasizes elsewhere that man is not defiled by what impinges on him from outside but by what finds its abode in his own heart. We are subject to the bad mental infections which surround us only when we have lowered our own moral and spiritual resistance by neglect of our own mental health.

When we consider what Mencius and Christ have to say about criticism of others, we should not be surprised to find Swami Rama Tirtha asserting that one of the most dangerous obstacles in the way of self-realization is criticism: criticism from within and criticism from without.

Perhaps we can begin to recognize what a challenging problem it is to deal with this polymorphic mental epidemic from which we are all suffering, and whose manifestations creep up on us unawares. It is worth trying to understand the matter in more detail. Criticism is a particularly good symptom to start with, because Swami Rama Tirtha has a great deal to say about it which may help us to understand the more fundamental spiritual dimensions of the problem.

Even Bertrand Russell recognized that 'our own age is... one in which envy plays a peculiarly large part'. He also believed that 'next to worry, probably one of the most potent causes of unhappiness is envy', and he goes on to say that:

> of all the characteristics of ordinary human nature envy is the most unfortunate; not only does the envious person wish to inflict misfortune and do so whenever he can with impunity, but he is also himself rendered unhappy by envy. Instead of deriving pleasure from what he has, he derives pain from what others have. If he can, he deprives others of their advantages, which to him is as desirable as it would be to secure the same advantages himself. If this passion is allowed to run riot it becomes fatal to all excellence, and even to the most useful exercise of exceptional skill.[7]

Anyone who doubts the truth of this statement should read of the problems Mozart and Haydn had with jealous colleagues. The planned performance of the early opera, *La finta semplice*, written by the twelve-year-old Mozart for Vienna, was successfully prevented from taking place at all by the other Court composers, fearful of a new and dangerous rival, and, eighteen years later, they again formed a cabal which almost succeeded in preventing the success of *The Marriage of Figaro* on its first night. Haydn suffered in the same way, in spite of enjoying the relative security of his established post with Count Esterhazy. He wrote to a friend that it was only the success of his journey to England in his sixties which at last silenced all those in Austria who had been speaking against him and denigrating his music throughout his life. These are not isolated or untypical examples. Tulsi Das, one of the greatest Hindi poets, remarks (presumably from experience): 'Rare are the poets who speak well of another's poetry'!

We must try and counter as far as possible these destructive effects of envy. Russell comments:

> Fortunately, however, there is in human nature a compensating passion, namely that of admiration. Whoever wishes to increase human happiness must wish to increase admiration and to diminish envy.[8]

Mozart's *Figaro* was an immediate and abiding success when it was put on in Prague, and the audience there adored him and his music. As a result his later opera, *Don Giovanni*, was written for Prague and was again fully appreciated there straight away, but, when it was later performed in Vienna, the Viennese were still critical, complaining that it was 'too learned—too much crowded with effects of scientific harmony'. Haydn was present at an assembly of composers and dilettanti at the house of Prince Radziwill in Vienna, which damned the opera with faint praise combined with outright criticism. Haydn sat silent through all this, but when he was finally asked for his opinion, said: 'It is difficult to decide among your various opinions. All I know is that Mozart is the greatest composer now existing'.

Later, when he himself was asked to write an *opera buffa* for Prague to follow on the success of *Don Giovanni*, he wrote in a letter that it would be possible only with an entirely new libretto:

> Even then it would be a bold attempt, as scarcely anyone can stand by the side of the great Mozart. For if it were possible that I could impress every friend of music, particularly among the great, with that deep musical intelligence of the inimitable works of Mozart, that emotion of the soul with which they affect me, and in which I both comprehend and feel them, the nations would contend together for the possession of such a gem. Prague ought to retain him, and reward him well too; else the history of great genius is melancholy, and offers posterity but slight encouragement to exertion, which is the reason, alas! that many hopeful and aspiring spirits are repressed. I feel indignant that this *unique* Mozart is not yet engaged at some royal or imperial court. Forgive me if I stray from the subject—but I love the man too much.[9]

Envy is the third of the seven deadly sins, and the first verse of the *Isha Upanishad* gives a warning against it when it says: 'Covet not what belongs to another'. So there is no doubt about its being regarded as a major ailment from the spiritual point of view. Envy masquerades behind many disguises and (as Russell points out) is clearly very closely related to competition. It may appear as a protest against injustice or a moral denunciation of the wickedness of others. Russell remembers from his own childhood one of their maids, who was a married woman, becoming pregnant and the staff being told she was not to be expected to lift heavy weights. The instant result, he said, was that none of the others would lift heavy weights, and any work of that sort that needed doing, the family had to do for themselves. The love of scandal and the belief in any story against someone else, even on the flimsiest evidence, is another frequent example of disguised envy, as is the wish to punish those who have committed a sin. In our own world the tabloids thrive on it, but that also is not a new phenomenon.

It is not difficult to imagine opening your newspaper and reading: 'Premier under suspicion of corruption. After meteoric rise during his career in government, leaked reports suggest that the Prime Minister has been secretly amassing a large fortune'. We would probably hardly spend a moment questioning the validity of such a report, although we might speculate as to which country this must be in. Italy or Japan perhaps? There is a strong temptation to accept without question something discreditable about others. We live in a hypocritical age which, on the one hand, prides itself on its permissiveness and the freedom of the individual, and, on the other, will acclaim the hounding of a Minister out of office for having an affair, in spite of the fact that it is recognized and accepted by virtually everyone that he was doing his job particularly well and was generally regarded as the best man for the job.

But it is, at any rate, instructive to find that essentially the same story of ministerial malpractice was being spread long before the days of newspapers, about a thousand years ago in Ghazni about the minister Ayaz, who was the favourite and right-hand man of the great ruler, Sultan Mahmoud. The evidence for the suspicion was that Ayaz kept a well-locked room to which he went every day. Nobody else was allowed to enter it. The other courtiers, who were no doubt jealous of Ayaz's influence over the ruler, went and told him of their suspicions and asked him to order them to break into the room and verify them. They confidently predicted it would prove to be full of the ill-gotten gains which Ayaz had appropriated. Ayaz had every reason to be avaricious, for he had begun life as a very poor man. He had been a shepherd when the Sultan had found him and taken him into his service, and he repaid this munificence by the faithfulness of the service he rendered to the Sultan. When the room was broken into, far from finding any treasure, the envious courtiers found only an old sheepskin coat and the rustic shoes that Ayaz had worn as a shepherd. He used to go each day to remind himself of his humble origin and of what he owed to God and the Sultan. The story is told in the *Mathnavi* of Jalaluddin Rumi[10], but (sadly) it is not the sort of story which would appeal to the editors of the tabloid newspapers as a way of increasing their circulation!

Russell writes:

> In old days people only envied their neighbours, because they knew little about anything else. Now through education and the Press they know much in an abstract way about large classes of mankind of whom no single individual is among their acquaintance. Through the movies they think they know how the rich live, through the newspapers they know much of the wickedness of foreign nations, through propaganda they know of the nefarious practices of all whose skin has a pigmentation different from their own... Why is propaganda so much more successful when it stirs up hatred than when it stirs up friendly feeling? The reason is clearly that the human heart as modern civilization has made it is more prone to hatred than to friendship. And it is prone to hatred because it is dissatisfied, because it feels deeply, perhaps even unconsciously, that it has somehow missed the meaning of life, that perhaps others, but not we ourselves, have secured the good things which nature offers for man's enjoyment...[11]

Russell comments that this feeling of strain and anguish, accompanying a sense that he has lost the way on the road of evolution,

> seems to have entered the soul of civilized man. He knows there is something better than himself almost within his grasp, yet he does not know where to seek it or how to find it. In despair he rages against

his fellow man, who is equally lost and equally unhappy. We have reached a stage in evolution which is not the final stage. We must pass through it quickly, for if we do not, most of us will perish by the way, and the others will be lost in a forest of doubt and fear... To find the right road out of this despair, civilized man must enlarge his heart as he has enlarged his mind. He must learn to transcend self, and in so doing to acquire the freedom of the Universe.[12]

Russell talks almost like a yogi at the end of this passage. What, then, is the yogic view as to the cure for envy or the over-critical attitude? Swami Rama Tirtha says that 'it is as easy to be prosperous as to be wretched, if only we can make the proper renunciations'. He quotes the old Vedic dictum: 'Sacrifice averts evil', and says that it is as true today as in the old days; only it is not the vicarious sacrifice of innocent animals that we need, but the sacrifice of our party spirit, caste feelings, jealousies, etc., at the altar of love, that brings heaven to us in this world.

In other words, if we examine the matter carefully, we will find that most of the ills of society and the so-called sins which are committed, are due to the absence of that deep fellow-feeling which will only prosper in a society where people treat their neighbours, not as alien beings, to be looked down on, feared or hated, but as fellow men and women. But this basis for a good society has to start with the education of the individual, and the cultivation, particularly in the young, of these simple but fundamental and immensely beneficial attitudes. From the spiritual point of view, this is a recognition of the truth that we are all members one of another and that there is the same spiritual essence hidden in the heart of each and every man.

Few of us would have any difficulty in deciding whether we would prefer to live with Iago or Sir John Falstaff, for the fat knight, for all his faults, was a great human being; hence, although he was a rogue, he spread happiness. No wonder he was one of Shakespeare's most popular and successful characters with the public—so much so that Shakespeare was forced to rush out an extra play about him by royal command. The quality of envy has the opposite effect; it is a cause of unhappiness in those who harbour it and it aims to increase the unhappiness of its victims. As such, it is one of the most unlovable and dehumanizing of feelings.

As has already been mentioned, Swami Rama Tirtha talks of criticism as one of the most dangerous obstacles in the way of self-realization, and he emphasizes that it is counter-productive both for the critic and for the person who is criticized:

> Because each party concentrates its attention on the faults of its neighbour,... this very concentration, based on doubt, acts as a malicious force to engender the objectionable characteristics. Call one a thief and he will steal is an undeniable truism....
>
> The energy we waste in judging others is just what is needed to make us live up to our own ideals.[13]

Swami Rama Tirtha is not facile or superficial in

what he says about criticism. He goes into the various ways in which it can manifest itself in some detail and shows the deleterious effects that it has. He is a wise physician of the mind, who knows all the signs of the troublesome disease he is describing, and the complications to which they lead. He recognizes that the spirit of criticism is mostly driven by an instinct to defend oneself from the fault that one is criticizing. And he recognizes too that (as he says) 'so long as the world has any room for improvement, the spirit of criticism and comparison will last'. But he makes an important distinction, which is worth noting, when he says:

> It is not the criticizing and comparing spirit which is undesirable...[nor is it] possible to eradicate [it], but the *venom* in it, which is giving to the parties concerned the sense of personality.[14]

Basically all sins and all immoral acts are rooted in individualism, or egoity, and if we are to overcome this problem once and for all, we have to reduce, and as far as possible eliminate, the selfishness in ourselves and others. It may seem like a counsel of perfection, but it can be expedited and very effectively approached through the means which the yogis give us. If we consider for a moment how selfishness distorts our view of things, we can understand something of what he means. For Swami Rama Tirtha puts it very directly: he points out that you see your own faults and you don't hate yourself for them; and that we should try and treat others similarly. If you see faults in them, avoid the faults but don't hate them for it.[15]

What matters is to escape from the narrow blinkered

outlook which we have if we are thinking selfishly. As he says:

> Let us fling aside the vulnerable little 'I' which alone makes 'sin' in ourselves and others; and, cured of all pain, we can look at all deeds and people around us with the scientific indifference and philosophic calm of a chemist or botanist, examining everything most dispassionately, accurately and minutely, with no fear of being entangled in the chemicals and plants under our inspection; like the sun as a witness (*sakshi*) helping all and watching all, the briars and the roses, the waste [ground] and the gardens, men, women, animals, plants, ants and clouds.[16]

This is the Yoga ideal.

There is a story told of two monks, who were travelling in the East when they came to a river which was in spate. As they were about to try and cross it, a girl came up. She asked them if they would help her to get across. One of the monks said without hesitation 'Yes. Jump on my back!', and he waded across to the other side with her. She thanked him and went off and the two monks continued their journey. The second monk walked on saying nothing for about ten minutes. Then he suddenly burst out: 'Why did you take that girl on your back. You know we shouldn't. We are monks. We are not meant to touch a woman'. The other monk simply turned to him and said gently: 'Brother, are you still carrying her?'

Envy and criticism is an example of mental bondage which can only lead to unhappiness, a demonstration of how man's mind and its lower propensities can become a prison if we do not take active steps to counter these tendencies, and it is one of the manifestations of the psychological illness which we mentioned and which is called spiritual ignorance by the yogis. It is to effect a radical cure of this illness in all its forms that Yoga is pursued.

18

Time for Thought*

Time is a subject which people are clearly interested in, for the book which has been at or near the top of the best seller list for the past three years or more is *A Brief History of Time* by Stephen Hawking. It is not an easy book to assimilate, but one which has obviously caught the popular imagination. This brief talk about time may serve as an introduction to a few of the ideas raised in the book in relation to the teaching of the yogis on the nature of the world of time, space and causation.

What is time?

St Augustine wrote: 'What, then, is time? If no one asks me, I know: but if I wish to explain it to the person who asks, I don't know what it is.'

He was right, of course. It is difficult to define what we mean by time, and our ideas about it are somewhat confused. Augustine himself said that memory, perception and expectation make up all there is of time. In other words time consists of past, present and future, and we know of the past because we remember it, we know the present because we perceive it and we know the future because we anticipate it all the time, having learned to expect its arrival. Our sense of time does indeed depend on these three characteristics of our experience, but it is also true that all our actual experience is here and now in the present; it is here and now that we can remember what has been in the past, see

---

* A lecture given on 25th March 1994.

around us what now exists and expect the future. And our present expectations of what is going to come, are often based on our present memory of what has happened before.

But Bertrand Russell criticizes Augustine's view, because it equates the sense of time purely with our subjective experience of it, whereas he maintains that there must also be a time which is independent of us, the time of history and of physics and of the creation itself. From the scientific point of view, objective time, the time measured by physics and mathematics, is precise and accurate, whereas our sense of time is often vague, imprecise and subjective, so there must be a difference between private and public time. Public time is in general more reliable and accurate than private time. Perhaps this is the basis of the old Music Hall song: 'If you want to know the time, ask a policeman'!

Sir Isaac Newton makes this distinction very strongly when he differentiates between what he calls 'absolute time' and the notions of the common man about time.

> Absolute, true and mathematical time, of itself, and from its own nature, flows equably without regard to anything external, and by another name is called duration: relative, apparent and common time is some sensible, external measure of duration by means of *motion* (whether accurate or unequable), which is commonly used instead of true time: such as an hour, a day, a month, a year.

There is no doubt about our own sense of time being

fallible. I remember a German Professor, well-known for the meticulous punctuality with which he arrived for appointments absolutely on time and for not wasting a moment (we have Professors like that here too, incidentally!). He was coming from Düsseldorf in Germany to give a scheduled lecture to a large International Congress in Amsterdam in the early autumn a few years ago. The lecture was scheduled for between 2 and 3 pm, and the assembled audience was in place well before the scheduled start, but it was only at 2.40 pm that the speaker arrived, under the impression that he was a comfortable twenty minutes early for his talk, whereas he was actually forty minutes late! He had overlooked the fact that Holland and Germany changed from summer to winter time on different dates. This is a good example of the distinction between the imprecision and fallibility of our own sense of time and the objective measurement of public time.

How do we measure it?

But how do we measure time at all? If we consider it carefully, we shall find that (as Newton suggested) we take some periodic movement and arbitrarily adopt it as the measure of time. For instance, we can take the rotation of the earth about the sun (and measure it in years), or the moon about the earth (and measure it in '*moonths*' or months) or the earth about its own axis (and measure it in days and nights). You don't need any extra equipment for these measures which is why they have proved so very useful since early times, but to go further than this we need to devise some special implements to measure time.

For instance, the invention of the sun-dial enabled our fore-fathers to measure changes in the position of the sun, and to register, not only differences of day from night, but of the hour of the day too. This was an inconvenient method because you lost your ability to measure the hour when clouds obscured the sun or at night. The time taken for sand to fall in a sand glass or for water to empty from a water clock avoided this particular problem, but wasn't much use if you wanted to arrange with your friends when to meet, because they were coming from elsewhere and had no knowledge of your particular sand glass. And this illustrates another important point about time. It is difficult to measure and compare events at different places, or even to synchronize clocks, unless you have good communications between them.

Gradually mankind has discovered and adopted other better methods of measuring time. With the development of clockwork, following the discoveries of Galileo and Huygens, the swing of a pendulum, the oscillation of a spring escapement, and, in more modern times, the vibration of a tuning fork or the characteristic frequency of vibration of a crystal of quartz, have been incorporated into clocks or watches which improved our time-keeping. But we still have to synchronize our watches and make sure their batteries are not flat.

Rupert Brooke's memory of the old vicarage in Grantchester, near Cambridge, reminds us that even public time could be unreliable at times.

> Stands the church clock at ten to three?
> And is there honey still for tea?

The public time kept by Grantchester's clock was clearly memorable, but not much use in practice.

Better agreement on a common public time has become much easier since we developed reasonably reliable centralized clocks like Big Ben, whose striking of the hour was widely disseminated by radio, or, better still, the talking clock of the telephone system, which have provided much more practical ways of getting our times synchronized. The pips on radio and time signal on TV have improved the accessibility of public time, but we still have inconvenient changes to take account of in regard to different places on the globe.

But all this useful technology does not provide us with any means of measuring absolute time. Newton himself recognized that the existence of absolute time was an inference and not something that one could directly observe, because, just as all days are not of equal length, so (he pointed out) there may not exist anywhere in nature a truly uniform motion. In other words, even if we believe in absolute time in Newton's sense, we may not have anything to measure it with.

Different measures of time do not agree.

This becomes very clear if we compare one measure against another, for we soon find that there are discrepancies between the two. Take the rotation of the earth about the sun. If you measure the solar year by the passage of the seasons, it averages 365.2422 days from one vernal equinox to the next. This is the point when the sun crosses the equator in the spring and the day and night are of equal length, celebrated this year (1994) last Sunday on March 20th. But this so-called 'tropical year' is twenty minutes longer than the year measured as one complete orbit of the sun by the earth relative to the distant fixed stars, the so-called 'sidereal year' (365.2564 days). Why should there be such a discrepancy? It is due to the fact that the earth's axis wobbles in a circle and takes 25,360 years to complete one wobble and this leads to a slight change in the timing of the seasons, known as the precension of the equinox.

The month fares no better than the year. In the rotation of the moon round the earth, the time is different according to whether one measures it relative to the time from one new or full moon to the next, when it is 29.53 days, or as the time taken by the moon to complete one orbit around the earth relative to the distant fixed stars, when it is 27.32 days. One may add that the calendar month is now an entirely human creation, which no longer has any relationship to the moon's rotation. It represents the fairly typical result of a series of well-meaning but ill-advised attempts by successive governments to get the calendar sorted out. It is clearly a botched job, adopting all sorts of awkward corrections, such as months with anything from 28 to 31 days and leap years with an extra day every four years. To keep things reasonably sensible we have also had to adjust the calendar every few hundred years. The last major adjustment was in 1752, when eleven days were added to the year. This is why our legal year ends on April 5th rather than the 25th March.

Apart from all these considerations we now know that the speed of the earth's rotation is anything but constant; it varies slightly with the gravitational effects of the tides which are being slowed down by gravitational friction. This only requires a small correction of a few seconds or less after many years, but it would still be a cause of variability in our measure of time if we did not have any other way of doing it.

Our ideas of time change with our world-picture: the search for an absolute frame of reference for time and space.

Clearly all these causes of variability in the empirical measures of time would not matter at all if we had a fixed frame of reference against which to record all these variations—if we had something which represented a fixed point or grid against which we could measure time, and another fixed point in space against which we could measure the position of a particular spot within absolute space. This appeared relatively easy in the old days, before we knew too much. Aristotle's view was that the earth stood still in the centre of the world, and that the heavens circled round it, so we here could stand on *terra firma* and knew where we stood. Absolute time was time as we would measure it (not now perhaps because of the unreliability of water-clocks and sand-glasses, but as soon as we had developed ourselves really accurate clocks). And then any variability that we detected would be shown up as an error measured against our own absolute time and from our own absolute position in space.

Things began to get more difficult when Copernicus, Kepler and Galileo decided that it was not us on the earth, but the sun that stood still in the centre of the solar system, while the earth and the other planets circled round it. A great cosmic frame of reference was provided by what were called the fixed stars, existing outside the solar system and apparently remaining in the same position as the earth rotated under them. It was easy for Addison in the eighteenth century to see these fixed stars as evidence of a great and abiding framework of creation, an ever-present evidence of the absolute space and time which God had ordained for us to be in.

> The spacious firmament on high,
> With all the blue ethereal sky,
> And spangl'd heavens, a shining frame,
> Their great Original proclaim....
> What though, in solemn silence, all
> Move round the dark terrestrial ball;
> What though nor real voice, nor sound
> Amid their radiant orbs be found;
> In reason's ear they all rejoice,
> And utter forth a glorious voice;
> For ever singing, as they shine:
> 'The Hand that made us is divine'.

Here, to Addison, seemed to be what was wanted, a fixed order of things providing the framework of absolute space and time which Newton had posited.

Modern developments in the scientific world-picture have abolished all idea of an absolute time or space.

Unfortunately, modern scientific progress since then has finally put paid to all hope of finding any fixed reference point, either in time or space, to act as a frame of reference against which we can pin down accurately the instant that an event occurred or the exact position where it took place.

This was already becoming clear at the end of the nineteenth century, when Michelson and Morley made their puzzling observations on the speed of light, which always seemed to be the same for any observer, no matter how fast he himself was moving, nor in which direction. Then, an unknown clerk in the Patent Office in Bern suggested in 1905 that the new results could be explained if one were willing to abandon the idea of absolute time altogether. His name was Albert Einstein, and he altered our idea of time completely. [A similar suggestion was made a few weeks later by a leading French mathematician, Henri Poincaré.[1]] The Special Theory of Relativity of 1905 was developed by Einstein in a more comprehensive form in 1915, in his General Theory of Relativity.

Both Einstein and Poincaré were mathematicians, and neither showed much interest in experimental verification. Their ideas were very difficult to understand and took time to become generally known. But another major change to our conception of what the universe was like came from the direct observations of the American astronomer, Edward Hubble, in the 1920's. Before 1924, no-one had been entirely sure what the Milky Way was, although as long ago as 1750 Sir William Herschel had concluded from his careful observation of the position and distances of a vast number of stars in the Milky Way, that it was what we now call a spiral galaxy, a disk-like Catherine wheel of stars. Edward Hubble demonstrated in 1924 that ours was not the only galaxy and that there were some hundred thousand million other similar galaxies, each containing some hundred thousand million stars, separated by vast tracts of apparently empty space.

These observations were first brought to the notice of a wider public by Sir Arthur Eddington in his little Pelican book *The Expanding Universe*, which the speaker remembers buying and reading with intense interest soon after its publication in 1940. What Edward Hubble had shown was that the light from distant galaxies consistently showed a red shift, that is, a reddening of the colour of the light arriving from them, and that the amount of this shift was directly proportional to the estimated distance of the galaxies from the observer in light years. The red shift is an example of the Doppler effect, comparable to the sudden lowering of the sound of the horn of a passing car as it begins to move away from you. The light waves are being shifted towards the red end of the spectrum by the reduction in the frequency of the light waves which are arriving less often. From Hubble's observations it appeared that all the galaxies were moving away from us with a speed which became faster the further they were away from us. In other words the whole universe was expanding.

One of the consequences of an expanding universe is that there is absolutely no possibility of finding a fixed point anywhere in it. You may object that the point at the very centre of an expanding universe can be fixed and motionless (even though one may not be able to find out where it is). Unfortunately this is no longer so in the world picture arrived at in Relativity, for reasons which we will come to in a minute. But if everything is moving, we can't say definitely where anything is. To put it more precisely: where it is will vary with one's point of view, and there is no reason to prefer one view to another.

The idea of stationary objects is an illusion. Mount Everest is no more motionless than a hurricane. It is hurtling round roughly 25,000 miles every 24 hours on the earth's surface, and is being carried round the sun at a velocity of 18.5 miles per second, or (to put it in units of speed with which we are more familiar) 66,600 mph.

So is the wicket keeper at Lords who believes that he stopped the ball stone dead behind the wicket. So is the ball, whether we regard it as moving or not! We can see the difficulty more clearly when we see astronauts floating about in the rocket cabins on space missions. They look as if they are hardly moving and only relatively slowly, but that is because we are only seeing the infinitesimal relative *differences* in speed of movement between them and the rocket they are in! This is the world of relativity!

Stephen Hawking gives the example of a ping-pong ball being idly bounced up and down on the same spot on a table of an intercity train. From the passenger point of view, it is going vertically up and down, for someone on the side of the track seeing it through the window it has moved rapidly sideways each time it bounces.

To any observer on neighbouring galaxies, the whole earth and its galaxy are rushing away at breakneck speed!

As Russell says, 'The whole notion that one is always in some definite "place" is due to the fortunate immobility of most of the large objects on the earth's surface. The idea of "place" is only a rough practical approximation... it cannot be made precise'.[2]

But, in spite of all this, why can we not find a still point at the middle of the expanding universe? It is because, to echo Russell, Relativity demands a change in our imaginative picture of the world[3] and depends upon getting rid of notions which—however useful they may be in ordinary life—are inapplicable to the world revealed by Einstein's General Theory of Relativity.[4]

The expanding four-dimensional space-time continuum which contains the electromagnetic field of the energy of Nature can be likened to the two-dimensional surface of a balloon which is being slowly blown up. You can go in any direction in space-time but you will never find an edge, although you may eventually end up where you started. As Carl Sagan has put it, it is 'a universe with no edge in space, no beginning or end in time'. The three dimensions of space and the one dimension of time, are bent or 'warped' in another dimension by the gravitational influence of the matter in the universe, which represents a very high local intensity of the field. As a consequence space and time themselves are 'warped' or distorted in the vicinity of large masses like the sun or other objects, and the light gets correspondingly bent in that vicinity.

Thus, in developing the Special Theory of 1905 into the more General Theory of 1915, Einstein was able to explain gravity. But, to quote Stephen Hawking:

> Gravity is not [any longer] a force like other forces [as in Newton's explanation], but is a consequence of the fact that space-time is not flat, as had been previously assumed: it is curved, or 'warped', by the distribution of mass and energy in it... In general relativity, bodies always follow straight lines in four-dimensional space-time, but they nevertheless appear to us to move along curved paths in our three-dimensional space... The mass of the sun curves space-time in such a way that although the earth follows a straight path in four-dimensional space-time, it appears to us to move along a circular orbit in three-dimensional space.[5]

In this world picture, incidentally, there *is* no centre of the universe. It is not simply an expanding sphere, but a finite, but edgeless, continuum.

How easy life was in the good old days! Until this century the idea of time and space had been clear and simple and fixed. Any event could be pin-pointed as taking place at a particular point in space and at a particular instant in time. Space and time themselves provided an accurate, objective, absolute framework against which things could be pinned down. The clock, whether astronomical or mechanical, might be inaccurate, but Newton's absolute time and space were the real thing. Things moved in absolute space and that movement occupied portions of absolute time. You could pin down events by specifying where they occurred in space and when they occurred in time. But all this depended on a fixed frame of reference, and the developments in science—in particular the observations of Michelson and Morley on the velocity of light, Einstein's Special and General Theory of Relativity and the discovery by Hubble of the expanding universe—showed that everything in the world was in motion. There were no fixed points. And it was not that the universe was expanding in some absolute space existing outside it; space and time were an intrinsic part of the universe itself. The electromagnetic field with the space-time continuum *was* the universe and, as far as we could tell, nothing existed outside it.

> Just as one cannot talk about events in the universe without the notions of space and time, so in general relativity it became meaningless to talk about space and time outside the limits of the universe.[6]

Many of the firm conclusions from this new world view were strange and almost baffling to our common sense view of things. For instance, it was known from Clerk Maxwell's equations and the subsequent discoveries of Hertz and others that light waves were transverse vibrations of electro-magnetic energy travelling in a field and obeying the predictions of the equations, but the idea of any underlying medium or ether through which the waves were propagated was abolished by the observations of Michelson and Morley. Light simply propagated through empty space without having any detectable medium through which it could travel.

Einstein's theory, which triumphantly explained a vast body of the new observations, indicated that energy and matter were basically the same, and could be converted into one another. There was no difference basically between matter and the waves of electromagnetic energy. No wonder Russell could sum it up by saying that science had abolished substance from the world and what we were left with was 'Waves of probability undulating in nothingness'. Science had reduced the hard real world of the Victorians to 'an insubstantial pageant faded', leaving not a rack behind.

Nothing could travel faster than electromagnetic waves in a vacuum (186,000 miles per second or 300,000 km per second), but the speed of those waves was exactly the same for any observer, no matter how fast or slow they themselves were moving. It was as if each observer was himself or herself a fixed point within the time-spatial continuum containing the electromagnetic field.

'Local time' peculiar to each observer.

Space and time not only affect, but are also affected by, everything that happens in the universe.

This had the curious consequence that each observer had his own version of time, related to that of other observers, but not the same. It was as if the clocks which were carried at each point in time and space had their own particular way of keeping time.

Of course, all this makes little difference to us, because we are all stuck to one little portion of the universe, with its own family of reference frames, not significantly differing from each other.

It is only when one deals with large distances and starts to approach the speed of light, at 186,000 miles per second, that one begins to see the differences clearly emerging.

This is reassuring, because we don't expect to be in danger of doing anything of the kind! But physicists nowadays do accelerate particles to this sort of speed, and the results predicted by the Theory of Relativity are found to be confirmed. So we are not merely dealing with theory.

It is perhaps here worth reading an illustration of what the implications of relativity are with regard to time. This is a passage from Bertrand Russell:[7]

> I have been speaking so far as if there were, as used to be thought, one cosmic time for the whole universe. Since Einstein, we know that this is not the case. Each piece of matter has its own local time. There is very little difference between the local time of one piece of matter and that of another unless their relative velocity is an appreciable fraction of the velocity of light. The local time of a given piece of matter is that which will be shown by a perfectly accurate chronometer which travels with it. Beta-particles travel with velocities that do not fall very far short of that of light. If we could place a chronometer on a beta-particle, and make the particle travel in a closed path, we should find,

when it returned, that the chronometer would not agree with one that had remained throughout stationary in the laboratory.

A more curious illustration (which I owe to Professor Reichenbach) is connected with the possibility of travel to the stars. Suppose we invented a rocket apparatus which could send a projectile to Sirius with a velocity ten elevenths of that of light. From the point of view of the terrestrial observer the journey would take 55 years, and one might therefore suppose that if the projectile carried passengers who were young when they started, they would be old when they arrived. But from their point of view the journey will only have taken about 11 years. This will not only be the time taken as measured by their clocks, but also the time as measured by their physiological processes—decay of teeth, loss of hair, etc. If they looked and felt like men of 20 when they started, they will look and feel like men of 31 when they arrive. It is only because we do not habitually come across bodies travelling with a speed approaching that of light that such odd facts remain unnoticed except by men of science.

Of course, this is a total impossibility, because our bodies could not survive such an experiment (and we are, empirically speaking, creatures whose material bodies could only exist in a very restricted set of physical conditions peculiar to our tiny corner of the universe). But the implications as regards time are calculated in accordance with the General Theory of Relativity, which we now believe to rule our physical universe as a whole on the basis of clear confirmatory observations.

Common-sense view of space and time is vyavaharika-satta (part of the sphere of empirical reality).

The common-sense notion of time and space turns out to be alright for everyday life, provided we accept it and ask no awkward questions about it, but it doesn't clearly have much relationship with what one finds if one really goes into it. This coincides with what the yogis tell us about time and space and causation. It is (they say) *vyavaharika satta* (empirical existence), good enough for the everyday world of ordinary life, but appearing much more credible and sensible than it really is, and not standing up to scrutiny. This character of time and space was echoed by such Western philosophers as Kant, Schopenhauer and Bradley, who pointed out that there were irreconcilable self-contradictions in our ideas about time (what Kant called antinomies), while Bradley lays out in detail the reasons for concluding that time, space and causation can all three only be regarded as appearances of the events of experience and not substantial and abiding realities.

The world is jagat, the 'moving thing'.

The modern scientific picture of the world reminds us that the yogis have always spoken of the world as *jagat*, 'the moving thing' and have regarded it as a product of the energy or power of nature (*prakriti shakti*). There could be no clearer confirmation of the appropriateness of this name than our present picture of the expanding universe, in which one searches in vain for the possibility of a fixed point.

Or does one? What is odd about the picture of the universe arrived at in the Theory of Relativity, is that the velocity of light is always the same for any observer, no matter how they are supposed to be moving in the world. It appears as if the one still point of reference in the world of time and space is here and now. Here and now we judge the simultaneity of events in different places, but our judgements are always complicated by the fact that we are not there and then when the events elsewhere occur. We have to wait for the arrival of the information, and the nearest we can get to observing there and then is to judge what we see here and now and make allowances for the time it has taken for the information to arrive. In relativity there is an innate ambiguity about the idea of simultaneity when applied to events in different places and there is a parallel ambiguity about the concept of the distance between two bodies at a given instant. Everyone effectively carries their own clock and this is affected by local events. Space and time in relativity are no longer independent and absolute measures, against which we can judge things; they are (as Stephen Hawking says in his book) things which not only affect, but are also affected by, everything that happens in the universe.[8] In the General Theory of Relativity 'space and time are now dynamic qualities: when a body moves or a force acts, it affects the curvature of space and time—and in turn the structure of space and time affects the way in which the bodies move and the forces act.'

Looking for the still point: the absolute beyond relativity.

But it is worth remembering in this context some words of one of the founders of Quantum Theory, Max Planck, who writes in his *A Scientific Autobiography*:

> In order to preclude a likely misunderstanding I have to insert here a few explanatory remarks of [a] general character. In the opening paragraphs of this autobiographical sketch, I emphasized that I had always looked upon the search for the absolute as the noblest and most worth while task of science. The reader might consider this contradictory to my avowed interest in the Theory of Relativity. But it would be fundamentally erroneous to look at it that way. For everything that is relative presupposes the existence of something that is absolute, and is meaningful only when juxtaposed to something absolute. The often heard phrase, 'Everything is relative', is both misleading and thoughtless. The Theory of Relativity, too, is based on something absolute, namely, the determination of the matrix of the space-time continuum; and it is especially stimulating to discover the absolute which alone makes meaningful something given as relative.

Our every starting point must necessarily be something relative. All our measurements are relative. The material that goes into our instruments varies according to its geographic source; their construction depends upon the skill of the designer and toolmaker; their manipulation is contingent on the special purposes pursued by the experimenter. Our task is to find in all these factors and data, the absolute, the universally valid, the invariant, that is hidden in them.[9]

Hidden in the here and now of each and every observer is the still point which provides the real source of reference for the empirical experience of relativity—of time, space and causation. Empirically his body and mind may appear to be sunk in the realm of relativity, because these instruments of experience are created by *prakriti*, the energy or power of nature, but the whole of nature and the world of relativity are supported on the underlying Reality, whose nature is Consciousness Absolute. This is the real element hidden in the heart of each and every being.

The yogis teach us that the region beyond time, the timeless region, is to be sought within the mind, rather than in nature. Because time, space and causation come into existence with the mind and the world, all being contained within the realm of relativity. But the mind can transcend empirical experience in *jnana*, enlightenment.

The same spiritual truth is hinted at in St John's Gospel, when Jesus taught the people in the temple: 'Your father Abraham rejoiced to see my day' and his listeners said: 'You are not yet fifty years old, and have you seen Abraham?', to which he replied: 'Verily, verily, I say unto you, Before Abraham was, I am.'[10]

It was an echo of the voice of God speaking to Moses from the burning bush in the Old Testament, and saying: 'I AM THAT I AM. Say to the children of Israel I AM hath sent me to you'.[11]

The Lord declares in the *Bhagavad Gita*:

> As the mighty air, moving everywhere, abides in space, know thou that in the same manner all existences abide in Me.
>
> All beings, O son of Kunti, pass into Nature (prakriti), which is my own, at the end of the world-cycle (or kalpa); and at the beginning of the next cycle I send them forth...
>
> Under My guidance, (the energy of) Nature (Prakriti) gives birth to all things, moving and unmoving, and by this means, O Arjuna, the world revolves...
>
> The great-souled, who abide in the divine nature, knowing Me as the imperishable source of all beings, worship Me with an undistracted mind.[12]
>
> O Arjuna, the Lord abides deep in the heart of all beings...[13]

Beyond the world of relativity—of time, space and causation, which the yogis call *jagat*, 'the moving thing'—there is the Absolute, the matrix or substratum of the space-time continuum. To know it is the aim and object of the Yoga of Self-knowledge.

In the words of the Psalmist:

> Be still and know that I am God.[14]

19

Searching for the Good Life*

In a recently published biography of the economist, John Maynard Keynes[1], Robert Skidelsky points out that one of the major problems which had been preoccupying the intellectual life of Cambridge since the nineteenth century, was to discover some basis for the good life—or to put it more technically, an adequate theory of ethics—to replace Christianity. As he points out, Victorian society relied heavily for its inspiration on evangelical religion. The political, social and economic reforms for which the Victorians are justly renowned were largely based on it. They believed in the sovereignty of the individual, but thought that he should live his life and make his choices on Christian principles.

Many of the great social reformers, like Elizabeth Fry, William Wilberforce, Florence Nightingale, Gladstone, and even a number of the founders of modern socialism, like Beatrice Webb and her nephew, Stafford Cripps, based their whole philosophy on a profound Christian faith. But, with the advent and steady advance of a purely secular tradition, originating in Bentham and the Utilitarians, and later in the rise of Marxism, combined with the shock of Darwin's theory of evolution, the traditional religious beliefs were soon in crisis and decline. This change in mood was captured early in the mid-nineteenth century by Matthew Arnold (1822-1888) in his poem 'Dover Beach', part of which runs:

* A lecture given on 29th October 1993.

Come to the window, sweet is the night air!
Only, from the long line of spray
Where the sea meets the moon-blanch'd land,
Listen! you hear the grating roar
Of pebbles which the waves draw back, and fling,
At their return, up the high strand,
Begin, and cease, and then again begin,
With tremulous cadence slow, and bring
The eternal note of sadness in...

...The sea of Faith
Was once, too, at the full, and the round earth's
  shore
Lay like the folds of a bright girdle furl'd.
But now I only hear
Its melancholy, long, withdrawing roar,
Retreating to the breath
Of the night-wind, down the vast edges drear
And naked shingles of the world.

Ah, love, let us be true
To one another! for the world, which seems
To lie before us like a land of dreams,
So various, so beautiful, so new,
Hath really neither joy, nor love, nor light,
Nor certitude, nor peace, nor help for pain;
And we are here as on a darkling plain
Swept with confused alarms of struggle and
  flight,
Where ignorant armies clash by night.

These words seem even more true today than they

were when they were written, more than a hundred years ago. And they well express the growing feeling among the thoughtful in the last century that life had lost its clear anchor in the traditional faith of their forefathers.

As a result, many mid- and late-Victorian intellectuals were pre-occupied with the quest for some alternative ground for morals. They needed an ethical philosophy to provide for a secular age, and two of the main lines along which this was sought, concerned, on the one hand, the good of the individual and, on the other, the good of society-as-a-whole. Those who still believed in the guidance of conscience, put their trust in the intuition of the individual to discover good motives and to recognize bad ones, while those who, like the Utilitarians and John Stuart Mill, thought that the important good was the good of society as a whole, put their trust in pursuing the ideal which Jeremy Bentham had promulgated, that of 'the greatest good of the greatest number'. Communism appeared to offer one solution along these lines, and socialism a watered down version of the same general principles. In the Liberal tradition some people hoped that a more scientific knowledge of economics and social engineering would produce a good society.

Maynard Keynes himself, who was a brilliant economist and a life-long Liberal, spent much of his professional life trying to improve the conditions of his fellow men through the development and application of more powerful economic theories. At the same time he was also a member of the Bloomsbury group, who thought that art, literature and culture in general were one of the main areas where the individual could find his version of the good life. In this sense, Maynard Keynes had a foot in both camps, and Skidelsky points out that he spent his life zig-zagging between the two.

It is fairly easy to see the flaws in the attempt of a secular society to base morals on either the individual or the social ideal. Even the best of intentions by the individual do not necessarily produce the best results. We may have a very sincere and deep desire to do good, but fail to possess the wisdom to carry it out in practice. We can all recognize what C S Lewis meant when he said of a woman do-gooder:

> She was one of those women who spend their whole life doing good to others. You can recognize the others by the hunted expression on their faces.

But those who put their trust in making the goal of ethics the good of society—or at least the greatest good of the greatest number (as Bentham put it)—soon found the difficulties confronting them in determining how you measured this, let alone achieved it. The American millionaire who gives generously to the arts or charity—often at negligible cost to himself because it is tax allowable!—may apparently do a great deal of good to a lot of people objectively (Andrew Carnegie's Library in Glasgow, for instance, must have helped innumerable poor students over the years, particularly before public libraries became generally available), but we can't see it as being anything like as morally admirable or valuable as the self-sacrificing efforts of someone who does social work among perhaps relatively much fewer of the poor or the deprived, or a volunteer who risks his or her life bringing desperately needed medical aid or food to some of the suffering peoples of Bosnia or Somalia. As Deussen remarks:

> Europeans, practical and shrewd as they are, are wont to estimate the merits of an action above all by its objective worth, that is by the resultant profit for (their) neighbours, for the multitude, or for all men. He who has obtained the greatest results by this standard passes for the greatest man of his time; and the widow's mite is never anything more than a mite. But this objective worth of a good action is too entirely dependent on the favourable or unfavourable character of an environment, on mental endowment, on position in life, on the accessory forces of trade and other accidents, to be capable of serving as a standard of moral value. Such a standard must have regard rather to the subjective worth of an action, which consists in the greatness of the personal sacrifice which is involved,... and consequently in the degree of self-denial (*tapas*), and self-renunciation (*nyasa*), which is exhibited in the action, whether in other respects it be of great or little or absolutely no value for others.[2]

Deussen is surely right about this. And it is because of its shining quality of self-denial (*tapas*) and self-renunciation (*nyasa*) that all of us recognize the moral grandeur and unique character of what Mother Theresa has done for the dying and destitute in Calcutta. This point is important because it shows clearly that it is within the mind of the individual, who strives for the good, that we must look for the basis of the good life.

What then is the good which man should follow and what is it good for? The nature of a good life is still a burning question both for us and for the society in which we live today. Few people would disagree that the respect for ethical values has been steadily eroded in the last hundred years or more. As Einstein wrote to a friend in Zurich during the First World War:

> How is it possible that this culture-loving era could be so monstrously amoral? More and more I come to value charity and love of one's fellow being above everything else... All our lauded technological progress—our very civilization—is like the axe in the hand of the pathological criminal.[3]

Twenty-nine years later, in 1946, he was writing in America to another friend, the psychiatrist, Dr Otto Juliusburger, who had, like himself, escaped from Nazi Germany to the States:

> I believe that the horrifying deterioration in the ethical conduct of people today stems primarily from the mechanization and dehumanization of our lives—a disastrous by-product of the development of the scientific and technical mentality. *Nostra culpa!* I don't see any way to tackle this disastrous shortcoming. Man grows cold faster than the planet he inhabits.[4]

It is clear, then, that our society still lacks a firm and clear basis for morals and needs one ever more urgently. It therefore seems worth-while considering what Yoga has to say on the subject.

It has sometimes been maintained that there is no ethical teaching in the Upanishads or in the later Yoga classics. A well-known Buddhist scholar, Mrs Rhys Davis, was provocatively promulgating this view about sixty years ago, and Dr Shastri was at pains to refute it. In fact, even a cursory reading of the Yoga classics shows it to be complete nonsense. Many of you will remember the well known verses from the *Katha Upanishad* (I.ii.1-2):

> One thing is the good, while another is the pleasant. These two, serving different ends, bind men; happiness comes to him, who, of these, chooses the good; whoso chooses the pleasant forfeits the true end.
>
> Both the good and the pleasant approach the mortal; the intelligent man examines and distinguishes them; for the wise man prefers the good to the pleasant; while the ignorant man chooses the pleasant for the sake of his body.[5]

The later works on Yoga are no less specific about the importance of the good life. In the second chapter of the *Bhagavad Gita*, Arjuna is told that, as a *Kshatriya*—a warrior prince—it is his duty to fight in a just cause and that he will incur sin if he does not carry it out. In the third chapter Arjuna asks Krishna what it is that drags a man on to commit sin, even against his better judgement, and is told that it is desire, born of the energy of passion, which is the source of all sin. Greedy and insatiable, arising from the senses and the mind, it clouds our vision, as smoke conceals the light of a fire. The reason for restraining the raw desires of the senses by self-control is that they delude us and destroy our capacity for thinking clearly. They are, in the words of the *Gita*, 'destructive of knowledge and wisdom'. It is only by gaining mastery of our mind that we can conquer this enemy within the citadel of our own personality.[6]

All this teaching makes clear that it is we ourselves who should have the greatest interest in cultivating the good life, because it is primarily we ourselves who suffer the consequences either of doing or not doing so. It is not a question of some abstract social ideal, like the Utilitarians' doctrine of the greatest good of the greatest number. It is a question of our own future life and whether we are building the basis for our own future happiness and progress or the reverse!

Nowadays it is fashionable among Western philosophers and thinkers to regard ethics as having no rational basis. The argument (spoken or unspoken) runs something like this:

> There is no such thing as the absolute good. It is all a question of value judgements and these vary from individual to individual. Different societies have different ideas of what is right and wrong, and even more so do individuals within societies. Therefore this vague idea of goodness has no real basis in any clear notion of what the good is. Everything is relative.

It is no wonder, with this idea floating around, that the standard of decency and morality in society at large has deteriorated so appallingly in the present century. In the West, as the old Christian ideals of good and evil have been eroded, so the levels of crime and violence and inhuman doctrines, justifying genocide or the use of bombs, poison gas or napalm against innocent civilian populations, have increased. But the idea that virtue is only concerned with value judgements and is without a firm basis is an eloquent testimony to the blind ignorance prevailing in the world at large. In Vedanta the basis for the practice of virtue is absolutely clear and its object is also clear.

Furthermore, whatever the thinkers may say, the ordinary man in the street has an innate sense of the existence of right and wrong and of the individual's responsibility for his own decisions. Each and every individual feels that he has freedom of choice and that he is in some sense accountable for what he chooses to do. This is not a question of crime and punishment in the judicial sense. The law is a very blunt instrument and many people who are guilty go scot-free because there is no adequate evidence to convict them. But they cannot avoid their moral responsibility. What one has chosen to do freely and consciously is part of what one is now, and one is accountable for it. One is not, of course, accountable in this sense for all the desires which arise in one's mind; it is only those desires which one has chosen and actually willed to act upon, which one can be said to be guilty of. That guiltiness is felt by the person themselves and is something of which they feel ashamed.

This is an interesting and significant aspect of our everyday recognition of good and evil, because it shows that in following one or the other, we are actually in some senses divided against ourselves. It is of course implicit in our feeling of freedom that we should be able to choose between opposites. Otherwise we are not free. But there is also a sense in which, as the *Gita* says, it is only reluctantly that we give way to our lower desires, as if compelled by force. The great Jewish philosopher, Spinoza, spoke about passion as something which arose in the mind, almost like an alien force, in whose hands we were passively swept along, willingly or unwillingly abrogating our own control of the mind and letting the desire take over from our wiser self. The *Bhagavad Gita* says the same:

> The mind which yields to the roving senses, carries away his knowledge, as the wind carries away a ship on water.
>
> The senses forcibly carry away the mind, even while the individual is striving to control them.[7]

People like to castigate the Creator of the world, maintaining that if he is the source of all the good that is in the world, he must also be the source of all the evil that is in the world. But a god who allows man freedom of choice, albeit within certain limits, must provide the possibility of the wrong choices being made. Dr Shastri says in his book, *Wisdom from the East*, that there is no devil but the soul which is still in spiritual ignorance and hasn't yet learnt wisdom. When we think about the careers of Hitler or Stalin, we can well understand this. There are individuals who, like Iago, deliberately choose to adopt the creed 'Evil be thou my good', but their fate is unenviable. In the sixteenth chapter of the *Gita*, the characteristics of good and evil men are described, and it is pointed out that the choice of evil leads to darker ignorance and to what may be called hell, which is, as much as anything, a state of darkness of the mind and certainly a state of bondage, while the good life leads to knowledge and wisdom and the freeing of the soul from the shackles of ignorance. But the good life is not the final end of human life, nor is it intended to be a permanent resting place for the human soul; it is a preparation for enlightenment.

In the *Katha Upanishad* we are told that:

> He who has not desisted from evil ways, who is not tranquil, and who has not concentrated his mind, cannot reach the Self through right knowledge.[8]

This verse shows clearly the Vedantic view about the purpose of virtue—about what the good life is good for. It is the means to enable the mind to acquire wisdom and ultimately, to know the spiritual truth.

This is an important point. Vedanta does not regard virtue or the good life as an end in itself. It is a means to an end. Only when the mind has been brought under control and is devoted to the higher values can we begin to escape from the strait-jacket of crude individualism and self-centredness and awaken to the understanding that we are all members one of another, that the good of others is also in a real sense our good—that we are all children of one God.

There is also a danger in thinking that virtue is an end in itself. As the *Katha Upanishad* indicates, it too can become a binding force. In other words, it may lead man from one form of egoity to another, from one sin to another, if we do not realize what we are doing. There is a saying of a Chinese sage which puts this pithily: 'Your goody-goody men are the thieves of virtue'.

In our own Christian tradition, we recognize that virtue too can increase our sense of self-importance and individualism, as it did in the case of the Pharisee who had the feeling 'I thank God that I am not as other men are'. It is a form of subtle egoity, well depicted by T S Eliot in his play *Murder in the Cathedral*, where the Tempter comes to Thomas à Becket offering him every worldly advantage in terms of wealth and success, which Thomas indignantly refuses. The Tempter leaves him with the words:

> I leave you then to your higher vices,
> Which will have to be paid for at higher prices!

Among the seven deadly sins, not the least is pride, the sense of being in a position to despise those who are not as good as you are.

The ethical ideal in Vedanta is a means to an end, and that end is nothing else but self-knowledge. The basis of all morality, as the British philosopher F H Bradley realized, was the need for self-realization. The reason why the mind is divided against itself when we take moral decisions, is that we are choosing between the lower and the higher self. We are choosing whether to follow the baser instincts of the mind—which is effectively to hand over control of our destiny to the blind forces of nature—or to take our stand on reason and wisdom and to follow our better self. As the *Gita* makes clear, evil is that which leads to darker ignorance. In the sixteenth chapter there is a graphic description of the two choices: the life of the higher self (the good life, as we should call it), and the life of the lower self. And it is said clearly there that the life of the lower self leads to bondage and ultimately to the hell, which is the region of darker ignorance, whereas the virtuous life of the higher self leads one to freedom and enlightenment.

In moral decisions we get the feeling of what we ought to do, whether we decide to do it or not; it seems like a theoretical ideal, but this ideal self is our real self, dimly sensed through the faculty which we call conscience. The pursuit of the good life is a constant process of self-transcendence and self-realization.

Seen from this point of view, it is clear that a sin does not characterize any member of a particular list of specified acts, like a criminal offence, but involves in the real sense the state of mind and heart in which such an act is performed. Swami Rama Tirtha puts it in a form of a vivid analogy: the same number differs in its effect according to whether it is to the left or right of the decimal point. On the left it leads to an increase in the value of the number by which it is multiplied, while on the right it actually reduces the value of the result. What would not be a sin to a moral baby can become a great sin when perpetrated by one who knows a good deal better what he is doing. But this doesn't mean that there is anything arbitrary about virtue and vice. It is a question of whether it leads to greater self-transcendence or not, or (to put it more simply) whether it follows the guidance of our higher or lower nature. To kill someone is certainly wrong, but we cannot ascribe the same moral opprobrium to those who plotted to assassinate Hitler in 1944 or to someone who ends the life of someone whom they love who is suffering from a painful and incurable disease, as we do to someone who abducts and kills a child to extort money or to gratify their lust.

Desire may be the great enemy of man when it is an unbridled force within the mind, and we can well understand the *Gita* speaking of it as the source of all sins. But, when harnessed and sublimated, it is also the source of great creativity. The fact is that desire is the manifestation of the life-force, and, as our teacher so often told us, the life-force and love-force are one and the same. Operating on the plane of the senses, the instincts are blind and serve the purposes of Nature, which are careless of the interests and concerns of the individual. He who abandons himself to following his raw instincts truly becomes a demon in human form, as the *Gita* says.

Julian Huxley maintained in his writings that, with the advent of man, the process of evolution, which we see proceeding blindly in Nature, moves onto a higher plane and becomes self-conscious. It is man himself, through his conscious efforts, who becomes the controller of his own future evolution, and he does so by harnessing the love-force, which is the life-force, in the search for self-realization and self-transcendence. Man's ultimate quest is for true self-knowledge and it will only end when he has discovered his true nature. This is the message of Vedanta.

Swami Rama Tirtha tells the story of a Victorian clergyman in the Church of England who read about the deaths of Darwin and T H Huxley and began to think about their fate and to wonder whether they had gone to heaven or hell.[9] He said to himself: 'These people did not commit any crimes, and didn't appear to be sinners. But they didn't believe in the Bible or Christ and they certainly weren't Christians. They must have gone to hell'. But then he found that he couldn't make up his mind that that was right. 'They were good men', he said to himself. 'They did some good in the world and certainly didn't deserve hell! But in that case, where did they go?'

Thinking it over in this way, he fell asleep and dreamt a wonderful dream. He saw that he himself had died and had been taken up to the highest heaven, where he found all the people who used to go to Church with him. After a time he asked one of the celestial attendants about the scientists, Darwin and Huxley, and was told that they were in the lowest hell. He asked whether he could be allowed to pay just a short visit to see them there and perhaps to explain to them the heinous crime they had committed in not believing to the letter what was said in the Bible.

After some inevitable fuss and trouble over such an irregular request, permission was eventually obtained from higher authority and he was given a first-class railway ticket valid for the journey to the seventh Hell. (Swami Rama adds here that it was natural that he should dream of travelling by rail, because he was used to it from his waking life.) It was a long journey, because there were many intermediate stations between the highest heaven and the lowest hell, and at each stop things got worse and worse. By the time he got to the lowest-hell-but-one, he could hardly bear it. The heat was insufferable and such a stench was coming through the carriage window that, in spite of covering his face and nose with his handkerchief, he almost passed out. All the time there was the sound of weeping, crying and the gnashing of teeth by a multitude of voices. He was by this time thoroughly repenting his decision to come, but the train went on and soon he was astonished to feel the train stopping again at a relatively silent station and to hear the station loudspeaker announcing for the convenience of passengers 'All passengers for the lowest Hell alight here! This is the terminus'.

He could hardly believe his senses, because there was no smell and the temperature was mild and pleasant. Everything looked clean and inviting. He had expected the lowest hell to be worse than any of the others, but he found a place which in some ways almost rivalled the highest heaven. There were magnificent gardens full of sweet-scented flowers, over which wafted fragrant breezes. He saw a tall man and called out to him and when he turned he recognized that it was Huxley. They shook hands and, after a few words of introduction, he asked Huxley if this was indeed the lowest hell. 'Oh yes', replied Huxley, 'it undoubtedly is. And very nasty it was when we got here! You weren't wrong in expecting what you did. It was the most undesirable place that one could conceive of. For instance, over there were swamps of filthy water; and over here was a mountain of dung. We also had areas of burning sand and molten iron. But after we arrived here we gradually set to and used the water to cool the iron and by exercising our ingenuity managed to start making some useful implements out of it. We found that the dung was invaluable for manuring the soil and produced the wonderfully fertile gardens which you now see. It took time, of course, but everything you see here now was produced in that way.'

Swami Rama Tirtha comments on this story that the lowest hell already contained all the materials necessary to create the highest heaven. All that was necessary was to rearrange them and use them wisely. In the same way, he says, we can make this world a hell for ourselves by ignorance and stupidity, but we can also make a heaven out of it. You cannot destroy the energy of Nature which is in you, which, if followed blindly, leads one to commit innumerable sins and follies, but you can use it constructively to create something really worth-while, to transform your personality and discover the good life.

NOTES

In the Notes which follow, all the references to the lectures and writings of Swami Rama Tirtha refer to The Complete Works published as *In Woods of God-Realization*, 8th Edition, by the Rama Tirtha Pratisthan, Sarnath Varanasi, India. Vol. 1. 1956; Vol. 2. 1957; Vol. 3. 1957; and Vol. 7. (Notebooks) 1990.

1
The Relevance of Yoga for Modern Western Society

1. Erwin Schrödinger, *Mind and Matter*, Cambridge University Press, 1959, pp 53-54.
2. Aldous Huxley, *The Perennial Philosophy*, Chatto & Windus, London, 1946.
3. Schrödinger, op. cit., pp 54-55.

2
The Religion of the Future

1. Hogarth Press, 1928.
2. From the lecture on 'The Secret of Success' given in Tokyo in October 1902. Published in *In Woods of God-Realization*, Volume 1, pp 113-122.
3. Sir John Woodroffe, *The World as Power: Reality*, Ganesh & Co, Madras, 1921, pp 6-7.
4. H P Shastri, *The Heart of the Eastern Mystical Teaching*, Shanti Sadan, London, p 56.
5. From a lecture on 'Religion' delivered at the Shanti Ashrama, Muttra (Mathura), published in *In Woods of God-Realization*, Volume 2, pp 174-175.
6. From 'The Present Needs of India' in *In Woods of God-Realization*, Volume 3, pp 175-176.

7   Cited by J W N Sullivan in *Aspects of Science* (First Series), Jonathan Cape, London, 1927, p 52.

8   See 'The Spirit of Yajna' published in *In Woods of God-Realization*, Volume 2, p 209.

9   Op. cit., pp 210-211.

10 *In Woods of God-Realization*, Volume 2, p xi.

11 See 'The Secret of Success', *In Woods of God-Realization*, Volume 1, pp 122-154.

12 'Informal Talks', *In Woods of God-Realization*, Volume 3, pp 158-159.

13 From Swami Rama's note on 'The Present Needs of India', sent to Swami Shivagan Acharya of Shanti Ashrama, Muttra (Mathura). *In Woods of God-Realization*, Volume 3, pp 176-177.

14 Max Planck 'Religion and Natural Science' in *A Scientific Autobiography and Other Papers*, Williams & Norgate, London, 1950, p 187.

15 'The Law of Life Eternal', *In Woods of God-Realization*, Volume 1, p 230.

4
The Inner Enquiry

1   M V Waterhouse *Training the Mind through Yoga*, Shanti Sadan, 1964, p 68 and p 105. The author was one of the earliest pupils of Dr H P Shastri after his arrival in England in 1929 and succeeded him as Warden of Shanti Sadan in 1956.

2   Bertrand Russell *Portraits from Memory*, pp 206-207; cp. *The Conquest of Happiness*, pp 76-77.

5
Attentive Silence

1. Lionel Giles *Musings of a Chinese Mystic*, John Murray, London, 1947, p 49.
2. Cited in J Angelet-Hustache *Master Eckhart and the Rhineland Mystics*, Harper Torchbooks, New York, 1957, p 60.
3. *Taittiriya Upanishad*, II.4.1.

6
The Meaning of Life

1. Swami Rama Tirtha's lecture on 'Maya or the When and Why of the World', *In Woods of God-Realization*, Volume 3, pp 26-29.
2. M V Waterhouse *Training the Mind through Yoga*, Shanti Sadan, 1964, p 132.
3. Swami Rama Tirtha *In Woods of God-Realization*, Volume 2, p 164.

7
No Time Like the Present

1. Bertrand Russell *Human Knowledge: Its Scope and Limits*, George Allen and Unwin, 1948, pp 19-20.
2. Op. cit., p 22.
3. Erwin Schrödinger *Mind and Matter*, Cambridge University Press, 1959, p 62.
4. H P Shastri *The Heart of the Eastern Mystical Teaching*, Shanti Sadan, 1948, p 205.
5. Op. cit., p 153.

6 Swami Vidyaranya *Panchadashi: A Vedanta Classic,* translated by H P Shastri, Shanti Sadan, 2nd edition 1965, Chapter VI, verses 49-50.
7 Op. cit., Chapter I, verses 6-8.
8 *Henry IV*, 5.4.81-83.
9 Swami Rama Tirtha *In Woods of God-Realization,* Volume 3, p 25.
10 Op. cit. pp 26-29.
11 Bertrand Russell *History of Western Philosophy*, pp 86-87.
12 Swami Rama Tirtha *In Woods of God-Realization,* Volume 3, p 35.
13 Op. cit., p 36.
14 Op. cit., pp 36-37.

8
Exchanging Complements

1 Niels Bohr, *Atomic Physics and the Description of Nature,* Cambridge University Press, 1934, p 2. Cited in Fritzhof Capra, *The Tao of Physics*, Wildwood House, London, 1975, p 55.
2 Werner Heisenberg, *Physics and Philosophy,* George Allen and Unwin, London, 1963, p 42. Cited by Capra, *The Tao of Physics*, p 51.
3 Capra, *The Tao of Physics* (see note 1), pp 54-55.
4 Capra, op. cit., p 16.
5 Sir John Woodroffe *World as Power: Reality*, Ganesha & Co, 1921, pp 24-25.
6 Swami Rama Tirtha *In Woods of God-Realization,* Volume 3, p 50.
7 Op. cit., p 38.

8 Op. cit., pp 28-29.

9 *Brihadaranyaka Upanishad*, 3.4.2.

9
A Good Koan

1 *Recollections of Wittgenstein*, Edited by Rush Rhees, Oxford University Press, 1984, p 3.

2 Op. cit., pp 82-83.

3 Katha Upanishad, 1.2.2.

4 Bertrand Russell *Human Knowledge: Its Scope and Limits*, George Allen and Unwin, 1948, pp 415-416.

5 F H Bradley *Ethical Studies*, 2nd edition 1927, Oxford University Press, p 313.

6 Op. cit., from Note on page 324.

7 *Recollections of Wittgenstein*, op. cit., p 83.

8 A N Whitehead *Adventures of Ideas*, Pelican Books, 1942, p 305.

9 Op. cit., p 306.

10 Op. cit., p 307.

11 See, for instance, Helen Dukas and Banesh Hoffmann, *Albert Einstein: The Human Side*, Princeton University Press, 1989, pp 66-71.

12 Whitehead, op. cit., pp 336 and 292-293.

13 Op. cit., p 337.

10

Reconciling the Contradictions

1. *Hamlet*, 2.2. 289-313.
2. *Upadesha Sahasri* XVI. 44.
3. David Hume *A Treatise on Human Understanding*, Open Court Publishing Co., Chicago, 1927, pp 246-247.
4. Op. cit., p 247.
5. Op. cit., p 263.
6. *Upadesha Sahasri*, XVI. 31.
7. *King Richard II*, 5.5.31-41.

11

An Example of Greatness

1. One is reminded of the recent reprimand suffered by the present-day Lord Chancellor, Lord Mackay, another devout member of a small Scottish Church which had seceded from the Presbyterian Church, for attending the Memorial Services of two Roman Catholic colleagues.
2. See, for instance, *In Woods of God-Realization*, Volume 2, pp 277-278.
3. Matthew 6.25-34; Luke 12.22-34.
4. By the word 'particular' here, Faraday, of course, means 'made up of particles'.
5. Cited in J G Crowther *British Scientists of the Nineteenth Century*, Kegan Paul, 1935, pp 110-111.

12
Seeing is Believing

1. Cited in Kenneth Walker, *The Story of Medicine*, Hutchinson, London, 1954, p 312.
2. Matthew 9.20-22; Mark 5.25-34; Luke 8.43-48.
3. Mark 10.46-52.
4. Luke 17.11-19.
5. Mark 9.17-29.
6. H P Shastri *Teachings from the Bhagavad Gita*, Shanti Sadan, p 83.
7. Figure 13 is reproduced with acknowledgements to Time-Life Inc.
8. *Panchadashi: A Treatise on Advaita Metaphysics* by Swami Vidyaranya. Translated by H P Shastri, Shanti Sadan, London, 1965.
9. James Frazer (1908) 'A New Visual Illusion of Direction'. British Journal of Psychology. Volume 2, part 3, January 1908, pp 307-320 +Plates I-IX.
10. Bertrand Russell *Human Knowledge: Its Scope and Limits*, George Allen and Unwin, 1948, p 174.
11. Op. cit., p 172.
12. Op. cit., p 172.
13. This point has been considered further in the earlier chapters on 'Exchanging Complements' and 'Reconciling the Contradictions'.
14. Russell, op. cit., p 109.
15. Op. cit., p 110.
16. Op. cit., p 162.
17. Op. cit., p 170.

18 Op. cit., p 110.
19 Swami Rama Tirtha *In Woods of God-Realization*, Volume 3, p 92.
20 Bertrand Russell *The Conquest of Happiness*, George Allen and Unwin, London, 8th Impression, 1943, pp 76-77.
21 Swami Rama Tirtha, op. cit., p 92.
22 Op. cit., pp 92-93.
23 H P Shastri, Paper on 'Mental Health', dated March 1949.
24 H P Shastri *Meditation: Its Theory and Practice*, Shanti Sadan, p 19.

13

Tolstoi's Questions

1 It should be remembered that earlier in the year, the peaceful, pro-democracy, protest demonstration, led by the Chinese students, had begun on April 15th 1989. This led to the Chinese Government declaring martial law on May 20th and to the brutal crushing of the protesters by the so-called People's Liberation Army on June 3rd and 4th. Hundreds of the participants were killed and an estimated 10,000 injured. The arrest of many of those involved was followed by summary trials and executions and a strict clamp-down on the Chinese Press, amid widespread international condemnation. In Eastern Europe, Soviet-style Communism was clearly in rapid decline from 1989 onwards and finally collapsed by the end of 1991.

2 *Bhagavad Gita*, III.38-39.

3 Op. cit., V.22.

4   Tolstoi's words are quoted from the 1902 translation by N H Doyle used in Stefan Zweig's *The Living Thoughts of Tolstoi*, 3rd edition, 1945, Cassell, p 23.
5   Op. cit., pp 24-25.
6   Op. cit., p 25.
7   Op. cit., p 25.
8   Op. cit., pp 26-27.
9   Op. cit., p 27.
10 Op. cit., p 28.
11 Op. cit., p 28.
12 Op. cit., pp 29-30.
13 Op. cit., p 31.
14 Op. cit., pp 32-33.
15 Op. cit., pp 35-36.
16 Op. cit., pp 37-38.
17 Op. cit., pp 38-39.
18 Op. cit., pp 39-40.
19 Op. cit., p 42.
20 Cited by Bertrand Russell in *Roads to Freedom*, Unwin Books, London, 1966, pp 41-42.
21 Russell, op. cit., p 42.
22 H P Shastri *The Heart of the Eastern Mystical Teaching*, Shanti Sadan, 1948, p 257.
23 Shastri, op. cit., p 228.

14
Living in Truth

1. Václav Havel *Living in Truth*, translated by Paul Wilson, Faber & Faber, London, 1987.
2. Václav Havel *Letters to Olga*, translated by Paul Wilson, Faber & Faber, London, 1988, pp 23-24.
3. Op. cit., p 31.
4. Op. cit., p 33.
5. Op. cit., p 48.
6. Op. cit., p 48.
7. Op. cit., p 57.
8. Op. cit., p 61.
9. Op. cit., p 62.
10. The words are, in fact, spoken by Edgar, the legitimate and honourable son of Gloucester, who has been maligned and disinherited by the machinations of his illegitimate and unscrupulous half-brother, Edmund. Edgar, disguising himself as a mad beggar, returns to help the father who has turned against him, but who has, through ill-fortune, been blinded and turned out of his home by Edmund, the son he trusted, in league with Lear's treacherous daughters, Goneril and Reagan. *King Lear*, Act 4 Scene 2.
11. Václav Havel *Letters to Olga*, op. cit., pp 347-348.
12. Op. cit., pp 349-350.
13. Op. cit., pp 351-352.
14. Op. cit., pp 352-353.
15. Op. cit., pp 353-354.
16. Op. cit., p 355.

17   Op. cit., pp 356-357.
18   Op. cit., pp 358-359.
19   Op. cit., p 360.
20   Shri Shankara's *Direct Experience of Reality*, verses 78 and 87.

15
Learning from Experience

1   Cited in *Arnold J. Toynbee: A Life* by Professor William McNeill, published by Oxford University Press, 1989, p 225.
2   McNeill, op. cit., p 224.
3   Arnold Toynbee *A Study of History: the One-Volume Illustrated Edition*, a new edition revised and abridged by the author and Jane Caplan, Thames & Hudson, 1972, p 477.
4   The material in this lecture on both Toynbee's life and thought is largely taken from the excellent recently published biography by Professor William McNeill. See note 1 above.
5   McNeill, op. cit., p 28.
6   McNeill, op. cit., p 30.
7   McNeill, op. cit., p 94.
8   McNeill, op. cit., p 96.
9   McNeill, op. cit., p 95ff. Those who are interested in finding out more about some of the other leading ideas in Toynbee's great work can choose between reading the original book in ten volumes (Vols I-VI, Oxford University Press, 1934-1939; Vols VII-X, 1954; Vol XII *Reconsiderations*, 1961) or the beautifully illustrated one-

volume reduction which Toynbee himself published at the end of his life (1972), which is now published in paperback by Thames and Hudson (1988). See note 3 above.

10 McNeill, op. cit., p 156.

11 McNeill, op. cit., pp 43-44.

12 McNeill, op. cit., p 44.

13 McNeill, op. cit., p 90.

14 This refers to the suicide of his son Tony in 1939.

15 McNeill, op. cit., p 144.

16 McNeill, op. cit., p 176.

17 McNeill, op. cit., p 185.

18 McNeill, op. cit., pp 187-189.

19 McNeill, op. cit., p 233.

20 McNeill, op. cit., pp 219-220.

21 McNeill, op. cit., p 221.

22 McNeill, op. cit., p 256.

23 Toynbee *A Study of History*, 1972, op. cit., p 346.

24 Toynbee, op. cit., pp 497-498.

25 'The ineffable is accomplished here.'

16

The Mind in Society

1. *Bhagavad Gita*, III.35.

2. Swami Rama Tirtha *In Woods of God-Realization*, Volume 7, p 153.

3. H P Shastri *The Heart of the Eastern Mystical Teaching*, Shanti Sadan, London, 3rd edition 1979, pp 48-49.

4. Bertrand Russell *The Conquest of Happiness*, George Allen and Unwin, London, 1943, p 220.

5. Cited in Dukas and Hoffman (eds) *Albert Einstein: The Human Side*, Princeton University Press, 1989, p 82. See also chapter 19, ref. 4.

6. Bertrand Russell *Portraits from Memory*, George Allen and Unwin, London, 1958, pp 168-172.

7. Op. cit., p 172.

8. William McNeill *Arnold J. Toynbee: A Life*, Oxford University Press, 1989, p 221.

9. Russell *Portraits from Memory*, op. cit., pp 170-171.

10. *Bhagavad Gita*, III.12.

11. Op. cit., III.16.

12. Op. cit., III.11.

13. H P Shastri *Teachings from the Bhagavad Gita*, Shanti Sadan, London, 2nd edition 1945, p 16.

17
A Critical Ailment

1. *The Times*, 20th November 1993.
2. *The Times*, 2nd December 1993, p 20.
3. From Swami Rama Tirtha's lecture on 'Criticism and Universal Love', *In Woods of God-Realization*, Volume 2, p 234.
4. *St Matthew*, 22.37-39.
5. Lionel Giles *The Book of Mencius*, John Murray, London, 1945, p 75.
6. Luke 6.37-45.
7. Bertrand Russell *The Conquest of Happiness*, George Allen and Unwin, London, 1943, pp 85-86.
8. Op. cit., p 86.
9. Quoted from Edward Holmes' *Life of Mozart*, the first English biography of the composer, originally published in 1845. Edited by Christopher Hogwood, The Folio Society, London 1991.
10. *Mathnavi of Jalaluddin Rumi*, translated by R A Nicholson, Volume 2, Luzac and Co, London, 1934, pp 111-129 *seriatim*.
11. Russell *The Conquest of Happiness*, pp 93-94.
12. Op. cit., pp 94-95.
13. Swami Rama Tirtha, Volume 2, op. cit., pp 229-230.
14. Op. cit., p 233.
15. Swami Rama Tirtha *In Woods of God-Realization*, Volume 2, p 94.
16. Op. cit., pp 233-234.

18

Time for Thought

1. Stephen Hawking *A Brief History of Time*, Bantam Press, London, 1988, p 20.

2. Bertrand Russell *The ABC of Relativity*, Kegan Paul, London, 1925, p 7.

3. Op. cit., p 1.

4. Op. cit., p 5.

5. Hawking, op. cit., pp 29-30.

6. Op. cit., p 33.

7. Bertrand Russell *Human Knowledge: Its Scope and Limits* George Allen and Unwin, London, 1948, pp 290-291.

8. Hawking, op. cit., p 33.

9. Max Planck *A Scientific Autobiography* Williams and Norgate, London, 1950, pp 46-47.

10. John 8.56-58.

11. *Exodus* 3.14.

12. *Bhagavad Gita*, IX.6-7,10,13.

13. Op. cit., XVIII.61.

14. Psalm 46.10.

19
Searching for the Good Life

1. Robert Skidelsky, *John Maynard Keynes: I. Hopes Betrayed 1883-1920*, Macmillan London, 1992.

2. Paul Deussen, *The Philosophy of the Upanishads*, Dover Publications, New York, 1966, p 364.

3. Letter of 6th December 1917 to Heinrich Zangger, cited from *Albert Einstein: The Human Side*, selected and edited by Helen Dukas and Banesh Hoffman, Princeton University Press, 1989, p 88.

4. Op. cit., p 82. From letter of 29th September 1947. The reader may remember that part of this comment of Einstein's was also quoted in an earlier lecture in this book (p 284). It can be compared with the strikingly similar point made by another great scientist, Erwin Schrödinger, in the passage quoted on p. 29 at the beginning of the lecture on the Vedantic View of the World.

5. *Katha Upanishad* 1.2.1-2.

6. *Bhagavad Gita* III.36-43.

7. *Gita* II.67 and II.60.

8. *Katha Upanishad* 1.2.24.

9. Swami Rama Tirtha *In Woods of God-Realization*, Volume 1, pp 92-95.

INDEX

Aaron, 30, 31

Abbott, Benjamin, 152, 155, 157-158

Absolute *see* consciousness, absolute

absolute time, 101, 316, 318, 320, 325

accountable, 81, 342

action, 46, 59, 67, 131, 144-145, 159, 167, 179, 203-206, 223, 229, 256, 290, 338; and reaction, 144-145; fruits of, 5, 29, 43, 67, 156, 159, 290

actor (in play), 9

Addison, Joseph, 319

Adhyatma Yoga described, 5

admiration, 263, 302

Advaita, 5, 8-9, 11, 21, 90

aesthetic perfection, 128

agitation, 49

agnostic, 112, 269

ahimsa, 231

ailments, 298

Akbar, 189

Allah, 17

Allnut, B W, 235

ambition, 31, 32, 215-216, 266, 289

Ames, Adelbert, 190

Ampère, André-Marie, 156

anaesthesia, 174

anandamaya kosha, 176

annihilation through death, 277

antahkarana, 39

antinomies (Kantian), 329

antisocial, 283

anubhava, 109
anxiety, 67-68, 283
appearance, 37, 39, 105, 106, 109-111, 127-130, 136, 138-140, 145, 194
approximation, 64
Aquinas, Thomas, 121
Archimedes, 148, 282
argument and debate, 64
Aristarchus, 241
Aristotle, 43, 121, 240, 242
Arjuna, 68, 163, 234, 276-277, 286, 333, 340
Arnold, Matthew, 334
asceticism, 18
astronaut, 238-239, 322
atheism, 14, 27
Atman, 90-93, 143-145, 201, 249-250, 260
Atma Bodha, 238
atomic theory, 108, 166, 168
Augustine, 121, 216, 312-313
authoritarian, 44, 62
authority and authorities, 13, 16, 19-23, 25, 42, 44, 62-63, 119, 161, 229, 240, 242, 251, 274, 348; Catholic, 242
automaton, 74, 77, 80
autosuggestion, 209
avidya, 130, 243
Baird, John Logie, 44
Bakunin, Mikhail, 228-230
beauty, 79-80, 119, 127-131, 171, 279
Beckett, Samuel, 239, 247
Beethoven, Ludwig van, 27, 46

behaviour, 73, 104-105, 120, 122, 135, 202, 206, 296
behaviourism, 77
belief, 2, 26, 49, 62, 170, 177-179, 186, 189, 193, 199-207, 214, 218-219, 294, 304
believers, 223, 224
benevolence, 233
Bentham, Jeremy, 334, 336-337
Bergson, Henri, 3
Berkeley, George, 101, 137, 143-145
Bhagavad Gita see *Gita*
Bible, 22-23, 151, 348
bliss, 41, 80, 91, 93, 110, 130, 281
Bohr, Niels, 101, 103, 104-105, 107
Bolshevik, 228
bombs, 282, 342
bondage, 83, 288, 310, 344, 346
Bottom (in *A Midsummer Night's Dream*), 141
Bradley, F H, vii, 8, 81-82, 89, 106, 108, 110, 111, 121, 123-125, 145, 329, 345
Brahman, 249, 260
Braid, James, 173
brain, 88, 184, 190, 192, 194-196, 198, 233, 278
Brande, Wiliam Thomas, 160
breakdown, 267, 279
Bream, Julian, 63
breath, 50, 54-55, 59, 69-70, 229, 335
Breuer, Joseph, 175, 178
Buddha and Buddhism, 9, 15, 22-24, 108, 231, 273   *see also* Zen
burying thoughts, 208
Butler, Samuel, 134, 296

capacities, 263
capitalism, 227
Capra, Fritzhof, 103, 354
Cartesian *see* Descartes, René
catch-phrases, 262
catchy tune, 293
causal sheath, 176
causation, 92, 93, 95-97, 106, 108, 110, 113, 200, 312, 329, 332-333
cerebral cortex, 194
Chairman Mao, 30
challenge, 239, 268, 291
change, 2, 12, 24, 32, 35, 91, 105, 165, 179, 189, 193, 219, 226, 228, 234, 248, 273, 281, 284, 287, 317, 318, 320, 323, 334
Charcot, Jean-Martin, 174, 175, 178
charity, 18, 169, 170, 298, 339
Charles II, 176
Charter 77, 244
Charvakas, 5, 14
Che Guevara, 30
chidabhasa *see* consciousness, relative
Christ, 22, 23, 124, 132, 151, 154, 163, 177, 234, 235, 286, 300, 348
Christian, 14, 22, 24-25, 162, 163, 214, 223, 234, 269, 271, 273, 286, 294, 299, 300, 334, 341, 345
Chuang Tzu, 64
Church, 20, 27, 29, 151, 152, 163, 170, 223, 233, 234, 265, 269, 295, 315, 347, 348, 356
Cicero, 241
circulation, 278, 290, 306

circumstances, 162, 166, 194, 219, 221, 234, 238, 243, 247, 248, 250-251, 267

civilization, 218, 234, 267-269, 290, 306; seven stages of, 269

clocks, 100, 200, 315-316, 324, 330

coherence criterion of truth, 200-201

Coleridge, Samuel Taylor, 261

Common Prayer, Book of, 236

communion, 18, 170, 270, 271, 277

complementarity, 105, 107

computer, 73, 74, 77, 292, 293

concentration, 4, 25, 49-50, 55-56, 59, 72, 308

concept, 97, 122, 201, 238, 296, 330

conception, 72, 101, 123, 168, 247, 280, 287, 320

conflict, 8, 19, 125, 239, 243, 271

conformation of appearance to reality, 127-130

Confucius, 230

consciousness, absolute (beyond mind), 9-13, 26, 36-40, 48-50, 71, 76-77, 79, 89-95, 97, 99, 110-114, 120, 125, 126, 130, 140, 143-145, 162, 200-201, 209, 243, 256-258, 260, 274, 277; beyond relativity, 330-333, 341; consciousness, relative, (a reflection in mind), 39-40, 50, 89-91, 113, 115, 138, 140, 173, 213, 276; states of *see* mind, states of

conservation of matter, 102

consideration, 11, 35, 252, 284

contemplation *see* meditation

contempt *see* habit

continuum, 324-326, 331, 333

contours, 180, 184-185

contradiction, 50, 101, 107, 123-125, 133, 144, 224-225

conventions, 8, 122, 123

conviction, 16, 51, 92, 128, 162, 218, 225

Copernicus, 241, 319
correction, 251, 318
corruption, 300, 304
creed, 18, 25, 27, 343
Crimean War, 216
Cripps, Stafford, 334
criticism, 143, 214, 227, 232, 241, 274, 292, 296-297, 300-301, 303, 308-310
crystal, 89, 315
daily life, conduct in, 54, 289
Darwin, Charles, 47, 348
Davy, Humphry, 153-160, 162
Dawkins, Richard, 293
De La Rive, Auguste, 157-158
death, 12, 14, 38, 44-45, 141, 173, 176, 215, 222-223, 225, 235, 264-265, 270, 276, 277
decency, 341
dehumanization, 285, 339
Delphic oracle, 239
democracy, 213
Descartes, René, 100, 137, 143, 145, 201, 240
desire, 32, 43, 45, 63, 94, 126, 130, 142, 154, 205, 212, 213, 218, 232, 243, 289, 337, 340, 343, 347
despair, 103, 132, 225, 240, 306-307
deterioration, 284, 286, 339
Deussen, Paul, 11, 338
devil, 343
devotion, 18, 281
dharma, 279
dhyana, 57, 115

dialectical process, 101, 111, 133

difficulties, 1, 44, 56, 66, 106, 161, 337

direct experience, 9, 21, 109-110, 126, 248, 258

Direct Experience of Reality, 109, 248

discoveries and discovery, 22, 42-43, 45, 81, 100, 150, 155, 159, 162, 165, 168, 242, 248, 315, 325

discrepancy, 125, 239, 317

disembodied, 74, 240

disillusionment, 46, 132

dislocation, 129-130

distortion, 129, 185, 190

distraction, 53, 224

disturbance, 65

divine right, 213

dogma, dogmatism, 24, 26, 28, 57, 110

do-gooder, 337

Doppler effect, 321

dragon, 56

dream, 7, 84-85, 141, 348

drug abuse, 232, 295

Drury, M O'C, 118, 126

Ecclesiastes, 236

Eckhart, Meister, 66, 69

economics, 265, 336

economy, 25, 68, 160

Eddington, Arthur, 6, 321

education, 42-44, 148, 155, 158, 171, 225, 265, 287, 294, 298, 306-307

Edward the Confessor, 176

effort, 41, 46, 50, 52-54, 59, 147, 162, 219, 253, 287

effortless, 50-52, 59

ego, egoism, egoity, 29, 31, 55, 67-68, 80, 107, 122, 135, 137, 139-141, 144, 146, 249, 260, 309, 344-345

Einstein, Albert, 47-48, 102, 103, 118, 150, 284, 286, 320, 324, 327, 339

electricity, 149, 152, 164-167, 169

electrolysis, 165-166, 169

electromagnetism, 101-102, 136, 150, 162-163, 169, 323, 325-326

electrons, 34, 104, 136, 202

Eliot, T S, 345

Elliotson, John, 174

empirical realm, 5-7, 9, 39-40, 47, 58, 69, 78-82, 90, 93, 96-97, 99, 104, 107, 109-110, 112-113, 123-124, 130, 133-135, 141, 144-145, 200, 216, 238, 250, 318, 329, 332

energy, 52, 55, 90, 136, 206, 281, 298, 308, 323-326, 329, 332-333, 340, 350; nuclear, 102, 282; packets of, 102

enlightenment, 9, 10, 57, 77, 82, 232, 260, 298, 332, 344, 346

enquiry, 10, 27, 34, 42-46, 48-49, 51, 57-59, 63, 65-66, 165, 171, 222, 238, 240, 242, 250

environment, 80-81, 127-128, 208, 243, 269, 281, 298, 338

envy, 292, 297, 301-302, 304, 307-308, 310

epidemic, 292, 301

equality, 233-234

equanimity, 45, 54

Erewhon, 134, 296

Esdaile, James, 173

ethics, 8, 40, 118-121, 123-127, 337, 341

evil, averted by sacrifice, 307; capacity for, 286; character and conduct, 135, 216, 226, 288, 300, 341-344, 346; consequences, 222; Creator as source of, 343; hatred of, 288; King's, 176; life as, 226;

evil (cont.)
   of different names of religions, 24; of indiscriminate charity, 170; of lesser beauty inhibiting greater, 127; of poverty, 176; of suffering and death, 225; resisted by force, 231 *see also* good and evil

Exodus, 30

expectation, 186, 203-204, 312

external world, 75, 89, 93, 107, 137, 139, 144

extremism, 45

facts, 21-22, 119, 166, 178, 186, 188, 193, 199, 263, 328

failings, 133, 250

faith, 2, 4, 20, 22, 28, 51, 99, 158, 162-163, 167, 170, 177-179, 214, 216, 223, 224, 227, 234, 273, 275, 334-336

falsehood, 55, 128, 129, 212

false gods, 31, 40

Falstaff, Sir John, 308

fame, 156, 173, 176, 216-217, 221

fantasies, 75, 294

Faraday, Michael, 150-171, 264

Fascism, 232

Father Poppiewsku, 233

Faust, 222, 248, 277

feelings, 1, 93, 107, 119, 154, 161, 204, 217, 219, 242, 280, 285, 289, 307-308 *see also* mind

finite, 70, 92, 95, 108, 110, 113, 126, 223, 256, 260, 324

focus, 50, 53, 62, 187, 194, 196

fraternity, 233

Frazer, James, 198, 357

Frederick the Great, 214

freedom, 46, 81-82, 94, 134, 230, 232-233, 249, 259-260, 268, 296, 305, 307, 342-343, 346

French Revolution, 46, 213, 233
Freud, Sigmund, 7, 14, 32, 122, 175, 178
fruits of action *see* action, fruits of *and* good fruit
Fry, Elizabeth, 334
galaxy, 85-86, 321, 323
Galileo Galilei, 148, 150, 242, 315, 319
Gandhi, M K, 231
Gay-Lussac, Joseph Louis, 156
genocide, 341
gentleness, 68
Geyl, Pieter, 275
Gita, 16, 45, 67-68, 147, 152, 159, 163, 233-234, 240, 244, 279, 286, 289-291, 333, 340-341, 343, 345, 347
Gladstone, William Ewart, 334
God, 9, 12, 14, 17-18, 20, 26, 29-30, 64, 66-67, 79-80, 87, 99, 113, 131, 141, 170, 205, 209-210, 214, 227, 255, 271-273, 275, 284, 287, 299, 305, 319, 332-333, 343-345; death of, 14 *see also* consciousness, absolute
gods, false *see* false gods
Goethe, Johann Wolfgang von, 27
golden calf, 30
good, 28, 30, 31, 46, 57, 68, 221, 222, 231, 237, 240, 261, 286-288, 294, 295, 297, 298, 317, 336, 338-344, 344, 346, 350; and the pleasant, 122, 340; behaviour, 122; fruit, 309; greater, 135, 290; highest, 121-128, 298; influence, 272; koan, 115-130; life, 334-350; pupil, 62; servants, 42; teachers, 67
good and evil, erroneous ideals of, 341; recognition of, 342-343
Good Samaritan, 287
Gospel, 177, 226, 234, 286, 300, 332
government, 42, 123, 212, 230-232, 234, 296, 304

grace, 10, 67, 160, 170, 254, 284

gratuitous violence, 295

graven images, 30

gravity, 97, 150, 238, 242, 254, 324

greater good, 133, 290

greatness, 79, 147-171, 338

group, 61, 62, 163, 201, 217, 237, 265, 268, 278, 283, 293, 294, 336

habit, bad, 49; its effect on vision, 183, 187; of blaming others, 296; of contempt, 215, 292, 295, 297; of meditation, 53; of mind control, 7; primitive, 29

half-truths, 87, 132-133, 154, 212, 230

hallucinations, 75

Hamlet, 131-132

happiness, 32, 41, 141, 215, 219-220, 225, 250, 302, 308, 340-341

harmlessness, 231

Havel, Václav, viii, 233, 243-260, 282

Hawking, Stephen, 312, 322, 324, 330

Haydn, Joseph, 302-303

health, 3, 167-168, 177, 208-209, 281, 284, 300

Heard, Gerald, 11

Hegel, Georg Wilhelm Friedrich, 133, 261, 285

Heidegger, Martin, 255

Heisenberg, Werner Karl, 101, 103-104

hell, seventh, 347-350

Helmholtz, Hermann von, 168, 190

Henry IV, 94

Herschel, William, 321

Hertz, Heinrich, 325

Hipparchus, 240

historian, 262, 264-267, 275

history, 18, 20, 27, 43, 77-78, 86, 133, 150, 173, 175, 177, 211, 231, 261-264, 266-269, 271, 273, 275-276, 285, 303, 312-313; unwillingness to learn from, 262

Hitler, Adolf, 31, 283, 343, 347

Hotspur, 94

Hubble, Edward, 320-321, 325

Hume, David, 3, 9, 107, 137-140, 143, 145

Huxley, Aldous, 11-12

Huxley, Thomas Henry, 348-349

Huxley, Julian, 347

Huygens, Christian, 315

hydra, 38

hypnosis, hypnotism, 173-176, 178, 206-209; by conduction and induction, 206

'I', the real, 56, 58, 92, 256-258, 332-333, 345

Iago, 308, 343

Ibsen, Henrik, 142

idealism, moral, 1, 31-32, 229; subjective, 101, 144

identity, 34, 36, 80, 93, 107, 125, 137-138, 144, 165, 248, 253, 256; with God, 80

see also self, knowledge and realization of

idols, 30

ignorance, 8, 58, 64, 95, 166, 225, 243, 249, 260, 311, 342-344, 346, 350

illusion, 14, 32, 40, 45, 81, 91, 186, 190, 196, 198, 209, 236, 239, 322

impartiality, 1, 16, 87

imperishable, 17, 333

indecision, 170

individualism, individuality, 31-32, 34, 36, 40, 68-69, 249, 283, 309, 344, 345

indoctrination, 43-44

indulgence, 1, 45, 80, 132, 226

infection, 292-294, 298

inference, 88-89, 110, 204, 316

infinite, 83, 92, 110, 112, 113, 131, 138, 223, 250

inner balance, 28; enquiry, 42, 48-49, 57-59, 250; life, 8, 276; light, 260; revolution, 249; source, 54, 248; spirit, 248; strength, 233, 248; unity, 286; voice, 254

insight, 20, 32, 57-58, 66, 252, 254, 271, 298; flash of, 83, 125, 132-133

interaction, 165, 279

interdependence, 278

interpretation, 61, 103, 130, 179, 184, 192, 196, 199, 202, 273

intuition, 129, 210, 336

iodine, 156, 165

Iraq, 282

irresistible force, 221

Isha Upanishad, 304

Isherwood, Christopher, 11

Islam, 17-18, 223

jagat, 329, 333

James, William, 3, 9, 20, 76-77, 173, 198

jet air propulsion, 43-44

jiva, 90, 91, 193

Joseph, 142, 264

Jowett, Benjamin, 264

Juliusburger, Otto, 339

Jupiter, 242
Kant, Immanuel, 3, 78, 81, 96, 106, 121, 139-140, 143, 145, 329
Katha Upanishad, 120, 340, 344
Kelvin, Lord, 65
Kena Upanishad, 9, 99
Kepler, Johannes, 241, 319
Keynes, John Maynard, viii, 334, 336-337
Kingdom of Heaven, 124, 154
King's Evil, 176
King William III, 177
knower, 77, 143, 145, 201
knowledge and wisdom, 285, 344
knowledge of self *see* self, knowledge and realization of
koan, 58, 107, 109, 115-130
Koran, 17
Krishna, 68, 340; as flute-player, 68-69
Kropotkin, 228
language, 3, 22, 70, 73, 75, 109, 118, 125, 202-205, 255
Lao Tzu, 64, 68, 230-231
law, 33, 91, 134, 166-167, 228, 230, 269, 274, 275, 287, 299, 342
laws and institutions, 22
laws, historical, 263; mechanical, 268; natural and spiritual, 25, 27, 265; of hygiene, 298; of motion, 100-101, 150; of time, space and causation, 110; scientific, 41, 201
Leibniz, Gottfried Wilhelm, 12, 101
Leonardo da Vinci, vii, 22
levelheaded, 246
Lewis, C S, 337
liberation *see* self, liberation of

light waves, 86, 321, 325
likes and dislikes, 7
linguistic analysis, 72; description, 108-109, 203
listening, 24, 51, 63, 65, 243
Locke, John, 106, 136, 139
Longfellow, Henry Wadsworth, 147
Louis XIV, 176
love, 19, 56, 58-59, 63, 75, 79-80, 93, 99, 122, 137, 155, 157-158, 162, 215, 234, 247, 272, 280, 288, 299, 303-304, 307, 335, 339, 347
lust, 347
Macbeth, 132
Macedonians, 270
Madariaga, Salvador de, 234-235
Mafia, 232
magnetism, 164-165, 168, 172
map-making, 108
Maria Theresa, 172
Marcet, Mrs, 149
Marx, Karl, 228-229, 232-234, 263
Marxist, 123, 211, 214, 233
masses, 169, 213, 224-225, 230, 324
master passion, 266
materialists, 14, 240
mathematics, 15, 38, 50, 116, 127, 222, 313
Mathnavi, 212, 305
matter, conservation of, 102
matter/mind dualism, 100-114
Maugham, Somerset, 11
Maxwell, Clerk, 20, 150

Maya, 78, 91, 94-95, 97-98, 193, 236

Mazzini, Giuseppe, 264

meaningless, 2, 72, 74, 77, 80, 133, 221, 226, 325

measure, 47, 86, 218, 299, 313-316, 318

mechanical laws, 268

media, 228, 292, 295-297

meditation, 21, 25, 49-59, 171, 208-210, 288, 289

megalomania, 274

memory, 4, 35-36, 39, 85-86, 88, 94, 153, 175, 179, 186, 202, 204, 205, 207, 293, 312-313, 315

Mencius, 299, 300

Mephistopheles, 94

merging, 49-50, 59

Mesmer, Friedrich Anton, 172-173, 176, 178

Mesmerism, 173-174

messages, 86, 194-195

metaphysics, 3, 9-10, 32, 40, 99, 168

Michelson and Morley experiment, 47-48, 169, 320, 325-326

military service, 230

Milky Way, 87-88, 321

Mill, John Stuart, 264, 336

mind, balanced, 45; contents and functions of, 6, 7, 32, 37, 39, 45, 49, 56, 66, 81, 89-90, 94, 122, 125, 135-141, 143-145,158-159, 166, 175-176, 186, 193-194, 199, 201-202, 204-206, 220; emptying 225, 268, 270; control and purification (i) *analogies*, the cup, 66; heated iron ball, 90; filling a sieve with water, 57-58; polishing a mirror, 66 (ii) *method*, 7-9, 31, 32, 41, 43, 45, 47, 49-60, 66-67, 83, 91-92, 231, 233, 288, 307, 309, 311, 332-333, 338, 340-348; differs from a computer, 73-75; fallibility of, 238, 260; illness of, 134, 292-311; in society, 278-291; is not the self, 240, 249;

mind (cont.)
  latent impressions and impulses, 7, 49, 55, 68, 89, 94, 136, 137, 176, 179, 193, 196, 206-207, 280; laziness of, 44; life of, 7, 75, 76, 137, 178, 179, 199; neurotic, 67-68; peace of, 253, 254; states of, 43, 45, 47, 49, 75, 77, 93, 107, 202, 204, 217, 219-220, 270; unreliability of, 174-176, 206, 208, 212, 293, 294, 296; viruses of, 292
mind, unconscious, 7, 39, 59, 72, 175, 179, 182, 206, 207, 217, 238, 253, 283; burying thoughts in, 209
  see also consciousness *and* matter/mind dualism
ministerial malpractice, 305
misconception, 136, 141, 146
misfits, 280
mistake, 21, 47, 130, 141, 226, 249, 253, 260
morality, 8, 29, 120, 123-124, 130, 154, 214, 216, 230, 250, 252, 254, 294, 296, 298, 300, 304, 338, 341-342, 345-347; Victorian, 122, 289, 334, 336 *see also* permissiveness
Moses, 30, 32, 332
Moslem, 24
Mother Theresa of Calcutta, 234, 338
Mozart, Wolfgang Amadeus, 173, 302-303
Muhammad, 22, 23
Müller, Max, 11
Murray, Gilbert, 266, 269, 274
mysticism, 12, 20, 24, 111, 179, 269
myth, 120, 274
names and forms, 70-71, 144
napalm, 342
Napoleon, 46, 156
narrowness, 280
nations, 227, 267, 273, 303, 306

Natural Philosophy, 149, 152, 155, 170
Nature, power of, 329; return to, 230
Nazism, 31, 212, 339
neighbour, 279, 288, 299, 308
neti, 97, 98
Newman, Ernest, 141
Newton, Isaac, 33, 100, 148, 150, 313-314, 316, 319
Newtonian physics, 48, 101
Nietzsche, Friedrich, 230
night, 60, 103, 141, 147, 218, 302, 315, 317, 335
Nightingale, Florence, 334
nirvana, 275, 277, 287
noumenon, 106, 140
Novarra, Domenico Maria, 241
nuclear bombs and explosions *see* energy, nuclear
offering, 68, 154, 290, 345
OM, 55, 58, 70-71
Oppenheimer, Robert, 11, 104
optical illusions, 186
orthodox creeds, 269
Palach, Jan, 233
Panchadashi, 51, 89, 92
parables, 79
paradox, 11, 38, 105, 132
participant, 107, 276
particles, 34-35, 72, 102, 104-105, 136, 165-169, 202, 327
passion, 261, 266, 301-302, 340, 343
passive resistance, 231
Pasternak, Boris, 27
Patmore, Coventry, 212

Pavlov, Ivan Petrovich, 194

Peel, Robert, 170

Peer Gynt, 142

perception, 89, 130, 137, 140, 144-145, 176, 179, 190, 199, 202, 258, 312

periodicities, 241

perishable, 17-18, 24

permissiveness, 120, 122, 305

personality, 4, 9, 68-69, 106-107, 109, 113, 133, 135, 148, 155, 171, 213, 233-234, 282, 309, 341; transformation of, 350

perspective, 89, 180, 248-249, 258, 285

photons, 102

place, 10, 17, 25, 35, 47, 68, 76, 86, 91, 97, 99, 127, 133, 138, 145, 166-167, 182, 257, 268, 274, 284, 302, 314, 320, 324, 327, 344, 349

plague, 298

Planck, Max, 26, 101, 331

planets, 33, 100, 172, 241, 319

plurality, 11, 37, 39

Plutarch, 241

Poincaré, Jules Henri, 320

point, fixed, 318, 322, 326, 329; still, 323, 331-333

poison gas, 342

polishing, 66

political agitators, 234

politicians, 282

Pope, 1, 233

Popper, Karl, 77, 78, 81

pop culture, 294

positive, 20, 228, 246-247, 275, 287, 289

posture, 50
potential, 41, 132, 280
powerlessness, 281
power desires, 31
Prakriti Shakti, 329
precedence, 19, 68
preconceptions, 46-49
prejudice, 7, 24, 44, 55, 57, 65
preoccupation, 24, 94, 266
Prince Albert, 170
Prince Radziwill, 303
principles, 76, 99, 100, 104, 121-122, 134, 138, 148, 152, 214, 234, 243, 261, 262, 266, 282, 289, 334, 336
progress, 3, 111, 202, 208, 219, 232, 268, 273, 285, 320, 341
proletariat, 232, 263
propaganda, 44, 228, 233, 306
properties, 36, 103, 105, 144, 164, 167
prophet, 159, 208, 274
psychiatrists, 134
psychologists, 183, 207
Ptolemy, 240-241
public opinion, 227-228
punctuality, 314
purpose, 77, 91, 96, 113, 202, 279, 280, 291, 344
Pythagoreans, 240
Quaker, 111, 152
qualities, 89, 105-106, 110, 136, 139, 144, 166, 330
quanta, 102
Quantum Theory, 101, 331
Queen Anne, 177

Queen Victoria, 151, 264

questions, 1, 2, 6, 8-10, 22, 37-38, 63, 73, 84, 96, 98-99, 113, 117, 130, 211, 220, 222, 256, 287, 329

Rama Tirtha, 14-23, 26-28, 41, 43, 70, 78, 83, 94-99, 110-111, 142-144, 148, 154, 205-206, 208, 280, 288, 289, 298, 301, 307-309, 346-347, 350

rays, 29, 54-55, 102

reality defined, 33

red shift, 321

reflection, intellectual, 51, 137, 194; of image, 39-40, 296

reintegration, 277

rejection, 132

relationships, 106, 110, 139, 144, 256

relativity, 47-48, 87, 93, 101, 110, 113, 150, 169, 320, 322-325, 327, 328, 330-332 *see also* consciousness, relative

relaxation, 49-50, 54, 56, 59, 236

religion, religious, 1, 2, 5, 8-11, 13-28, 32, 45, 83, 123, 125, 151, 162, 170, 178, 269, 271, 273-275, 280, 294, 334

renunciation *see* Self, renunciation of

responsibility, 134-135, 253-254, 259, 342

results *see* action, fruits of

return to Nature, 230

revolution, industrial, 265; scientific, 150, 242, 249, 259-260, 265; social, 45-46, 213-214, 229-230, 233, 259-260

riddle, 58, 107, 115 *see also* koan

right and wrong, 20, 122, 296, 341-342

Rousseau, Jean-Jacques, 213, 230

Royal Institution, 153-156, 158, 160-162, 170

Royal Society, 159, 165, 168, 174

Royal Touch, 176

Rumford, Count, 160

Rumi, Jalalu'ddin 212, 305

Ruskin, John, 264

Russell, Bertrand, 3, 59, 87-89, 96, 116-117, 121, 127, 179, 186, 199-207, 283, 285-288, 301-302, 304, 306-307, 313, 323, 326-327

Russia, Russian Revolution, 42, 46, 211-235

sacrifice, 1, 5, 290, 307, 338

Saddam Hussein, 282

Sagan, Carl, 323

saints, 18, 79, 277

Sakharov, Andrei Dmitrievich, 123, 233

samadhi, 52

Samaritan, 287-288

Sandemanian, 163

Schopenhauer, Arthur, 3, 11, 329

Schrödinger, Erwin, 11, 13, 29, 32, 38, 88, 101, 104, 135, 239

science, 5, 13-16, 20, 22-26, 28, 30, 32, 39, 44, 72, 87-88, 99, 104, 106, 111-112, 118-119, 135-136, 149-150, 153-159, 162, 167, 170, 201, 226, 239, 265, 326, 328, 331; seventeenth century, 100, 136, 242

scripture, 21 *see also* Veda

Searle, J R, 72-75

sectarianism, 19, 280

secular, 2, 272, 334, 336-337

Segovia, Andrés, 63, 66

self, better, 345; -deception, 221; evidence, 201; higher, 135, 345, 346; ideal, 123, 346; -interest, 31; knowledge and realization of, 40-41, 81-83, 90, 95, 99, 123, 128-129, 135, 171, 239, 291, 301, 308, 345-347; liberation of, 77-78, 81, 98; lower, 122, 346; naked, 276; perfection of, 133, 253; preservation of, 133; renunciation of, 338;

see also consciousness *and* mind

sensation, 88, 109, 179, 186, 194, 199, 201
sense world, 94, 280
sensory messages, 194
sensuality, 216
Sermon on the Mount, 25, 299
Shankara, 5, 21, 40, 89, 97, 106, 109, 140, 142, 144-145, 240, 248
Shanti Niketan, 231
shape, 34, 105, 136, 155, 180, 190, 192, 195, 207
Shastri, Hari Prasad, 4, 45, 49, 63, 79, 209, 262, 291, 340, 343
Shri Dada of Aligarh, 17, 56, 57, 90, 235, 280
Shruti *see* Scripture
silence, attentive, 51, 60-72, 319
sin, 277, 304, 310, 340, 344, 346
Skidelsky, Robert, 334, 337
skills, 26, 42
sleep, deep (dreamless), 98, 173, 209, 283; *see also* mind, unconscious
Social Contract, 213
social ideal, 337, 341; justice, 234
socialism, 334, 336
society, Yoga in, 1-13
sociology, 62, 283
Socrates, 45, 60-61, 234, 282
Solzhenitsyn, Alexander, 123, 233, 282
sound, 65, 69-70, 77, 86-87, 93, 132, 289, 319, 321, 349, speed of, 87; waves, 86
Soviet society, 123
space, 17-18, 48, 85-97, 101, 106, 108, 110, 113, 122, 126, 168, 180, 182, 200, 312, 318-326, 329-333
see also time and space
Spencer, Herbert, 99

Spinoza, Benedict de, 121-122, 133, 343
spiritual, reality, 9, 41, 79, 113-114, 240, 249, 272, 273, 276; traditions, 9, 65, 79, 83, 104, 111, 123, 283, 294
spoken dialogue, 60
Stalin, Josef, 46, 282, 343
states, totalitarian, 31, 211, 227, 273
stories, 6, 56, 95-96, 141, 145, 189, 304-306, 310, 347, 350
study, 10-11, 16, 21, 24, 51, 76, 78, 88, 110, 116, 174, 207, 224, 228, 236, 240, 247, 255, 262-263, 266-267, 269, 275-276
sub-atomic physics, 103-105
subconscious *see* mind, unconscious
suffering, 91-92, 134, 141-142, 169, 212-213, 225, 240, 252, 273, 276-277, 298, 301, 338, 347
Sufis, 66
suggestion, 40, 57, 174-176, 178, 180, 186, 190, 199, 205-209, 320
sun, 29, 33, 66, 69, 86-87, 93, 158, 167, 241, 248-249, 310, 314-317, 319, 322, 324
supernatural, 119, 125
superstition, 26, 223, 274
super-ego, 122
symbiosis, 278
symbols, 17, 68, 74-75, 79-80, 277
Tagore, Rabindranath, 231
T'ai Chi, 104, 277
tapas, 338
teachability, 69
Teachings from the Bhagavad Gita, 291
technological progress, 339; skills, 43-44; society, 30
television, 43-44, 292
Tempest, The, 84-85

tension, 50, 55, 67-68

Teresa of Avila, garden analogy, 52-54,

testimony, 201-202, 204, 243, 342

texts, 21-22, 56, 120

Theresa, Mother, of Calcutta, 234, 338

Thomas à Becket, 345

thought *see* mind

Thrasymachus, 61

time, 312-333; absolute, 313, 316, 318-319; changing ideas of, 318-319; definitions of, 313-314; future, 85, 87-88, 90, 92-94, 162-164, 202-203, 205-206, 248, 263, 282, 286, 312-313, 341, 347; local, 326-328; measurement of, 314-318; past, 19, 25, 36, 84-90, 92-94, 161, 179, 186-188, 225, 261-263, 269-270, 312; present, 15, 25, 47, 84-99, 111, 114, 124, 126, 161, 202-203, 295-296, 312, 313, 319, 329, 341; private, 312-314; public, 313-316; 323; still point beyond, 323, 331-333

time and space, common-sense view of, 329; former view of, 324-325; modern scientific view of, 326-330; space-time continuum, 325, 331, 333

Tolstoi, Leo, 132-133, 211-235

totalitarian regimes, 31, 45-46, 48, 211, 232-233, 243, 250

Toynbee, Arnold, ix, 262-270, 272, 275-276, 283, 287

traditions *see* spiritual, traditions

transcendence, 32, 40, 45, 79-81, 113, 133, 307, 332, 346-347 *see also* consciousness, absolute

treatment, by hypnosis 173-175; of current social mental ailments, 292-311; of people by totalitarian regimes, 227, 243;

Truth, living in, 236-260

Tulsi Das, 302
Tuscany, Grand Duke of, 157
Tyndall, John, 162, 169-170
tyranny *see* totalitarian regimes
ultimate reality *see* consciousness, absolute
unconscious *see* mind, unconscious
undogmatic attitude, 269 *see also* dogma, dogmatism
unity, 19, 33, 35, 37-40, 64, 90, 93, 104, 124, 138, 140, 143-144, 235, 279, 286, 291
universal, benevolence, 233; outlook, 283, 286
universe, 9, 17, 69, 72, 83, 95-96, 100-101, 115, 126-127, 139, 145, 193, 238-242, 249, 276, 307, 320-330
unpredicted discoveries, 43
Upadesha Sahasri, 135
urges, 176, 283
Utilitarians, 334, 336
vacuum, 66, 273, 326
value judgements, 119-120, 127, 341-342
variable, 33, 35
vasanas, 7
Veda, 5, 99
Vedanta Light, 79
venom, 309
verification, 4, 6, 320
vichara, 46, 57, 59, 171
virtue, 235, 249, 260, 342, 344-346
vision, 6, 8, 32, 40-41, 57, 235, 269, 286, 288, 340; rajasic, 212
Volta, Alessandro, 157
Voltaire, 213
vrittis, 55

Wagner, Richard, 229
waking, 7, 36, 45, 270, 281, 348
Waterhouse, Marjorie, 54, 78-79
waves, 69, 86, 102, 104, 136, 145, 169, 202, 219, 321, 325-326, 335
Webb, Beatrice, 334
Weil, Simone, 126
Whitehead, Alfred North, 127-130
Whittle, Frank, 44
Wilberforce, William, 334
wisdom, 22, 29-32, 91, 134-135, 155, 199, 212-213, 219, 234, 283, 285-287, 291, 294, 298, 337, 341, 343-345
Wisdom from the East, 343
Wiseman, Richard, 176
witness, 90-92, 107, 140, 143, 177, 310
Wittgenstein, Ludwig, 116-118, 124-126, 186
Woodroffe, Sir John, 16, 110
wooing the Lord, 69
world view, 101, 325
worship, 17, 25, 30, 79, 273, 283, 333
yajna, 21, 289-290
Yajnavalkya, 113
Yin and Yang, 105-106, 277
Zen, 57, 66, 109, 115
Zoroaster, 22

Vedanta Classics
translated by A J Alston

ŚAṀKARA SOURCE BOOK
A new approach to the texts of India's greatest philosopher and interpreter of the Upanishads

This work in six volumes brings together the main texts of Śaṃkara, freshly translated and grouped systematically into topics. Each section is introduced by a passage of explanation, and the Notes aim to serve both the specialist and the general reader.

1. Śaṃkara on the Absolute
2. Śaṃkara on the Creation
3. Śaṃkara on the Soul
4. Śaṃkara on the Rival Views
5. Śaṃkara on the Discipleship
6. Śaṃkara on Enlightenment

THE THOUSAND TEACHINGS OF ŚAṀKARA

The **Upadeśa Sāhasrī** is an unconstrained exposition of Advaita Vedanta, and the one independent work accepted by all authorities as undeniably written by India's greatest scriptural commentator and philosopher.

REALIZATION OF THE ABSOLUTE
Naiṣkarmya Siddhi of Sureśvarācārya

Sureśvara was an immediate disciple of Śaṃkara, whose aim in this work is to provide 'a compendium containing the essence of the entire Upanishadic teaching'.

Key Books on Yoga

by Hari Prasad Shastri

THE HEART OF THE EASTERN
MYSTICAL TEACHING

WISDOM FROM THE EAST

SCIENTIST AND MAHATMA

MEDITATION – ITS THEORY AND PRACTICE

THE CREST JEWEL OF WISDOM
*translated by A J Alston
with Dr Shastri's commentary*

★

by Marjorie Waterhouse

TRAINING THE MIND THROUGH YOGA

THE POWER BEHIND THE MIND

WHAT YOGA HAS TO OFFER

★

by A M Halliday
FREEDOM THROUGH SELF-REALISATION